Private Eye, Secret Spy

Private Eye, Secret Spy:

My Life as Britain's Most Controversial PI.

By Ian D. Withers

Contact@IDWithersPI.com
January, 2021.

This book is dedicated to:

Phyllis, my sorely missed late wife and best friend.
A promise fulfilled.

Stuart, my late brother and business partner for the first twenty years.
We shared so many adventures.

Acknowledgements

My daughter Debbie, and sons, Andy, Johnnie and Jamie
Growing up with a very often absent father

The researchers, who were invaluable digging up old news reports,
dates and places

Jacqui, Charley, Gennine and Kaitlyn

Daughters-in-law: Natalie, Seychelles and Leanne, South Africa

The readers, commentators, critics and helpers

Shirley Withers, Helen Withers, Maureen Clarke,
Jim and Shirley McCullins, Julie McCullins
and all other volunteers who assisted in any way on this enterprise.

Jason Johnson – Editor

Jason faithfully transformed my
250,000 word report
into finished manuscript.

JasonJohnsonWriter.com

Contents

PROLOGUE

THE car arrives fast on my drive and I don't know who it is. A second car right behind it, braking firmly. Then a third. I look outside. Doors are being flung open all over the place. Suddenly people everywhere. Now a van pulling up behind.

What on earth?

I open the front door. Men and women, fifteen, maybe twenty—armed, fanning out around my property. Two are looking right at me, coming my way. I stand still, poker face, my mind searching for answers. They're all in suits, clean-cut, clean cars. The two stride right up.

'Good morning officers,' I say.

'Ian Withers?'

'Yes.'

He says he's a sergeant, Police Service of Northern Ireland. A warrant into my hand.

'These officers will be searching your home,' and they're already all over the garden.

'For?'

For anything connected to 'the 1985 murder in London of Gérard Hoarau,' he says.

'Ah,' I say.

He says he's here at the direction of the Counter Terrorism Unit of the Metropolitan Police.

'Do not go anywhere,' he adds. 'An officer from the Met will speak to you shortly.'

1

I sit in the kitchen, coffee mug in hand, read the broad scope of the warrant as strangers fill my home. I thought they might come one day, but by appointment.

I'd been National Security Advisor to the Republic of Seychelles in 1985. Hoarau led a hardcore dissident faction. It hired mercenaries over and over to oust the left-wing government and seize power. My job was to derail his efforts and I did so. Over and over.

Police are tearing through my bedroom, pulling open drawers in the study, bagging up documents and laptops and mobiles and flash drives and tapes and CDs.

That killing was thirty-three years back. I'm seventy-seven, retired. Why have they come today? Why now? Last night I was in Cyprus, arrived home about seven hours ago. Had they been waiting for me? Could they have known I'd been writing this memoir? Did they think I might have jotted down some clue to cracking the case?

Gérard Hoarau never understood discretion. He talked openly with his contacts in public places, discussed military manoeuvres and funding all the time. He repeatedly exposed his own plans right into my ears. His killing was horrific, raked with automatic gunfire on his doorstep one November day in London. His supporters blamed me. They put posters on walls saying I should die too. They never knew he was my single best intelligence source. His death forced me to relinquish my contract with Seychelles, forced me to reshape my life, changed everything for my family. Whoever benefited from that murder, it wasn't me.

Another man paces into my kitchen. He says he's from the Metropolitan Police Counter Terrorism Command and asks me to stand.

'Ian Withers,' he says, 'You are under arrest on suspicion of conspiracy to murder Gérard Hoarau in November 1985 in London. You do not have to say anything but it may harm your defence if you do not mention when questioned something which you later rely on in court. Anything you do say may be given in evidence.'

I'm to be taken to the counterintelligence interrogation unit in Southwark, southeast London. Criminal psychologists will be working with my interrogators, isolating and exploring my words, my movements, the patterns of my memory, trying to unlock the secrets they suspect I've been guarding all this time. They play the evidence gathering game there with a mastery that makes the bad guys tremble. But I won't be trembling. I have nothing to hide.

I collect my medications, other bits and pieces, and in a couple of hours I'm in the sky again, two women and a man escorting me over the Irish Sea. I look at the cold, grey water below, lean back.

My mind soothes to thoughts of Seychelles, those extraordinary years. What a place to live, to work, to love. The warm embrace of the Indian Ocean, the heavenly Kreol food, the easy spirit of the islands. There's an old cast-iron clock tower in the little capital there that tells a time all of its own. It'll hit the hour and chime, then chime that hour again a few minutes later. The locals sing:

> 'I'm going back to the Seychelles,
> 'Where the Clock Chimes Twice,
> 'I'm going back to the Seychelles,
> 'Isles of Paradise.'

Driven to Southwark, booked in, asked to wait for my solicitor, Steve Wedd.

How many times have I been arrested now? Not sure. I'd have to think about it. Arrested, beaten, imprisoned at home and abroad—I've had all of that and more. I've had my home ransacked by gangsters, my office bombed, had more threats and weapons aimed my way than I can count. I've been prosecuted four times by the Metropolitan Police, stood twice in the Old Bailey's number one dock, challenged and changed the way conspiracy law is applied. Over sixty years I've crossed the world to recover abducted children, bug millionaires, guard politicians, track VIPs, locate terrorists, flush out fraudsters. I've negotiated paths through war zones, set national news agendas, helped seal an international treaty, built a business with a reach spanning the globe. I've prevented murder, witnessed murder and uncovered murder but, as I'll be making clear to my inquisitors, I've never had any involvement in any murder.

My solicitor arrives. He advises me to say 'no comment' as much as I like. I shake my head, tell him I'll answer every question. Not only that,

I say, but I'll be writing it all down afterwards.

Along with so many other stories from my life and work, I tell him, this one's going in the book...

ONE

The Hong Kong Murder Plot (1974)

I DRILLED a small hole in the wooden saddle across the bottom of the door in the five-star hotel. Quietly as I could, I blew away the little mound of sawdust. Into the hole I placed a small probe holding a tiny wired microphone.

Over the coming hours, as guests slept, we lifted the sumptuous carpet in the spotless corridor inch by inch, feeding the thin wire underneath, replacing it as cleanly as possible. By dawn, after a night on constant alert for prying eyes, we had reached my room, number 1806. It was four along from the microphone site, number 1802. I fed the wire under my door, opened up, entered and locked. No one had seen us.

Inside, we again tested the Uher recording machines. All were working well. A setting ensured they'd automatically record every conversation in the target room. We expected significant talking to begin after the arrival of a person unknown from London. The guests in 1802 had referred to this person, in Cantonese Chinese, as the *secret weapon*. It was imperative that we established who this was.

Ahead of the mystery arrival, a meeting took place in that room. A translator assisted as the machines clicked into action and we listened. It was in that conversation we learned the identity of the *secret weapon*. It was an English barrister, John Balcombe QC, who would later become Lord Justice Balcombe. It was clear he would be representing the men we were interested in. A case was pending at the Hong Kong High Court. There had been some underhand business involving the men in 1802 and some colleagues. I'd been hired to find out more about them, what they were planning, what kind of characters they were. Enormous sums of money were at stake. I could not balls this up.

I'd arranged to put a surveillance team in the hotel lobby. Hours passed by and nothing. Then, around lunchtime, a little flurry of activity. Four Chinese men left 1802 and made their way down. A call from the lobby advised they had met with a man matching the description of *secret weapon* John Balcombe. I alerted our translator and Stuart, my brother. We gathered in 1806 just in time to see the machines begin to whirr.

Much was in Cantonese, but each of the Chinese men also spoke at times in English with the barrister. We were quickly able to get a handle on what was being planned. Ahead of the court case, the *secret weapon's* hosts were wondering if there might be a way to discredit the character of the witness—the British businessman who had hired us. It was an interesting start.

The conversation, clear as a bell, continued for a time before the translator turned to me. She was startled. She said the tone had completely changed among the men. They were now discussing how to 'dispose' of the witness. We all knew what it meant.

More details came. The men talked of using the 'same people' who carried out a job for them in Kuala Lumpur, Malaysia. My heart thumped. Just a few days before, a man working for my client's firm had been shot dead by persons unknown outside his office—in Kuala Lumpur. We had made an astonishing interception.

As the meeting closed and the translator left, I gathered her notes and carefully removed the tape. Like my life depended on it, I took it where my client was staying. I told him the news wasn't pretty for him personally, but it could change everything.

On the way back, I met Stuart in the hotel lobby. We were sure we'd cracked it, armed our client with some very powerful evidence of character. We had a strong coffee each before I went back to my room. I needed to pack up the machines, clear away the other little bugs and various bits and pieces I'd picked up in Hong Kong.

I put the key in the lock but, strangely, it did not work. I tried again, considered I may have put it in wrong, may have turned it wrong, but no. That key did not work. Could it be that—

People behind me in the corridor. I was about to turn. Then the barrel of a revolver pushed firmly into the small of my back. I froze. The stakes that had climbed high and fast were still climbing. I closed my eyes. Was I about to get shot?

The man spoke, a Chinese accent.

'Put your hands against the door,' he said, and I complied.

'Do not move,' he said, and I complied.

I had a pressing question. 'Who are you?'

'Inspector Tsan-Kwong Wong. Royal Hong Kong Police.'

That was something of a relief. I was, I hoped, less likely to get a bullet through me.

'How can I help you?' I asked, delicately as I could.

'We have some questions. Are you carrying any weapons?'

'No,' I said.

He pulled the barrel from my back. I breathed deep. He frisked me and put the revolver away.

There were six of them, all in plain clothes, all waiting around for me to return to the room. It was they who were able to open the door. They wanted to search inside. I wasn't happy and said so. Yet the recording equipment I'd brought from London, the various little bugs and gadgets I'd bought in the local shops, all the wires and spare tapes on my bed. It did look pretty suspicious. I'd been doing a lot of eavesdropping in various locations in recent weeks, but I wasn't going to tell that to Inspector Wong.

He looked it over. I suspected he had already seen it, that he had already had a poke around in my room. Had it been reported by a chambermaid? Or had someone rumbled our microphone wire under the carpet? Had the police been in and changed or somehow jammed the lock on my door?

Inspector Wong said, 'I'd like to ask you what this is all for?'

'I can't tell you anything,' was my reply. 'All I can say is that I am a private investigator acting on behalf of clients. I am in Hong Kong concerning a major civil matter in the High Court.'

'You're not allowed to monitor in a hotel like this,' he said. 'It is a breach of Hong Kong law.'

His aim, it became clear, was to find out who hired me. I wasn't about to tell him. However the answer he wanted was written on the uncashed cheque my client had given me for a round of expenses.

As the men were on the cusp of pulling my room apart, I said I was concerned. There was cash in the drawer, I said. Could I retrieve it before the strangers began their search?

The inspector kindly let me do so. As I collected the notes, I slipped the cheque in among them. While the men got on with their job, I stepped into the toilet, ripped it up, flushed it. HK$5,000 down the tubes.

Moments later there was a phone call to the room. The inspector let me take it. It was Stuart in the coffee shop, wondering where I was. I was relieved he too hadn't been nabbed, but I needed to let him know I had.

'I'm busy here with people,' I said, mouthing to the policeman that it was a call from someone at reception. 'I'm afraid I won't be down.'

I knew Stuart had got the message. But a moment later the police had too. Inspector Wong looked me in the eye as it dawned on him.

He snapped at his men, ordered them to the lobby fast. They knew I had not been alone and knew now that I had just tipped off the other man they wanted. The police needed at least one more suspect. I'd come to know they knew more about events in that hotel than they were saying. They were seeking to piece together a *conspiracy to pervert the course of justice* case ahead of the High Court trial. But it was too late for them to bag an all-important suspected co-conspirator—Stuart had left the building.

'You are under arrest,' I was told.

I was cuffed and driven the short distance to the police station. The senior officer in charge, an Irishman, introduced himself.

'Superintendent McMahon, Royal Hong Kong Police Anti-Triad Squad,' he said confidently. 'You are going to tell me who you're working for.'

'Well,' I said, 'We're going to fall out because I'm afraid I'm not.'

But who was I working for? It was a good question. It had taken time to find out...

The call came around 3 am. I had been fast asleep, cuddled up with my eight-months pregnant wife Phyl as a cold January took grip in England. A Chinese accent on the phone. He said I had been recommended.

'Can you come to Hong Kong right away?' he asked, his voice suggesting he was completely serious.

'Okay,' I said, cautious yet sensing adventure ahead.

'Bring as much monitoring equipment as possible to begin a critical assignment immediately,' he said.

'Okay,' I answered, but followed up by suggesting he would need to pay for the ticket.

Stuart drove me to Heathrow Airport. My mystery caller had said someone would leave an envelope at the check-in desk. He wasn't joking. A £1,000 cash advance and a roundtrip business class ticket to Hong Kong. I sent £500 back with Stuart for Phyl, to keep the home fires burning, and boarded the plane.

Just before touchdown, a hostess surprised me with a note. It said I was to take the Mandarin Hotel limousine outside the terminal and check in to my prepaid room. The limousine turned out to be a Rolls Royce. They don't cut corners at the Mandarin.

A little later a call came to request I attend a meeting in one of the suites. The door opened and four men were waiting. I recognised one right away, a short, slim, bald and smiley bloke of about sixty. He was a previous client, a sharp business operator, a jittery yet gracious man with ruthless confidence by the name of Jim Raper. We shook hands heartily. Jim was well-known in London through the seventies and eighties. He involved himself in various public companies as a specialist minority shareholder, meaning he would gradually take-over companies and sell off the assets—it's better known these days as asset stripping. Jim was a controversial figure, brilliant at his work but inevitably he ruffled feathers along the way.

I sipped on passionfruit juice as he explained. He said he was a shareholder and director of a huge international corporation known as The Faber Merlin Group. Its interests included hotels, mining, shipping, transport and salvage rights across the Far East. Around half its shares, he said, were owned by Chinese and the rest by Europeans. That delicate balance had led to an internal power struggle which resulted in the Chinese calling an extraordinary general meeting in London. And as all the European directors made their way, the location was switched at the last minute—the meeting was now taking place in Hong Kong. At the new venue, the majority Asian directors passed a resolution, backed by shareholders, suspending the European directors. In a single swoop, the Chinese had full control of the company.

As you can imagine, the Europeans weren't having it. They secured a High Court injunction in Hong Kong to freeze the company's activities. The whole mess was going to take a long time to resolve.

Jim said, 'I need to know what the Chinese group is planning. I need to know of anything we could use against them when it gets to court.'

He said whatever I needed, in terms of expenses or support, I would have it. But a warning followed. A lot of money was at stake, a lot of powerful people with connections all over the world were involved. He told me that a Chinese employee at the Kuala Lumpur office had been out for a coffee a while ago when a car pulled up alongside. He was shot dead.

First thing I did was call Stuart who worked with me at the time. I told him this was a tricky business and I could with my trusted colleague at my side. He flew over right away.

Together we drilled down as far as we could to get the names of everyone involved and work out where they were. The coming weeks saw us jetting all over the region, sometimes on the same planes as some of our targets, tracking movements and meetings where we could in Seoul, Singapore and all over Hong Kong. We used various sensitive microphone and briefcase tape recorders and captured conversations to begin building the picture.

When we began hearing of the arrival of the mysterious *secret weapon*, we knew we were close to the action. Their *secret weapon* would, as it happened, be staying at The Mandarin Hotel. A little negotiation with staff and I established room 1802 had been booked by our friends. I was moved to the nearest available room.

But none of this would be reaching the ears of my new pal, Superintendent McMahon of the Royal Hong Kong Police Anti-Triad Squad. He shrugged off my silence that day and had me sent to a police lock-up in a place called, pleasantly enough, Happy Valley. I was dumped in a large holding cell with about thirty others—the most recently rounded up pimps, pick pockets and petty crooks of Hong Kong. Funny enough, Happy Valley lived up to its name. They were all perfectly welcoming people. For four days I drank Chinese tea and, fighting the chopsticks, munched twice daily on chicken, fish and rice.

On March 13, 1974, I was taken to the island's Magistrate's Court. The police were seeking to remand me for fourteen more days while they worked to establish the conspiracy they suspected.

On the outside, as the media took an interest in the case, Jim Raper had got to work. He arranged for an outstanding lawyer, one Bernard Gunsten, to support me. Bernard advised that their case boiled down to my possessing radio transmitters without a licence. He said I should plead guilty, pay the fine, move along.

I took the stand as the police prosecutor showed the magistrate the evidence. The charge was put to me—*possession of a transmitter without a licence*. The prosecutor explained this was a holding charge. I should be held for another fourteen days while inquiries continued, he said.

My lawyer spoke. 'Your Worship,' he said wearily. 'In Hong Kong there is no such thing as a holding charge. Might the prosecutor provide some authority as to the legal basis of a holding charge?'

The prosecutor, a police officer, said it was a long-standing way of keeping somebody in custody while inquiries continued. Yet, as my lawyer pointed out, there were no law book references, no authorities, nothing official covering this matter.

Bernard said, 'My client wishes to plead guilty now to the offence charged. He is entitled to have his plea heard as quickly as possible and I see no reason why this cannot be heard today so he can get back to the UK.'

The magistrate mulled it over, turned to the police officer, asked if he had further evidence on any matters. None came.

I apologised to the court for my minor crime, the silly mistake of buying some cheap transmitters openly on sale in many local stores. I was fined HK$4,000.

It was going to take Superintendent McMahon a couple of days to get his finger out and return my passport. I headed back to the Mandarin where the manager asked to see me. He said the world's press had been camped out in the hotel for the last number of days and that it wasn't ideal. It was only then that we learned myself and my brother had made the newspapers in Hong Kong, the UK and elsewhere. All the talk was of a spying scandal at a five-star hotel, all these reports about my brother being on-the-run. The manager politely suggested I go to a less 'well-known' hotel. I checked in at the Hilton over the road under a false name.

Soon afterwards, I spotted some of the same police officers who had searched my room in the Mandarin milling around in the Hilton.

Of course…

They were to follow me, locate my brother, arrest both, play one off each other and build the conspiracy case they longed for. That would have suited my client's enemies down to the ground.

Double checking my hunch, I went shopping, to a restaurant, some other places—and my unwelcome buddies were close behind every step of the way.

Jim, who had assumed I'd be on my way home by this stage, set up a discreet meeting for me, him and Stuart in Kowloon. It took me an hour to shake off my escort by jumping on and off the Star Ferry but I made it. Unexpectedly, Jim arrived disguised as a woman. Or maybe more like a dishevelled transvestite. Stuart, hiding out in a B&B, showed up in more standard gear.

Jim's first words were of apology for his outfit and then for the position we were in. But he said the evidence we had secured gave him all the cards in terms of his court case, and that he was in our debt. He said the issue now was that we could be subpoenaed over our making of the recording of a conspiracy to murder him. As soon as my passport was returned I must, he said, fly to Bangkok. Stuart, who remained a wanted man, would surrender to police alongside Bernard and, assuming they could do little to him alone, he would fly to Taiwan. I'd meet him there later. The Hong Kong authorities could not subpoena us from Taiwan. And besides, Jim's firm had a few nice hotels there.

The police did grill Stuart when he walked into the station after my safe escape, but he made no comment and they let him go. At Jim's insistence, and expense, we later lived it up as free men at a five-star hotel in Taipei for a fortnight before making our way home.

Later reports told how the Faber Merlin case had been settled out of court. Few knew that the background included the recording of a recognisable Chinese male voice discussing, in the presence of an English QC, a plan to murder Jim Raper. He went on to receive almost two million shares in the British company Saint Piran, just over one-third of its issued share capital, as part of the settlement. In turn he relinquished any further interest in Faber Merlin.

A few months later we met him in London. He had already paid us handsomely, but said he wanted to pay us again. He asked us to think of it as a 'cash bonus'. It was enough for Stuart and I to buy a small hotel in Brighton, the lease for a busy pub in Worthing and a house in Sussex. A house each, that is.

And, for good measure, I splashed out on a personal ambition—a sublime light-grey Daimler Sovereign. Stuart got himself a beautiful wine-red 4.2 litre Jaguar.

There was still cash leftover. I was thirty-three. I'd never had as much money in my life. Despite getting dragged through the papers, this independent private investigator thing had never felt more promising.

TWO

The Path to PI (1940s/50s)

ADOLF Hitler tried to blow my family to Kingdom Come in the war. The London street where we lived was hit during the Luftwaffe's relentless bombing when I was little more than a baby. A house just down the road was flattened. Everyone inside was killed. We were told in the times ahead that the children there had been moved to the countryside just before. I knew it wasn't true.

I'd been born about twenty-five miles from the capital in St Albans, Hertfordshire, a quiet, pretty little English city. My mother was moved out of London after becoming pregnant. I arrived in 1941 and was quickly christened. They rushed it along in those days. The infant mortality rates were already sky high and, I suppose, no one knew which family might be wiped out next.

My first memories are of our family life at 138 Stanley Road in Carshalton, a small house in that scarred suburb of south London. I was the first of three brothers destined to take over the family business, a third-generation building contracting concern with a yard in Mitcham Junction.

In those war years, my dad was called up and posted to an RAF bomber station in Lincolnshire because of his skills. He was one of the forgotten heroes of the day. He never flew, never risked being shot out of the skies, but his hands refined and maintained the magnificent machines which helped propel the British towards victory. Aircraft would return mauled by enemy gunfire and unsung engineers, like my dad, made them fit for the fight once more. I'm forever proud of what he did in those terrible times.

My mum, despite the severe rationing, worked wonders to ensure me and my little brother Stuart were kept fed, entertained and loved right through those same difficult days. At times my grandmother or an aunt would show up with some eggs or a brace of rabbits or my dad would arrive with real bacon, the odd steak and even a toy or two when he got a rare pass from duty. Yet it was my mother who was always by our sides while air raid warnings screamed out into the night. I remember her being cool under pressure, how she would lead us confidently to the small iron, brick and concrete bomb shelter in the back garden. We would sit close under the grey military blankets, the small space low lit only by paraffin lamp, and wait for the horror of war to rain down again. The recollections are vivid.

That bombing which killed our neighbours left the street fogged with dusty, oily smoke and rubble, the air heavy with a sense of despair. I remember my mother was weeping uncontrollably as she picked me up and held me tight. She was unable and unwilling to explain the enormity of what had happened. Like many loving parents of those times, she saw no choice but to bottle up the madness of it all to protect puzzled minds.

In the years that followed, my dad's business, D Withers & Sons, really began to thrive. We ended up moving to an historic gatehouse named The Lodge in Hackbridge, between Mitcham and Sutton in south London. Stuart and I relished the large back garden where dad's stores of sand, ballast and gravel became our adventure playground. It was clear even then that he wanted us to apprentice into the building trades, to become the fourth Withers generation to inherit the business.

I was fifteen when he took me from Carshalton West School. Instead of formal education, he placed me with a Wimbledon joinery firm called Duffels and signed me up for a one day a week course at the local college. He told me the combination of on-job training and study would secure me a City & Guilds Certificate. Then he gave me a bike and told me to get on with it. In the meantime, so did he. To the surprise of everyone, a third brother, Charlie, arrived that same year.

I didn't like my new life. I was something close to an indentured servant at Duffels, labouring under a contract that gave me no reasonable way out. Dad would bellow me out of bed at 6.30 am, send me off on the forty-minute ride to working days that bored me witless. It got a little better the following year when I was able to go back and forward on my new AJS 500cc motorbike, but the journey was always more fun than the job.

In 1960 he gave me another shove, this time into the ranks of the Territorial Army, the part-time British Army Reserve force. He said it was the patriotic thing to do, an unrivaled way to get some real discipline into one's life. He said I had a habit of thriving through difficulty, that I was the kind of lad who fell 'into cesspits and came up smelling of roses,' and was sure I'd be fine. So I duly signed up with the Army's 624 Light Anti-Aircraft Regiment in Morden, Surrey. My number was, is, and forever will be 23741406.

In the meantime, I figured out that to break free from the grind at Duffels I would need to get that City & Guilds Certificate sooner rather than later. I changed colleges, studied harder and, two years earlier than the planned five, secured the qualification. I quit the firm right away.

I hadn't much else going on so, despite reservations, joined the family business. It didn't work out so well, and I had expected as much. My father's two partners, his brothers, did not relish the idea that the young and inexperienced me would be heir to the family business. It all got a little heated between my dad and uncles. There was the odd exchange of punches in the backyard, black eyes and bloody noses in the workplace, days of foul moods and dirty looks—an early lesson in the ways of family businesses.

But I was loving the TA. I relished the move from physical training into the more challenging military exercises. As with everyone else, I got shouted at a lot, ordered around all the time and told to work harder, but I can't say I was unfamiliar with any of that.

After a while, I was transferred to the RT Unit which specialised in radio communications. We were sent zooming off on motorbikes and fast vehicles ahead of our mobile radar units and anti-aircraft guns. The missions were to get behind 'enemy lines' in the fields and mountains of the west of England. We'd set up surveillance points in the hills, use binoculars to spot incoming aircraft (in our case, drones), radio back the target coordinates. The guns would lock on and, if we'd got it right, blow them out of the sky. Of all the things in my life at the time, this was the most thrilling.

One of the more memorable ventures was in Bude, Cornwall, after a few of us secured passes to explore the town. Inevitably, we ended up in the pub. A kindly barman introduced us to Scrumpy, the brain-mashing local cider. Some hours later I came round while being angrily shaken by a clergyman. I looked at him baffled, head pounding, as he barked, 'What the hell do you think you're doing?' I had to look around to find out. Beside me, on the steps of the vicarage, lay a fully asleep yet half-dressed young lady. She was, awkwardly enough, his daughter. I was reported, confessed the lot and was confined to barracks for three days. But it was worth it. Probably.

Unexpectedly, my honesty around that event led to me being promoted from Gunner to Lance-Bombardier. And the step forward meant I'd get paid a little more too. Relishing the new position, I became more and more involved in the TA. But although it was part-time, my weekend disappearances on exercise were causing conflict back at the firm. That bothered me. I wanted out.

Aged 19, I teamed up with Tony Dent, a fellow apprentice I'd got to know at Duffels, and we launched our own business—Building Joinery Services, or BJS. Stuart had been away in the Merchant Navy and, after a voyage on the seven seas, also signed up with the new company.

The timing was good. The swinging sixties were getting underway, a post-war building boom was in full flight and Prime Minister Harold McMillan had told us we had 'never had it so good.' At the same time, the government was rethinking military budgets and unfortunately my 624 Light Anti-Aircraft Regiment Royal Artillery got the chop. I was transferred to an infantry regiment, the City of London Battalion, Royal Fusiliers, where I trained up as an Army Light Rescue Instructor—a skill-set seen as important in an era when the threat of nuclear war was moving into the picture. Promoted to full Corporal and with two years in the TA under my belt, I was later offered a place on officer training. I loved the TA, thought about it long and hard, but BJS was on the rise. It was one or the other. With a heavy heart, I left the British Army.

Across London, with the buoyant economy of the day, rundown back street property was morphing into yuppie apartments and townhouses. Myself, Tony and Stuart knew it was time to make the most of it. Before long we were working every day and night of the week, and most weekends too.

In late 1961 we quoted on a contract to convert a substantial old property at 99 Clarendon Road, Bayswater, into four small luxury apartments. The client was a man by the name of John White and, foolishly, we assumed he was as straight with us as we were with him. He asked us to complete the conversion fast so his company, John White Construction, could recoup their investment.

Over five months we threw everything we had at the job. We brought in tradespeople galore—labourers, plasterers, electricians, plumbers, bricklayers and higher-end craftsmen to get it just right. John White duly paid our interim bills and we had no concerns.

Prospects good, money in the pocket, my life belting forward, I began seeing Rita and we knew we were falling for each other. We decided to make the most of all that was going on and get married. In those days you needed parental consent to get hitched if you were under twenty-one. Maddeningly, in an unnecessary blow to my independence, my dad said no. But nothing could stop the march of time. I moved in with Rita at her parents' home in New Malden and, in the spring of 1962, after I turned twenty-one, we were wed. Wonderful news followed soon after— our first baby was on the way.

One day in the middle of that year John White didn't show up. We had no cash to pay the workers. We tried, but couldn't reach him. We shut down the site. I went to the bank to request an urgent loan, but they said no. Thankfully my father-in-law came to the rescue, stood in as guarantor and the bank relented.

But it was a bad situation. More a case of *roses to cesspits* than the other way around. Two weeks passed and we still hadn't heard back from White. We had been plunged into a £2,000 debt with no idea what to do. Tony, Stuart and I met. I said I was going to sort this. Whatever it took, I would take time out and find the elusive Mr White.

There was no social media or online resources back then. If you wanted to track someone down, you had to get numbers, make the calls, pound a few streets. I knew little about the man, only that he was from the Sutton area. It was enough to start with. I asked around, kept my cards close to my chest, approached a few people, said I was an old friend, a one time colleague, an old classmate from school. I was aware I was telling what you might call a *white lie*, but I had no issue with it. I was setting out to right a wrong. Being economical with the truth in order to chase down someone who had abandoned their obligations was fine by me. In fact, PIs have a word for it—*pretexting*. I didn't know the term at the time, but it was about to become very significant.

So, via pretext, it didn't take long to narrow the field. I'd heard Mr White still lived with his folks, that he was likely to be at the family home. I found out where they lived and went for a look. It gave me a real boost to know I was close to getting our man.

I called Stuart, told him to meet me there. Two cars would be better than one. Off I went, parked myself close by and waited. After a few hours, White showed. He walked out of the house, got into his car for the two or three mile drive to Wallington. Our plan was to box him in, me in front and Stuart behind—and it worked. Our runaway client broke down right away, told us of his troubles. It wasn't pretty. We took him to a nearby cafe and bought him a coffee, talked it all over. Despite our success in locating him, we had no chance of getting the money we needed to secure the building firm.

My baby was on the way. We were up to our eyes in debt. I had to make a decision.

'I have to go,' I told Stuart and Tony. 'I need a job.'

That night in 1962, dejected and troubled, with no real idea of my next step, an advert in the paper caught my eye.

'Wanted: Trainee Investigators—ring Kingston Detective Agency.'

THREE

Learning the Ropes (1962/63)

Pretext—noun.

A pretended reason for doing something that is used to hide the real reason.

Cambridge Dictionary.

'Now! Now! Get here now!'

Barrie Quartermain, my boss. This was my cue. My job: on his command I was to climb out of the attic pronto, dash into the bedroom, witness the errant husband in action with his secretary.

I'd heard the couple talking below, had an idea at what stage they were at in their bonding, knew I had to be ready. But after a few hours up there in the dark, pouring sweat, breathing stale air and busting for a pee, I wasn't as finely tuned as I'd hoped to be. It was 11 pm. My limbs were a muddle.

At Barrie's shout from below, I leapt to my feet, ducking to avoid the rafters, adrenaline surging as I made my dash for the exit. Then a crunch—my shoe (left one, I think), straight through the ceiling. The couple in the bed below were terrified. Splinters, plaster and dust rained down. In a panic I tried to rescue my wayward foot, but it got worse. The whole leg plunged downwards. Then the right foot lost its place, the right leg following. In a second, half my body had crashed into the room below. I don't remember if I yelled or screamed or if they yelled or screamed, but someone did.

The poor couple was stunned; the image I saw was like a freeze frame of them in early copulation, faces agog. Barrie, hiding in another room and figuring I'd blundered, burst through the door. Blinding flashes followed as he snapped the pictures. He only just avoided having my legs in the frame.

And then a moment where everyone looked at everyone else.

'What the hell,' said the rudely interrupted husband, 'is going on?'

His job done, Barrie took hold of my legs, guided me downwards and onto the bed. I arrived sheepishly between the couple before, as politely as I could, I removed myself from the bed.

Barrie told the man we were 'inquiry agents' acting on behalf of his wife. She suspected, Barrie explained, that the man was using the family home for his ongoing fling with his secretary. As he and his mistress continued to stare in disbelief, Barrie added that the actions taking place in the bedroom, up until the moment we arrived, would be reported to his wife's solicitors.

I stood there, coated with dust, wondering if it was possible to drop dead from embarrassment.

Barrie nudged me. I looked at him.

'My colleague,' he said, 'will ask you some questions.'

It all rushed into my head. I had some lines to say. I cleared my throat as four wide eyes turned to me. 'Sir,' I said, 'I'm obliged to tell you that you do not need to say anything unless you wish to do so, and anything that you do say may be used in divorce proceedings. Would you like to make a statement in writing, admitting your adultery?'

The man and his not unattractive conquest stayed fixed on my youthful, yet blushed and dusty face. Their body language under those sheets, or lack of it, made it plain that both were stark naked.

The householder's first point was, reasonably enough, that I had just wrecked his ceiling. We let him vent for a bit about that, knowing he would get to the issue at hand.

'And okay,' he said, rage subsiding, 'I understand why my wife let you in here.'

He said the marriage had been over for years and admitted the lot. He added that our intervention would serve to speed the formalities along.

That done, his secretary gracefully removed herself from her boss's bedroom, disappeared to get dressed, went downstairs and, very thoughtfully, made everyone tea.

An uncontested divorce followed. The man's wife, who had headed off with the kids for the weekend, was delighted. She later invited Barrie and I to lunch at the Savoy Hotel in London. The ceiling issue, she said, was not an issue.

I recovered from my embarrassment by telling myself it had been a lesson in life. Stay alert because, like it or not, every chance to take a step forward is also a chance to put your foot in it.

That day, a few months before, when I had spotted the advert had already changed my life. And it would change it a good deal more in the years ahead.

'Wanted Trainee Investigators—ring Kingston Detective Agency.'

I'd been thrilled just to see it. The chance to train up as a Private Investigator? Just the thought had lifted the cloud from above my head. I'd checked my watch right away. It was 9 pm. But, heart drumming, I called anyway.

A woman spoke, cut-glass accent, 'Kingston Detective Agency. May I help you?'

'Yes,' I said, very professionally, 'I'd like to apply for the trainee position.'

'Fine,' she said, curtly, 'come at 10 am tomorrow for an interview.'

I arrived bang on time at *Kingston Detective Agency*, 92 Tudor Drive, Kingston Upon Thames. I expected an office yet this was a semi-detached private house. A pleasant-looking homely lady opened the front door. She told me she was Pat, wife of the owner, PI Barrie Quartermain.

Nothing inside was as I'd imagined from the outside. The front of the property, upstairs and down, had been converted to offices. The place was a hive of activity. People were working at desks, opening and closing grey filing drawers, typing reports, taking and making calls. A glass-fronted cabinet to one side was filled with impressive-looking cameras, zoom lenses, tape recorders and other gadgets essential to the trade. I was thrilled, but gave nothing away. And besides, I was not alone. As I waited in the hallway as instructed, the bell rang again and again and again. Every few minutes another young man would arrive, another pair of eyes to be surprised by what lay behind the front door.

Mrs Quartermain walked me upstairs and into a luxurious office. It was truly astonishing. I found myself looking at quilted ceilings, chandeliers, silk wallpaper, plush red carpets, beautiful antique furnishings, numerous ornaments and artifacts from around the globe—it was totally over the top.

Yet, despite the surroundings, the room was dominated by an imperious, gleaming desk that took up a third of the floor-space. Behind it, on a chair only a man of great confidence could sit, was the captain of the ship—Barrie Quartermain. Known to many as BQ, he was a sleek, fit, lean, slightly receding and somehow jovial-looking man of about forty. He was already smiling broadly as I entered and I smiled broadly back. He asked me to sit, advised me to relax and I told him I would.

He got straight down to business. He said his firm had been running for ten years, that it had three areas of work.

One: General investigations. Miscellaneous work, charged by the hour.

Two: Commercial investigations. Mainly locating debtors and repossessing assets for banks and utilities. Fixed fees paid on results.

Three: Media work, arranged through a sister company, *Kingston News Agency*. Mostly involved chasing up leads from national newspapers. Payment based on the newsworthiness of the story.

And now it was my turn.

I told him I'd been in the TA, said I had gathered intelligence while on military exercises and that this, I was sure, was useful in terms of turning my hand to the work of a PI. I told him too about finding John White, that I had been adaptable during the search, that I had used instinct and intuition to find out what I needed to know. I added, at the end, that it had been rewarding in itself just to locate him.

BQ gave nothing away but I felt it went well. I was excited while driving back to New Malden, wondering what might be ahead if it worked out.

As the day closed, a call from BQ's Commercial Manager, Valerie Jackson.

'Please report to work tomorrow at 9 am, Mr Withers,' she said. 'You have secured a trainee position.'

Over tea and toast at the Quartermain's, Barrie introduced me to Mike Linguard, who was also starting on a three-month trial. He said we'd be working at the commercial end of things. Each agent, he said, had their own patch in London and each was expected to work it exclusively and vigorously. In short, I would be tracking down people like my old friend John White—people who had fled from debts or absconded with secured property. I had to get them either to pay up or hand over their cars, TV sets or whatever they had defaulted on.

Two locations needed covered. Mike took south east London, where he had grown up. I was given west London. I didn't know at the time that, due to a higher number of transients, short-term renters, and sometimes hard-to-track migrants—mainly Irish, African and Caribbean, it was an unpopular patch with other agents. But I was happy enough. I knew the ground to some extent having worked with locals for five months on the John White project. The only immediate issue was that west London hadn't been serviced for weeks—there was a lot of catching up to do.

At first I was guided by Valerie. We packed files into her car and set off for debtors' doors. The job was to find out if the person was there and, if not, to find out where they'd gone. And all the way along, it was wise to hide true intentions—there are few occasions when debt collectors are wise to say they're debt collectors. It was all about thinking on your feet, adapting to circumstance, winning people over.

Just two days later, Valerie waved me off with fifty cases to crack. I knew it was a heavy load and that I was unlikely to make major inroads in a short time, but I was damn sure I was going to do as good a job as I could. After thinking about tactics, I went first not to the doors on the list, but instead to a pub in Ladbroke Grove, close to Bayswater. I'd been in there often with Tony and Stuart. Most of the punters were Africans or Jamaicans and we had taken on quite a few during the John White job.

After some quiet conversations, I had piqued the interest of one or two people—some new faces, some I already knew. A few agreed to help me find some people. No one needed to know why and I didn't volunteer much about what I was up to. What I was clear about was that every little bit of usable information would be rewarded.

In the days that followed, things weren't working out. Many debtors had pre-planned their disappearance, made a good job of covering their tracks. And there was a natural suspicion about me, a random bloke calling at doors and asking questions. I found it a little frustrating, found myself questioning how sure I was about the quality of my instincts in terms of this trade. After all, this was many people's idea of hell—chasing down debtors, being the unwelcome guy in unwelcoming places. Had I made a foolish decision?

I trudged back to the pub in Ladbroke Grove, unsure about how I was feeling about all of this, my wife and our future child on my mind. I had asked for help with thirty-five of the fifty cases and hoped for at least a handful of decent leads. As I went to collect up what I could from that, I was stunned. I left the pub that day with thirty new addresses. It was nothing short of an astonishing result. Just when I needed a lift, I was lifted sky high. My gut feeling had been right. My patter and pretext had won over and focused minds.

Off I went, knocked the right doors, often stunned the people I'd been looking for. If I wasn't getting the person themselves, I was getting the next best thing—a close relative, partner, friend. When I wasn't collecting cash, I was collecting televisions and a host of other items, filling up my minivan in no time.

As a trainee, I was paid a flat rate of £10 a week and took ten percent commission for each successful trace. Ever after paying off my invaluable sources at the pub, my wage had rocketed. My boss was chuffed, the firm's clients were delighted.

So out I went again. I kept on working, kept on knocking the doors, kept engaging my contacts, charming whoever I needed to charm. I didn't let up and, when it came to results, it showed over and over again. Each Friday Barrie would beam as I submitted my positive traces. He happily handed me my fees and commission.

'If you keep this up Ian,' he said, 'you'll be a manager before you know it.'

I used the phone to reach neighbours and subjects, sourcing numbers from wherever I could get them—contacts, snitches, phone books, electoral lists at public libraries, post offices, even police stations. One useful method was to find the debtor's previous street address in the register of voters, then get the names of near neighbours. From there, I'd go to the phone book to see if I could get a few numbers, ring them with a suitable story, ask if they knew where my friend or workmate or relative had gone.

I can't say it was all good fun—far from it. The successes were great and, now a young father to Debbie, it felt good to be moving up the ladder. Yet I was always working alone in what could be tense situations. While a lot of people were polite and held their hands up, I was also coming up against people who were at testing times in their lives, who were at their wit's end. I faced aggressive people, daytime drunks and others who had little time for the repo man. I was routinely threatened, shoved around a little and that wasn't exactly what I wanted from a day's work. Yet while I might not have been what you'd call a bruiser, I was a sturdy enough bloke. I'd laboured on building sites, been in the thick of army training, had a long-running interest in sailing that kept me fit. I could handle myself if needed. In fact, as one or two people found out, I was pretty handy at judo too. I'd kept it up at a local club since leaving school and could remain vertical when it counted.

Yet in the end, the best way through for a man in my position was to always be calm, always be polite and always show sympathy for the debtor's predicament. And then to make sure they understood they had an obligation to meet and that I could be a hard man to get rid of.

I learned ways to sweet-talk car keys into my hand or a television into my van, succeeding to the point sometimes that debtors would offer to help carry the large and heavy TV's of the era to the ground floor. Pleased with myself, I agreed to that once or twice. And they'd pretend to trip, cause the TV to fall and crash its way downstairs as the gas-filled tubes exploded and showered the place with glass. Another lesson learned.

My territory began to expand from west to north and eventually into east London. I was aiming high every day, building a network district by district. Pretexting was becoming second nature to me, learning the dark art on the job, being bullish and confident about whatever it was I needed to say to get whatever needed done. I think back and can say for sure that I never really thought I was being in any way underhand, never that I was playing fast and loose with ethics. I was on the trail of people who knew what would happen if they welshed on a deal.

After a few months, Barrie invited me out on other general investigations, usually at nights or weekends. Much of it came down to cheating spouses—husbands or wives needing the proof of adultery that the courts required to grant a divorce. It was not enough to say two people were locked together in a hotel room for eight hours. We needed evidence, and no evidence was stronger than a snap of a half-naked couple in the sack. I look back sometimes uncomfortably on that part of it all, but the way the law worked was less than ideal. The wronged spouse needed the court for a divorce and the court needed the evidence to grant it. As often happened, the court made a point of telling men like me that it was not impressed with our methods, while the relieved spouse couldn't thank us enough—even if I had made an Ian Withers-sized hole in their ceiling.

From there BQ promoted me to Commercial Investigations Manager at his new offices in High Street, Kingston upon Thames. This would put me behind a desk for the first time and I'd get to deal with the clients. I learned how to sell our trade to people in need, how to work out the fees, assign jobs to agents, vet results, prepare bills and reports for clients. I'd often work twelve-hour days in that role and it wasn't exactly riveting, yet it was central to the good running of the business and I took every detail on board.

At home, the issue with the loan to pay the debt left by John White was getting difficult. The bank was pressing my father-in-law for settlement and he was pressing me. The problem was I'd only been able to make a few repayments and full payment of the balance was still a way off. I'd been making better money than before, but my parental outgoings had increased and I didn't have much spare. It got me thinking about moving in a different direction, taking what skills I had learned and seeing if I could make them work in a steadier job with a clearer progression up through the ranks, a career that the average bank manager might look upon more favourably.

For the second time, an advert in the local paper caught my eye. Surrey Police were recruiting and, as serendipity would have it, had just dropped the height requirement from six feet to five feet eight. I might just make it.

I was called for an interview after a few days of home exercises in which I tried to make myself stand a little taller. I showed up at Mount Browne, Guildford, the headquarters of the Surrey Constabulary, with my head stretched up as high as it would go. There was an educational exam, a medical, a physical test and, a few weeks later, I was in.

Rita was delighted, saying it felt like a real step forward in terms of our independence as a family unit. We would have the opportunity to take a house offered by the constabulary as part of the deal and could now move out of the pressure cooker environment of her parents' house.

Barrie was disappointed and right away offered me more money. But my mind was made. I told him I had to do what I knew to be the right thing. After two instructive years with his firm, we parted on good terms.

As I left the office for the last time, he handed me an envelope—£100 cash.

He said, 'Your desk will always be here for you.'

FOUR

Police Constable Withers (1964/65)

A SUDDEN gear change. No longer was I duty-bound to act for clients, I was now under orders to act on behalf of the great British public. Every drunk shouting outside the pub, every motorist who drove carelessly or didn't pay their road tax, every suspicious-looking individual everywhere would now become of interest to me, *PC899*.

It turned out to be a great grounding for the investigative career that followed. A person can learn a lot about themselves when charged with arresting and detaining citizens, when first on the scene after a death, when they witness a man having passionate sex with a sheep.

My first arrest came after a few weeks on duty alongside an experienced copper called Eddy. We'd been paired after my training finished. My job was to walk and cycle alongside him as he imparted advice. Off we went to a host of incidents on our patch including minor accidents, traffic violations, burglaries, fights, sudden deaths and domestics. We had no way to communicate with the station other than via public telephones. When out and about, we would regularly dial in to check for updates. And, of course, between calls we were tasked with handling whatever we came across while plodding the beat.

The face of one young lad I had dealings with has remained with me all these years. His name was Lynne Tame and, very early on in my new role, I pulled him in after he failed to stop on his bicycle. There had been a stop sign, but he had ignored it, pedaled right onto a main route. Lynne was very unhappy with my intervention and chastisement, but he needed to be told. His name went into my pocket book and we left it at that. I didn't expect I'd ever see him again.

I learned quickly how useful those pocket books were. Issued to every constable, they became little goldmines of information when used right. There were fewer cars around in those days and it became second nature to record the number plates of vehicles being driven badly, parked illegally or spotted close to scenes of crimes. That could often be a real head start in terms of eliminating or confirming the presence of a vehicle when a fuller picture of what had been going on might emerge. In fact, I found jotting down numbers and other notes to be so useful that I put plenty of effort into developing the habit. It turned out to be nothing less than invaluable in the career that followed, and indeed in terms of writing this very book.

Anyway, much as I was absorbing all I could about life on the beat, in those early days I wasn't exactly filling up the station's holding cells with crooks.

Eddy turned to me one evening. 'I think you're ready to go out alone on tomorrow's early shift,' he said.

I wasn't so sure, but I'd give it a good go. I was about to thank him for his insights when he added, 'I am quite concerned, however, because we have been doing this for a few weeks together and in that time you haven't made a single arrest.

'Tonight is the last night I'm with you. I want you to make an arrest to determine that you know the procedure and the caution and to give me confidence you can handle things properly.'

We set off on foot, my eyes sharp, ears open and heart stout in search of a crime. I was determined to make an arrest yet the good people of Surrey seemed equally determined to stay on the right side of the law. As the night dragged on, neither of us saw anyone who needed nabbing.

Heading towards midnight, Eddy said, 'Come with me. I've an idea.'

I was intrigued. Arrests on demand? A place where wayward citizens gather to commit crime? We set off towards the cinema in Walton and, just as people were exiting after the last show, he pointed.

'You see the newspaper vendor's stand?'

I did.

'The vendor's gone home but leaves newspapers out and trusts people to put money in the slot. As sure as it rains in England, it won't take long for someone to grab a paper without paying.'

This sounded like a job for me.

Eddy went on, 'Arrest the first person who doesn't pay and that will get your name in the station daybook in red ink. When the inspector checks the book in the morning, he'll know you do actually exist.'

Moments later, a couple of students wandered from the cinema. I could see both were eyeing a paper with devious criminal intent. And, sure enough, both paused, took one each, and walked off.

'One moment please lads,' said I, pacing their way, my voice fulsome and authoritative. 'I just saw you take a newspaper from that stand without paying.'

A desperate face turned to me, a young man in shock. He said, 'But it's nearly midnight mate—they're out of date.'

'That's not the point,' I said. 'The newspaper belongs to the vendor who no doubt will receive a refund for papers not sold. I have no option but to arrest you for the larceny of the newspaper.' And then, for the first time, I followed up with the grave words, 'I must warn you that you do not have to say anything...'

I firmly grabbed an arm of each and marched them to the police station just along the street. They were cautioned and released and I had broken my duck. Yet, in truth, the surge of pride I felt in seeing *PC899* in red ink in the station daybook was flattened by the pang of shame I felt for ruining the night for two decent young men over such a minor issue.

As I settled into the role, I applied to the divisional motorcyclist section. I'd been on motorbikes since I was sixteen and it seemed like a great option. The bikes at that time were 500cc Triumphs, black with white fairings, *POLICE* emblazoned across the front. I had no problem during the test, got in straight away.

I relished patrolling the countryside, keeping an eye out for trouble, the relative romance and independence of riding around on a great looking bike. One day I was sent to Hersham Road in Walton on Thames, the scene of a serious road traffic accident. A motorcycle had slammed into a motorcar turning out from a side street. The bike was buried into the car door and the pillion rider had catapulted over the top. As I pulled up, the rider was being looked after but I couldn't see the other man anywhere. A few people had gathered, all in shock at what they'd seen.

'Where's the pillion rider?' I asked.

No one knew.

I looked at the hedging on Hersham Road. Some of it had been damaged just across from where we were. I pulled a few branches back and there lay a crumpled body. It was the cyclist I had ticked off in my first few days, the lad by the name of Lynne Tame. His neck had been snapped. My heart sank. I'd never seen anything like it. At least the young man had not suffered.

I was transferred to Chertsey Police Station, allocated one of two detached police houses beside each other in the pretty village of New Haw. A separate police office, complete with desk, filing cabinet, telephone and interlinking doors, had been built between the two homes. It was there that I really began to make inroads in paying the debt I owed to my father-in-law, thanks to the bankability of a job in uniform. And it was there that, in the summer of 1965, our second child, Andrew, came into the world.

One morning, when heading into Chertsey, I remember riding over a bridge when some people waved me down. They were focused on events in a field. At first glance it seemed to be a Wellington-booted farmer at his work, tending his sheep, but there was something about the way his body was gyrating…

It soon became clear. He had raised the rear legs of the poor sheep into the air and, in the middle of a wide open space, was brazenly and energetically thrusting away.

'Hey!' I yelled. 'You there, what are you doing?'

As if I didn't know.

The gentleman, committed to his lovemaking, took no notice. I called in the incident on the bike's two-way radio, scaled the fence and trudged through mud and dung to reach him as fast as I could. Children were among those watching this awful scene and I wanted to bring it to an end as fast as possible.

He turned, spotted me, withdrew himself from the baffled creature and dashed off while trying to tuck himself away. I didn't let up and caught him a little further along.

His first words were, 'Good morning officer.'

'What on earth do you think you're doing?' I fumed.

'I'm not doing anything.'

'I saw you with my own two eyes, sir. I'm arresting you for the offence of bestiality.'

I cautioned him, took him by the arm but he resisted. A little struggle ensued and both of us fell into the muck and sheep shit. Eventually I got him cuffed and dragged him to the roadside. He resisted all the way and the whole messy thing took much longer than it should have. People were laughing and cheering as I got him out of the field. And by this stage, one of the smiling observers was my sergeant.

'PC Withers,' he said, 'that is the most amusing arrest I have ever seen.'

Unfortunately, he wasn't feeling amused enough to let either of us into his car. In fact, he wouldn't even take a hold of the man so I could wipe the crap from my uniform. Shortly after, a van arrived to take the sheep shagger away. It turned out he was a psychiatric patient who had just fled from Chertsey's Botley Park Mental Hospital. Not in full possession of his senses, he faced no charges.

A mind-boggling thing to witness yet the depths to which human behaviour can sink can just keep on surprising. I won't forget the morning sitting at home when the police office bell rang next door. An enraged man and a girl, aged about ten, had arrived seeking help.

He said, 'My daughter has been sexually assaulted.'

I brought them into the office and, as Rita made tea, called CID given they investigated sex offences. No officers were available. I got on with taking the details.

The little girl and her friend had been approached by a young man on a red motorcycle two days before. He lured the child into the bushes and molested her. The girl had only just found the strength to tell her mum and dad. I got a reasonable description of the assailant and, at the request of CID, carried on with the investigation. I knew the offender had been riding a red motorcycle and was wearing dark blue. Could this be one of the uniformed Post Office riders who rode the red bikes?

I contacted the local sorting office who worked out there had been three telegram boys on duty. Only one had been working in the area in question. I called at his door, told him what I was investigating and he blushed. He denied all knowledge saying he hadn't been there that day. I took him to Chertsey Police Station, talked sympathetically with him and he broke down, admitted the crime.

It was the most significant investigation of my time in the police and I was proud to have seen it through. But I can't tell you how disappointed I was to learn the young man would not be prosecuted. Why? He was about to join the army, and a conviction would spoil his chances. I was appalled.

On saying that, I did let someone go myself after pulling him over for speeding. I told the man I'd tailed him for a while and he had been a whole 30 mph over the 40 mph limit. About to read him the riot act, I realised he had a police radio in the car.

I asked, 'Is this a police vehicle?'

'Son,' he said, 'I am your chief constable.'

It felt like a colossal blunder on my part and I apologised, let him drive on. A few days later I had a ticking off from an inspector for not reporting my boss. I explained I believed it was an on-duty police vehicle, although it turned out to have been his own car.

While still a probationary constable, I took the opportunity to get assigned to CID. It meant plain clothes and, most of the time, nine-to-five hours. I got comfortable quickly after being tasked with tracking down some bail-jumpers and missing migrants whose visas had expired. Instead of the standard door knocking at relatives' houses, I got myself a phone and a quiet corner of the station and went to work.

I found fast that many officials are only too willing to assist when the police call. And in terms of the people who feel the other way inclined when they hear the law on the phone, I involved myself once more in a little pretext or two. It was a questionable yet certainly useful tactic.

My successes went down well even among the hard-bitten and time-served members of CID. My confidence in being able to handle that end of the work buoyed me up and I got to thinking about my future.

And right about that time, an old friend called the station. It was Barrie Quartermain. He asked to meet for a chat and I have to say I was suspicious, a little concerned he might try to recruit me as a source inside the police. But he had other plans.

He had just bought out another detective agency in Surbiton, Surrey. It was, he believed, the largest commercial investigation agency in the UK and provided tracing, court document serving, repossessions and bailiff services across London and beyond.

He looked me in the eye and said, 'Would you like to be general manager of Southern Provincial Investigations Ltd? I'd start you on a two-year contract at £1,000 per year plus ten percent of the sales over a baseline each month. Your expenses will be covered, a car allowance paid and we would assist with a house.'

In 1965, a brand-new car cost around £600. A small house in outer London cost around £6,000. There was no doubt about it, £1,000 was a fine salary.

I asked for everything in writing and BQ obliged. I signed on the spot.

On my last day as a copper, my inspector wished me well with whatever lay ahead.

As I left the building he said, 'Ian. Always remember you were a police officer. Always act accordingly.'

It was advice I'd never forget.

FIVE

The Jeremy Thorpe Case (1965)

AT the end of 1965 I was back in civvies and back on the payroll for the irrepressible Barrie Quartermain. It had been a big decision to leave the police, a tricky one to negotiate given I had a young family. Yet I knew I had drive, good instincts and a confidence that was emerging like never before. And I knew too that Barrie saw these things in me and wanted to make the most of them.

After buying out *Southern Provincial Investigations Ltd* in Surbiton, he had persuaded the owners to hang on for a couple of weeks to show me the ropes. It was a thriving business, founded by married couple Peter and Iris Heims, with more than twenty employees on the books. They were relatively young, in their late thirties, yet I remember they were surprised at the even more tender nature of my years. Looking around on that first day, I was aware of being the freshest face on the team. But I stood tall and told the Heims that the firm they had nurtured was in safe hands. At least I hoped so.

Their business focused exclusively on commercial investigations—tracking down debtors. There was no surveillance, no investigations into infidelity, nothing that a private individual might order. They worked for banks, finance companies, utility concerns, solicitors and others. One wing, the cheekily-initialled Commercial Investigations Department, did the digging. The other, the Bailiffs' Department, did the retrieving. All bailiffs were court certificated with ID confirming their authority to levy, seize and auction off goods and property to recover rent and rates. To keep everything above board, I got myself certificated too.

Over the years the Heims had built up a mammoth resource of news-paper cuttings, court and debtor lists. Two people were employed solely to clip names from newspapers and elsewhere to add to the tens of thousands of alphabetical index cards. It was a vast and ever-growing archive, an invaluable private library for investigators. More often than not, when new cases arrived we already had some background on the people in question. When we tracked down the person and served notice, we'd send a bill to the client. And if we couldn't find them, there was no bill. Yet success was much more common than defeat. Such was the system that, with the help of partner agencies, there was geographically nowhere in the UK we could not reach. If people wanted to hide from their debts, they had their work cut out for them.

BQ would land up at my new Surbiton office from time to time to discuss business. Never one to be inconspicuous, he'd swing his Rolls Royce in the no waiting zone right outside. He'd spring into the office and throw himself into Peter Heims' armchair, even before Peter had left the firm. He'd beam broadly and entertain us all with the workings of his mind.

Surbiton, he said, would continue doing what it did best—commercial investigations. And Kingston, he said, would focus on miscellaneous cases for private individuals or businesses. He'd continue to run Kingston and get first dibs on the agents. That made sense given that commercial work tended to be less time sensitive than the other operations.

I told BQ I had plans to streamline the operation, that the filing process worked well but could be less unwieldy. I said I was sure I could make it all move along faster and, as a result, bring in more money. In fact, I had come up with an idea I named the Automatic Tracing System. It would ensure things flowed better and that the danger of overlooking or misplacing a file, as had been happening, would be cut to a minimum.

I ran the ATS past BQ and then by the rest of the staff. There were some quizzical faces and, I think, some whispered suggestions I might be getting ahead of myself, but I wanted to give it a go. That said, I never had to convince Barrie that it had potential. His faith in me was constant and I appreciated it.

It was around this time, on a cold November morning, that I took a call from him in my office.

'Ian,' he said, 'BQ here. An important meeting in Kingston this morning. Need you here.'

He was meeting, he said, a 'VIP client' who had advised him the issue was a 'politically related and sensitive matter.' He had no more information than that.

Although bogged down in perfecting the ATS and securing the support of the Surbiton team, I was ever ready to clear the decks if needed. Not long afterwards I was on the road to Kingston, about ten minutes by car.

Two men had already arrived. I remember the atmosphere in BQ's office, as I walked in, was slightly tense. He introduced me to a well-dressed, middle-aged chap called Peter Bessell, a Liberal Party MP for Cornwall in the south west of England. The other man, who was much younger, was not introduced to me. He did not speak during the entire meeting.

Bessell asked Barrie and I to give an undertaking that nothing said in the room would leave the room. We agreed. He said he was speaking on behalf of the Liberal Party. It was seeking to locate a young man who had been issuing threats to a rising star in the party and in parliament by the name of Jeremy Thorpe. He said the man claimed to have had a gay affair with Thorpe, the MP for North Devon. I knew little about politics but I knew information of that kind at that time was enough to destroy any political career in the UK. I asked if this was a blackmail situation, wondering if the police had been brought in. Bessell said it was. He said the man in question, twenty-four-year-old Norman Josiffe, also known as Norman Scott, was demanding money in exchange for his silence. He said the police had not been informed. It was very much expected, he went on, that Thorpe would become the next leader of the Liberal Party and, very possibly, a future British prime minister. The party was seeking at all costs to protect its man and avoid scandal. It was therefore not inviting the police into its confidence.

I understood. Things were changing in Britain at the time but homosexuality was still illegal and would remain so until 1967. And Bessell gave me no reason to think the allegation against his friend and colleague was anything but legitimate. From what I was told that day, I got the impression the relationship was over and that the other party had turned to blackmail because he was not happy about that.

Bessell said Norman Josiffe, aka Norman Scott, was in the horse business. He said there was a good chance he was in Ireland where he had worked before. He gave over the names of some people Scott knew as possible starting points. He said if we were able to find him, we should encourage him to go to a meeting that would be arranged involving Bessell in Dublin.

After around forty minutes, we shook hands. Bessell and his anonymous colleague left the office. It seemed clear that two firsts were about to happen in my life—going on a plane and going to Ireland.

A couple of days later I was above the Irish Sea and fired up with confidence about the mission ahead. The plane touched down in Dublin Airport and off I went to pick up my rented mini, the coolest car of the times, and cruised my way towards Wynn's Hotel off the city's O'Connell Street.

I wasn't expecting to see quite so many priests in one place but it seemed as if dog-collared clerics were the key clientele at Wynn's. Many were enjoying a pint or two of Guinness at the bar and, curious about the famous Irish stout, I dropped off my suitcase and did the same.

The next morning, a little worse for wear, I got to work. I secured all the Irish telephone directories I could get and, after working the phones, friendly as can be, I was told the whereabouts of Norman Scott. He was, it was claimed, working at a small racehorse training yard south of Wexford town, about eighty miles away.

Powered by a huge breakfast, I was back in the mini and on the road again, moving through the gears as I sped through the scenic countryside towards Ireland's southeastern corner. There was no problem finding Wexford, but the stables were a different matter. The signpost situation was not exactly cutting edge. I had to ask for directions again and again, got lost along winding roads to nowhere, was almost tearing my hair out when I found myself driving up and down the same flippin' road two, three and four times. And all the while I could only hope the information that brought me there in the first place was accurate.

In the end persistence paid off. I caught sight of the training yard. I jammed on the brakes, reversed to the entrance and guided the mini up a narrow lane towards the stables across from the main house. I parked up and looked around, taking stock of all I could see. I had a gut feeling I was in the right place.

After a moment, I spotted a lad mucking out one of the stables. I got out and approached. He was surprised when he clocked me. And it hit me right away—he matched the description of Norman Scott.

'Is Norman around?' I asked, without any explanation, curious as to how he would react.

'Who are you?' he said, clearly startled. Just three words but that accent was English, not Irish.

I said I needed to find Norman Scott, that I was to advise him of a meeting in Dublin involving a VIP. It was vital that the details were passed on. And he became yet more anxious.

'Wait here,' he said. I told him I would.

A couple of minutes passed and I found myself chatting to a couple of horses, stroking a few noses. A couple more minutes came and went. Then a few more. By now I had to consider if the young man had done something of a disappearing act. He had not passed me and I could see no other way out. Could it be that he was hiding inside the main house? Had he legged it over some fields at the back?

I took a wander around the yard and saw three other people tending horses and mucking out stables. I spoke to each but none knew of a guy called Norman. An English girl grooming a horse said there was an English lad around, that he was visiting for a few days. She said she didn't know his name. I asked if she might check if he was at the house and we wandered up. She went in and returned saying there was no sign. By now I figured he had made his mind up not to speak with me. There wasn't much I could do about that. Yet I was almost certain he was Norman.

I left the yard feeling a little glum and headed back into Wexford. I called Barrie with the news.

'Don't worry,' he said, 'You could hardly be expected to put him in handcuffs and bring him back. Just go back to Dublin, and we'll see what happens.'

As I navigated northwards, Barrie put in a call to Peter Bessell to let him know. Unexpectedly, he already knew I had approached Scott. For the young man had called Bessell, hugely agitated, and ranted at him down the phone. He accused him of sending someone to Ireland to kill him. The story was, he insisted, that if he had not made himself scarce

I would have murdered him. I can only assume he thought I would do this with my bare hands in the stable yard, with witnesses around, after driving around Wexford in a distinctive mini asking questions for half the day. It was the most bonkers allegation I had yet faced in my life. But it did give me some insight into the wild mind of Norman Scott.

Nevertheless, Bessell had been able to get him to calm down and arrange for that important Dublin meeting to take place. And as a result, the prospects for a potential future prime minister could be getting brighter. He was more than happy with how the job had worked out.

Chuffed, I got back into the car and headed for Dublin. It had been an unusual day, one that would have indirect implications in the corridors of power in the UK in the years ahead. But I couldn't have known that at the time.

As I drove north of Wexford town, I noticed an open horsebox at the side of the road ahead. A man was leading horses into a field. A motorbike coming from the other direction roared past just as I was closing in. One of the horses was startled. It bolted right into the road. I jammed the brakes but it was too late. My mini slammed into this beautiful creature. The memory is sketchy and difficult but this huge animal seemed to turn over on the tiny bonnet right in front of me. Its head punched the windscreen, scattering glass all around as my foot pinned the brake pedal to the floor. When the car finally stopped, I was breathless. It was a horrifying, haunting scene. The Irish police, or Gardai, arrived. And a vet was brought in to put the poor creature to sleep at the side of the road. I was there for three awful hours while everything was sorted out. For all of that time I was distressed and upset and, thinking back on it today, I feel the same.

Back in London, Barrie's big smile awaited me at the debrief. I explained everything, including about the accident, and we talked over what had been a memorable trip. He told me Peter Bessell had paid the bill in cash immediately on receipt and that he had sent along a personal note of thanks.

It emerged later that the meeting between the two men went ahead. They had agreed a payment plan which ensured Scott would not speak publicly of his relationship with Thorpe. At least for a while.

Two years later the youthful and dashing Jeremy Thorpe was, as Bessell had predicted, elected leader of the Liberal Party. But a little over a decade later his hopes of higher office went south. The erratic Scott did not stay silent and, as it all got messy, Bessell himself ended up spilling some unsavoury beans. He claimed that in 1968 Thorpe told him he wanted to draw up a plan to kill his former lover. In 1975 a suspected murder attempt was carried out on Scott, blowing the whole saga wide open. Thorpe was forced to resign, lost his parliamentary seat and was charged with conspiracy to murder. He was acquitted, in part because of the weakness of the evidence from his former colleague Bessell, but his life was in tatters. He died in 2014 amid allegations that the police had suppressed evidence in the case.

Yet that wasn't the end of my involvement in the Thorpe case. In the times ahead I would find myself working on many occasions for another Barrie, this one a very brilliant *Sunday Times* journalist by the name of Barrie Penrose. In the mid-seventies he and his co-writer Simon Courtiour approached me while researching their book, *The Pencourt File*. Among other revelations, it told of the extraordinary impact Norman Scott's actions had on UK politics. They asked if I could locate the young man once again, and I agreed. And they asked if I could locate and provide a background report on a man called Andrew Newton, the self-styled hitman who allegedly tried to murder Scott. In the event, he had shot Scott's Great Dane and not Scott after the gun jammed. He had been jailed for two years. I found both men and both were interviewed for the book.

My clients requested too that I find a way to plant recording equipment in the Surrey home of Jeremy's elderly Mother, Ursula. The only way to do this, I believed, would be to talk our way indoors and leave a sound-activated recording device. So off I went, pretexted that I was a journalist and was invited into her drawing room. I *accidentally* left my briefcase behind, out of sight yet very close to the sofa. Later the same day, Barrie visited and interviewed Ursula. He asked her some leading questions about Thorpe's relationship with Scott. After he left, as expected, Ursula phoned Jeremy. He wouldn't discuss anything on the phone, fearing it could be tapped and, as expected, drove to the house that evening.

Among other matters, which went on to appear in the book, they did discuss the locked briefcase left by the earlier visitor. Jeremy Thorpe was suspicious and tried without success to open it, but quickly gave up. The following day a courier arrived to collect it.

After locating Scott for the first time in 1964, I went back to work oblivious to my part in one of the biggest political scandals in modern British history. I was in a way consumed by my nifty new ATS given that it really was beginning to speed things up and ultimately earn more money for the Surbiton office.

And I was busy too with other office matters as, at the time, some issues with the police needed handling. In short, one of our agents had been arrested while attempting to repossess a car. It became clear the debtor had called the coppers in to stop the agent and, despite his ID being in order, he was taken in for questioning. Their actions stank.

I wasn't having it. Yet after I became involved, the situation escalated. I too was arrested and what followed would ultimately become something that dogged my career for many years to follow.

SIX

Cocktails, Competition, Convicts, Cops (1965-67)

THE mid-sixties. London was booming, swinging and gyrating like never before. I was in my mid-twenties, working hard and doing well in an industry that was itself on the rise. With more disposable cash in the average pocket, with more personal freedom than ever before, the demand for the services of the private eye was scaling new heights. An army of suspicious spouses, tabloid hacks, paparazzi and worried company bosses had got in line with the ripped-off utility firms, rental companies and banks who needed to know who was doing what and where they were.

Barrie Quartermain made the absolute most of it all. When he wasn't sailing around the West End in his Roller, he was instead in his left-hand-drive Cadillac, one of the most exclusive sights in London in itself. He had a taste for the high life, relished making money and he loved nothing more than splashing out on the finer things in life.

By day I'd be reviewing the work coming across my desk, handling operations for clients, dictating letters and generating bill after bill. From 7 am, I'd be reading the piles of updates on the latest cases across the city and far beyond. A secretary would bring me coffee after coffee, keep me fired up into the afternoon as inevitably more queries arrived, more demands for us to find people who did not want to be found. The database just kept on growing in that pre-digital age to the point that, at least in some areas of life, it was as if we must be rivalling the collective knowledge of MI5 or GCHQ.

By night, I wasn't getting home to Rita, toddler Debbie and baby Andrew as much as I would have liked. Most evenings BQ would ask for my company and/or assistance with a matter he had to deal with, and invariably it ended with a barrage of drinks.

We'd meet clients in top-class restaurants, be joined at the table by celebrities, influencers and key journalists of the era. More often than not you'd spot me cutting a dash on the town in a handmade suit and plain tie, clean shaven and richly scented with Old Spice. BQ, similarly bespoke, would be ordering overpriced bottles while the latest tunes from The Beatles or The Rolling Stones blared out. More often than not, I'd end up driving his high-end car home after he handed me the keys and collapsed, joyful and pie-eyed, on its back seat.

When not out and about, the party was at his place as he threw cocktail parties galore. He loved to show off his new home in Esher, Surrey, as he moved up in the world, and especially loved to show off his all-new swimming pool which my builder's hands helped create. Incidentally, he tried for a time to get me to buy his previous home but, to his annoyance, I never agreed.

Anyway, somehow, through it all, Barrie kept his business head on, kept seeking out and securing juicy contracts from people who had the kind of finances that would catch his eye.

But he was not the only leading PI boss in London. Anyone who knew him well knew of his distaste for his chief rival, Peter Merken. BQ was a most territorial businessman, offended and angered at the idea that other PIs were working his patch. He made no secret of it.

Peter Merken operated a West End agency called *Ace Detectives* and, in many ways, had a great deal in common with Barrie. They both courted publicity, both knew the value of getting their names in the public arena when it came to drumming up business. Indeed both were known to have used the same boast, each claiming at various times that they were businessmen first and investigators second. As to their way of doing business, each typically asked for as much up-front money as possible from their more well-heeled private clients. And each had their background bread-and-butter business, such as the commercial wing I was running.

And, of course, both skirted the legal borderlines when it came to some of their work. They had no issue with the fact that some of what they did took place in the grey area between the lawful and the downright dodgy. Indeed, it's safe to say they both enjoyed that side of their reputations.

It was in this upbeat, even febrile atmosphere that we plied our trade, pushing the boundaries here and there, trying to get the job done come what may and, where possible, score points off the other guy.

Between 1965 and 1967 I was in the thick of some of the most extraordinary cases in London. My ambition was unassailable, my competitive edge razor sharp, my skills multiplying. And when I got hold of whatever it was I needed in order to crack a case, I locked down like a vice.

I relished much of the work at the time, loved situations that tested me, that compelled me to adapt and develop. I'm thinking now of The Golden Nugget Casino, a well-known establishment at the time on London's Shaftesbury Avenue. It was owned by Mecca, a large UK gaming concern, and it was suspicious about money losses at its tables to the point where fraud was suspected.

BQ called me in, said I would be briefed about the workings of the tables by some senior figures in the company. After that, he said, I'd go undercover as a regular punter and seek to identify where the missing money was going.

Armed with insights, I got into character. Each night I'd arrive at 10 pm, collect £200 worth of chips set aside for me and play until closing time. As time passed I learned the dice game Craps, learned Blackjack and Roulette, figured out the slot machines, got what insights I could into the people who spent their nights there, whether employees or not. I have to say I lost most of the casino's money most of the time, but that was part of the learning process.

And at the end of each week I'd file a report on the dealers, their interactions with each other and with clients. As I grew more comfortable in an environment that I had never known before, my senses adjusted and my instincts began to develop.

I became intrigued, over a few nights, by the behaviour of a young female dealer on the American Roulette table. Night after night she would pay out winning bets to an elderly lady who always sat with a cup of coffee in front of her. The payouts typically included £50 cash chips, tokens which can be used on any table and swapped for money at any point. The lady consistently bet on a set group of numbers. She would push her stake onto the table, the dealer would take it and place it at the edge of the wheel. This kind of play is known as making *pattern bets*. It's when the punter repeatedly picks the same numbers but is given the all-clear to not have to lean over the table and place their chips on the same numbers each time, which slows things down.

The dealer would spin the wheel, the ball would drop and I got to noticing how, more often than not, the lady would be a winner. I realised that when the chips she won were pushed her way, the punter would scoop them up and, with first class sleight of hand, drop a £50 cash chip or two into the half-full cup. No one was any the wiser.

Once I had it worked out, I put security staff on standby. On my discrete signal, they swooped and, without identifying me, tipped the lady's coffee into a glass. There were four £50 chips in there. The lady was barred from all of Mecca's casinos and the dealer was prosecuted for fraud.

I became aware too of other funny business at the Craps table. If you don't know it, I'd describe Craps as a complex but often thrilling game where players bet with or against the house on the outcome of rolls of the dice. Central to this is the *stickman*, the typically exuberant individual who hands the dice to the shooter, calls the rolls and generally sets the pace of the game. I came to suspect that one or more of the Nugget's stickmen were pocketing cash chips.

When the casino closed one night, I kept watching as one of them met with other dealers and left. They were buzzing with that end-of-shift feeling and were no doubt heading off for a few drinks. It took me a little by surprise when, on the pavement just outside, one of them suddenly flipped himself into the air. He landed on his hands and spun around in what was an impressive, impromptu cartwheel. Unfortunately for him, when he was briefly upside down, gravity gave the game away. Casino chips poured from his breast pocket onto the footpath.

I dashed over to retrieve them—all £100 cash chips—as they rolled around at people's feet. The casino's doorman couldn't help but notice and bolted over. He grabbed the now upright dealer and called out to a policeman on the street. He was arrested on the spot.

Naturally enough, word had already been getting around that there was a spy in the camp and that light-fingered staff weren't going to get away with it anymore. And now, after retrieving the chips from the street, my cover was blown. I worked for one more night then bowed out of my gambling career. Soon after, the casino required staff uniform pockets to be stitched up.

Bizarrely, on the last night I worked there, I hit the jackpot on one of the fruit machines. As other punters gathered to urge me to pull the lever again, it locked. Bells and sirens filled the air and I was declared the winner of not just the £500 jackpot, but a double jackpot of £1,000. I collected the cash—a heck of a sum in the sixties—and, with a heavy heart, brought it to the manager. I said I had technically been there as an employee and should hand it over.

'No worries,' he said, 'you keep it—you deserve it.'

BQ felt much the same.

'Saves me having to give you a bonus,' he said.

The next day I bought my first new car—a 1967 Morris 1100, in dark green. I paid cash.

Some of the work involved teaming up with journalists, print and broadcast, who were chasing down some of the biggest stories of the time. Among the most memorable was a hard-nosed veteran *Sunday People* hack called Roy East, a man with one of the fiercest reputations in the UK press. The pair of us worked together undercover to expose some of the mysterious doings inside the Church of Scientology. We received death threats for our trouble. That seems to have been something of a running theme in the years that followed.

And there was the gifted BBC journalist Trevor Philpott, who investigated many suspected miscarriages of justice. In one case I was sent to find details on a suspect in the notorious A6 murder, one of the most chilling and high profile crimes of the era.

In 1962 a petty crook called James Hanratty had been one of the last men to go to the gallows before the death penalty was abolished. He had been convicted of the murder a year before of Michael Gregsten. The victim had been shot dead in a car on that main road in Bedfordshire. Gregsten's mistress, Valerie Storie, was raped, shot five times and left paralysed for life. She only survived because she played dead.

There was a great deal of public interest in evidence that the man who stole the couple's car had been a bad driver, that he was heard crunching through the gears as he drove away. Yet Hanratty was known to have been competent behind the wheel. Many high profile people, including the one and only John Lennon, felt the wrong man may have been hanged. I was asked by Philpott to find out what I could about a second suspect and the potential real killer, Peter Louis Alphon. I was able to establish that he was not known to be a driver at all, causing something of stir in legal circles. Yet it was never a clear cut case and, of course, Hanratty could not assist.

In 1997 amid mounting concern, the whole thing was formally reviewed. After an exhumation of Hanratty's body, DNA samples were compared with evidence from the scene. The results proved, the court said, that Hanratty was undoubtedly the killer. Yet supporters, citing theories of cross contamination, have never been convinced and questions persist to this day.

I worked with Philpott on the case of another murderer convicted on thin evidence, but Jimmy O'Connor had avoided the gallows. He had been due for execution in 1942, on his twenty-fourth birthday. At the eleventh hour the hanging was commuted and instead O'Connor, who always protested his innocence, was given life.

There had been a long legal battle which involved him working closely with barrister Nemone Lethbridge QC, famed for representing the Krays. My job, some fifteen years after O'Connor's release, was to covertly record an informal chat between the barrister and the man believed to have been the true killer. There was no definitive confession and the courts did not consent to issuing a pardon. Yet what came from that recording was enough to tip the balance in the minds of many.

In all of this time, BQ and I kept our eyes peeled. These kinds of jobs brought in good money for the firm and, perhaps more importantly, boosted our reputation. When people in a host of industries—legal, finance, media—needed discreet services, they had few recommendations to go on. As a result of the work we were doing, and who we were doing it for, we were able to get to the top of the list.

But BQ's constant rival Peter Merken was always there, always trying to get a handle on what we were up to and always seeking to lure potential clients from us to him. The result was that we worked harder, pushed further for results, promised we would do whatever it took to get the job done. It was maybe inevitable that both BQ's and Merken's increasing flirtations with the wrong side of the law would come to the attention of the police.

As for my own standing with the constabulary, well… put it like this…

I had quit the police to become a private detective; I was involved in probing murder convictions, questioning evidence gathered by the cops; I was involved in the explosive Thorpe case that rattled the top rank of society; I was a young man co-running one of the largest private investigation businesses in the UK at the behest of a man who was no stranger to London's boys in blue… so, as for me, I was perhaps treading on toes that didn't like to be trodden upon. I started to get the feeling that the Metropolitan Police didn't like me at all.

The first clear inkling came one sunny evening when one of the investigators had been arrested while trying to repossess a luxury car. The car in question had been leased, yet the customer seemed to believe he had been paying it off in installments. He did not own it but he felt he did. He ignored letters and phone calls, seemed offended by the idea that he did not own the motor. Repossession was the only option left.

Our agent had duly made his way to Esher, Surrey, only to be reported to the police. They would not listen to his explanation and he was arrested. He wasn't pleased. After they let him go with no decent excuse for having arrested him in the first place, we talked it over. I said I'd go with him to get the car. Armed with a set of keys supplied by the leasing firm, we made our way. We opened the car and rolled it gently out onto the street. Just as we were driving out of the estate, a police officer arrived on the scene. He said it was suspected we were stealing a car. I told him that was not the case.

The copper looked through the papers and had no choice but to accept what we were doing was above board. And then, looking around, he noticed my keys. I had a bunch of them on a chain—keys for the offices, house keys, car keys, the leasing firm's keys, all legitimately in my possession. He asked me about them and, a little surprised, I explained. Then he chose to arrest me. Under the 1916 Larceny Act of the time, I was detained for being in possession of housebreaking implements during the hours of darkness.

I did my best to politely explain that he was out of order, but his mind was made up. The agent was allowed to go on, the leased car was seized and I was taken in for questioning. Again, in the station, I explained the situation and, after a couple of hours, was released. A file was to be sent to the DPP for consideration. Eventually, we got the car back from the police.

A few months later, a policeman arrived at the office to serve me with a summons. They had decided, for reasons best known to themselves, that I should be prosecuted. I ended at the Magistrates Court in Kingston facing a charge under that archaic Larceny Act. My solicitor entered a not-guilty plea and the case was sent for trial. In the meantime my Bailiff Certificate, giving me authority to seize goods, was rescinded.

In due course, a jury was sworn in and the prosecution's first witness—the man who had leased the car—was put on the stand. I wasn't surprised that his evidence was demolished, nor that my lawyer succeeded in having him admit he shouldn't have had the car in the first place.

The chief prosecution witness was the police officer. He conceded I had shown him the repossession authority, that he had no doubt I was acting lawfully on behalf of my client and that I had the authority to repossess the vehicle. When pushed as to why he took issue with the bunch of keys, he was stumped. There was no good reason why I should not have had a single one of those keys in my possession. The judge stopped the trial. He said there was no case to answer. In the years ahead, attempted and actual prosecutions involving the Metropolitan Police would follow. I am as convinced now as I was back then that this was personal.

Back in the office, in 1967, I felt I was becoming a victim of my own success. The commissions I had been earning on top of my wage were substantial and I had started to get the strong feeling BQ felt I was being overpaid. The shine seemed to be coming off our working relationship.

He called me to his office one day, close to the end of my two year contract, and said it could not be renewed on the same terms. I felt that was unfair. I told him what he already knew—in my time as general manager *Southern Provincial* had tripled its sales, revenue and bottom line, that the client base had expanded considerably, that it had all helped him buy his new home. I felt I was being punished for that, and perhaps too for not buying his former house as he had pressed me to do many times.

He didn't seem to care. He wanted to strike a new deal, one that would see me earn less money, and it was patently unfair to me. I told him if he was sticking to his guns, I didn't want to renew the contract at all. BQ flew into a rage, barked at me like a crazed dog and told me to leave his employment right now.

I did just that.

In a way, perhaps just like his key rival, he had been losing his grip a little. In 1972, Peter Merken was arrested, prosecuted and convicted for conspiracy to pervert the course of justice. He had obtained private and confidential information on behalf of clients involved in divorce proceedings between 1964 and 1972.

Around the same time, in a separate case, Barrie Quartermain was arrested too. When he was bailed, he vanished. Eventually he was found hiding out under a false name in South Africa, still working as a PI. In 1974 he was convicted of *conspiracy to effect a public nuisance* by fraudulently obtaining confidential information from public authorities.

By that time, my career had moved on considerably.

SEVEN

Spying for South Africa (1968/69)

'IAN,' the *Sunday Times* journalist asked, looking me in the eye. 'Is it true you are party to a plan to plant drugs or pornography in the briefcase of a senior Amnesty International official?'

It was quite a question, especially from a man I'd call a friend. But, as I would come to know, well-placed allegations passed to influential journalists like Barrie Penrose can be useful in terms of muddying the waters. The answer, by the way, was no. But the information delivered within the question advised that people were seeking to discredit me. Disinformation, I would learn, came with the new territory in which I was working.

After breaking away from BQ, I joined forces with my brother Stuart in an agency of our own. He had quit the building trade some months after I did on learning how well things were going for me. He and his mate David Flowers launched a detective agency called *Christopher Robert & Co.* Stuart's middle name was Robert, his pal's was Christopher. They had built up something of a client base and, while with *Southern Provincial Investigations*, I had commissioned them for a number of jobs.

Now, out on my own in 1967, Stuart quickly offered me a partnership in his firm, based in south London's Carshalton Beeches. I was only too happy to accept. Using my client contacts, we got stuck into developing the commercial side and before long the business was on the up. As our working days grew longer and weekend breaks became more rare, David Flowers bowed out seeking instead a less hectic life. I couldn't blame him for that.

Stuart and I kept building. In early 1968 we moved to offices on the first floor of Lincoln House in Wallington. The place had two self-contained apartments. One became the new home for the agency. And we agreed that Stuart, who had just married Margaret, should take the other.

As well as the new premises, both of us also took on a pair of Alsatian dogs which had been cruelly abandoned by some idiot near where we were based. Mine was *Duke*, a challenging, aggressive, yet lovable chap who got on great with my kids. In office hours he liked to sit under my desk and, on occasion, growl at visitors. Stuart's dog was more of a barker and sometimes ran at the new arrivals into our office, pouncing on them, his tongue bared, before giving them a good licking. The place was not short on atmosphere.

We launched into a marketing campaign, including a press release offering easy payment terms for domestic clients with marriage problems. That idea caught the imagination of some journalists who liked the boldness of our invitation to fed-up spouses. It all ended up on the front page of a national title under the headline *"Divorce on HP"*. It was safe to say we had got our message out.

We sent mailshots to utility companies, banks, financiers, consulates and embassies. We talked up our debtor tracing services, told them of my past success rate. Looking back, it could be that we were among the early pioneers of something close to that well-known advertising refrain *No win, no fee*.

Hundreds of new assignments rolled in from across the UK, and the demands on our time rocketed. We took on two additional investigators—John Franks, a professional press photographer; and Phyllis Clarke, whom I had met in Belfast while on a job in 1966. And we took on Helen Gearing, a former divorce client, to help out with research and secretarial services.

Phyllis, or Phyl, was a first class store detective with an impressive record of catching shoplifters in her home city and in London. She was a talented operator, glossy-haired and beautiful, bursting with life and wonderful to work with. Indeed, around this time, especially with me working an immense number of hours, my relationship with Rita was beginning to depreciate. As we moved towards an agreement to separate, Phyl became very much my new love interest. And, as it played out, she went on to become my second wife.

Our team was in place and, once we were in motion, worked like a well-oiled machine. The clients kept calling and we kept coming up with the results. We rarely failed. In a short time our reputation for getting things done was rock solid.

One valuable new client was the aforementioned Barrie Penrose, who went on to become a lifelong friend. He had been an investigative reporter with the BBC before moving to *The Sunday Times*. We had worked together before on a number of assignments while I was with BQ and I was delighted to hang onto him after moving away.

Also around this time we began receiving requests for our services from, in effect, a number of governments from around the world. The High Commissions of New Zealand, Australia, Canada and South Africa were all asking for the same thing—could we track down UK citizens who had failed to pay what they owed?

At the time a number of passage schemes were in place to assist British people who sought to emigrate to Commonwealth nations. Perhaps the best known of these led to the creation of the term *Ten Pound Poms*, Aussie slang for the Brits arriving by boat after the war. In some cases these new arrivals changed their minds, repacked their bags and went back the other way. Yet the various governments had invested in bringing them there and helping set them up. They didn't like to see their money wasted. The High Commissions of those countries wanted us to track down *returners* and get them to cough up. We had a lot of work to do.

After a few months of successes, I was invited to a meeting at the South African High Commission in the magnificent South Africa House in London's Trafalgar Square. I could only assume it was to discuss doing more of the same. Inside, I was advised I would be meeting the attaché before a gentleman led me into a separate room and towards some bookshelves. He opened a hidden door between them which led into an office complex. I was introduced to the attaché, a thick-set man by the name of Piet Schoeman. From there, Schoeman guided me first through a series of corridors and down to a basement. It felt as if I was going somewhere secure and sensitive, and on arrival I could see I had been right. There was a bank of TV screens, a number of people were monitoring various locations, some were making quiet phone calls.

I was keen to hear what this was about but, at first, Schoeman arranged for coffee as we chit-chatted about minor matters for a while. The conversation led on to South Africa and touched on the apartheid regime. I knew, as every British child had learned, that his country was in the Commonwealth. I had some sense of an emerging unease between it and the UK, but I didn't really know much more than that. Neither the word *apartheid* nor the system were at all well known in the UK at the time. But Schoeman seemed to be keen to make a point about it, perhaps to gauge my reaction. In his soft-spoken Afrikaans accent, he said it was a way of government which allowed for the 'self-determination' of the various races of South Africa. I had nothing to say in response. So he moved on.

He said his country was having trouble with 'communist-backed terrorists,' namely the African National Congress (ANC) and Pan African Congress (PAC). He said each had supporters and funders based in the UK. He asked if I would be interested in researching these British connections.

It was a curious moment. A representative of a sovereign government was asking me to assist with an issue of national security. This was a direct and broad request to move to a new level of intelligence work. It was important stuff, he said, and it could save lives. And, he said, it would be fulsomely rewarded. I told him that I and my firm would be willing to do what we could.

The years that followed saw us take on all kinds of assignments from the South Africans as matters became increasingly fraught. These included gathering data on the movements, connections and plans of a large number of persons of interest.

One request led to my infiltration of the London office of the Anti-Apartheid Movement (AAM) to, quite simply, work out how they were able to issue mailshots on influential official House of Commons-headed paper. Many individuals and organisations had been invited to join commemorations into the 1960 Sharpeville Massacre, where South African police shot dead sixty-nine protestors, via this potentially influential stationery. There was no question that it gave the impression the UK parliament was endorsing the commemorations. Yet in reality the issue, and its outworkings, were a point of ongoing and unresolved fractious discussion among MPs.

To get access to the office, and specifically any printing equipment, I had to get the pretext right. It didn't take long to come up with the idea of making inroads in the guise of an equipment servicing engineer. After a few calls, I had secured entry and knew it was likely I would be given time alone just where I needed to be.

I was led over to the equipment and, sure enough, left to get on with my work. Right away I could see that a Gestetner duplicating machine had been loaded with a stencil and letter heads from the House of Commons. It had been pumping copies out by the thousand. There were boxes of them everywhere. I took some photographs and a couple of sheets, bluffed my farewells and met with Schoeman. He told me he hoped what we now knew could be turned into a scandal in the UK press. I knew what he was asking.

A couple of weeks later a British newspaper ran a story headlined: *"House of Commons supports A.A.M. Commemoration."*

An internal investigation followed which clamped down hard on the use of parliamentary letterhead being used for anything other than an MP's constituency business.

Meanwhile, in South Africa itself, tensions were escalating and the violence getting worse. As a result, Schoeman's workload became ever more complicated. He tasked us with following a host of high-profile anti-apartheid supporters in London—church leaders, politicians and others. He connected with a number of people in South Africa's security services who in turn provided me myriad detailed leads. Our agents took scores of photographs of meetings between MPs and activists and delivered them, with comprehensive notes, to our client.

Then one day, in late 1968, my old contact and frequent client Barrie Penrose called from his office at *The Sunday Times*.

'Are you running surveillance on a South African man currently visiting London?' he asked.

We were. But I denied it.

A half hour later, Barrie arrived at my office with a photographer at his side. It seemed clear I might be about to become a story myself.

He said some people from South Africa were being followed. They had taken down the details of the car, including its number plate. They had been in touch with the police. In short, two agents who were freelancing for our firm had been rumbled.

I made no comment.

Barrie said those being followed were involved with the AAM and Amnesty International. He went on to say he had information which named me as the main suspect involved in bugging some closed sessions of a conference organised by the UN Special Committee on Apartheid in mid-1968.

That was news to me.

It seemed, he said, that one of a number of agents who had worked with us had given my name as the man behind the bugging. That agent had apparently said I was in charge of UK operations for the South African government.

Again, more news.

'Ian,' the *Sunday Times* journalist asked, looking me in the eye. 'Is it true you are party to a plan to plant drugs or pornography in the briefcase of a senior Amnesty International official?' I was not and never would participate in such a scheme.

With Barrie Penrose and his trusty snapper right in front of me, I chose to say nothing at first. The details of my work, even though he had got them wrong, were between me and my client.

As the questions continued, I relented a little, threw my inquisitors a bone rather than a potentially suspicious silence. I admitted I had made some inquiries on behalf of the High Commissions of a number of governments, including South Africa. And I left it at that.

The Sunday Times published their interpretation a few days later. It said I was an agent of that country's newly-formed Bureau of State Security (better known by its no-nonsense acronym, BOSS).

Years later, a book called *Inside BOSS* by South African journalist Gordon Winter told of how pleased the secret service had been with the work conducted by *Christopher Robert & Co* and Ian Withers.

Another book, *On South Africa's Secret Service*, by Riaan Labuschagne, also claimed I was an agent for the Pretoria government who sometimes went by the name John Douglas.

In the eighties, when I began working in intelligence for the left-wing government of the Seychelles, I received a notification from the Immigration Department of the South African government. My right to enter that country, it said, had been withdrawn. I found that interesting given that I had never once set foot there, nor had any plans to do so.

I called South Africa House in London more out of curiosity than indignation. Piet Schoeman advised me, off the record, that this was to be expected. He said I had to consider that his country was a right-wing capitalist state. And he said my new client, the Seychelles, was essentially a Marxist state. The assumption could only be made that I was now in league with people and organisations which were banned in South Africa. His government, he said, would give no consideration to that I was an apolitical investigator for hire.

That said, in typical ex-cop fashion, I had kept a record of everyone I had dealings with in the South African security services. Ironically enough, my connections there would prove extremely useful in terms of my work in the Seychelles.

EIGHT

The Bug Business (1970s)

'*THERE is only one thing worse than being talked about,*' mused Oscar Wilde, '*and that is not being talked about.*'

Or, to put it another way, there's no such thing as bad publicity. Some might say it depends very much on what's being said. But, in my experience, Oscar was broadly right. Even bad news can have an upside.

As the press enjoyed spinning the idea that I was up to my neck in dirty tricks for South Africa, every instinct said both myself and *Christoper Robert & Co* would suffer. I had, of course, surveilled for South Africa. As an ambitious private investigator I had worked for other nations too, indeed for anyone who would pay good money for my services. Yet something of an exaggerated and uncomfortable fiction was being created around me. I needed to shake it off.

The priority was to reassure and protect our regular clients—the solicitors, finance firms and individuals who were the bread and butter of our business. In a first effort to show them we were responding to the publicity, we came up with a second company name and moved our work for existing clients under that new brand.

At first we went with *National Investigations Bureau*. But, as we sought to register it, there was an objection by the registrar to the term *national*. We appealed and they suggested *Nationwide Investigations* as an alternative. It would be the company name, or at least one of them, for the next fifty years.

But back to Oscar's observation. We were being talked about in ways we felt could damage us, yet the publicity itself was generating interest in the broader nature of our work. Being talked about was proving to be excellent advertising in some of the most useful places, not least among journalists themselves.

After a while it felt my number was on every newsdesk in the old Fleet Street of the day. Over a fairly short space of time the calls I was receiving morphed from queries about South Africa to requests for advice, for help and comment about news events in the UK. Out of that emerged some truly quality publicity which would aid the fortunes of *Christopher Robert and Co*, aka *Nationwide Investigations*, for years to come.

By 1968 Stuart and Margaret had moved out of our offices at Lincoln House to Sussex. At the time, he and I were constantly on-the-go, starting even earlier than before, getting home late at night. Ours was an intensive business where there were no shortcuts, where positive results took time to secure, where taking one's eye off the ball is the road to ruin.

And those results were being talked about as our satisfied clients became evangelists for our endeavours. We were taking calls all the time, routinely hiring agents, stocking up on equipment, compiling ever-expanding files, inviting clients inside for meetings.

Soon enough, despite the extra space in the office since Stuart moved out, we needed yet more. Unfortunately, between the long hours and the new travel situation, all of this took a toll on Stuart's marriage, as it had been doing with mine. He and Margaret separated and later divorced. Looking back, it is no lie to say we were putting everything we had into our firm.

We moved the agency to larger premises at Nelson House on West Street, Carshalton, south London. It was a grand, listed building and, it's said, a former home of Emma, Lady Hamilton, a mistress of Lord Nelson. Our first floor office had apparently been the bedroom where she welcomed horny Horatio back from his seafaring exploits. The story goes that he made use of a secret tunnel to the house which at one stage ran from a nearby convent. It all seemed very appropriate for our line of work. We liked to think it was all true.

As business blossomed, we moved our portfolios around a little more, looked into purchasing other agencies in the UK and Ireland in part or in full, into diversifying our own brand with the launch of more interconnected companies. Key among the newly-fashioned firms was

Christopher Robert & Co (Security Equipment) Ltd, arguably the first spy shop in London. We flung the doors open at the start of 1970 and lured in thrilled, cautious and curious punters alike with a host of electronic devices, phone tapping kits, body-worn recorders, mini cameras, clocks and ashtrays with built-in microphones and more. We were designing and selling items that were making great use of the developing technology, stuff that was not far removed from the kind of gear which was firing up the imagination in the James Bond movies of the time.

The man putting our pieces together, our very own Q, was hugely talented Post Office engineer Jim Firth. He had set up in business making all types of recording gadgets from his home and knew his trade inside-out. His most popular recorder was a discrete switching unit that could be attached to any phone-line. It would turn on and off as the handset was lifted and replaced. We marketed these as ATR's, Automatic Telephone Relays. We sold and leased them to a host of private clients, businesses and other agencies.

Also on board as a consultant was a bloke called Lee Tracey, a well-known security expert of the era. Lee could, and often did, boast of his not-insignificant links with UK intelligence agencies and police forces. And we hired a sales manager, Eric Levitt, to really help push our product line across Britain and beyond.

Between us all, we had the expertise, contacts and good old-fashioned moxie to drive aggressively forward into new markets, to reach further than any other British private investigations agency or spyware trader had done before. We researched every other agency that was out there, looked into all the devices on the market and made sure we were the best. We weren't just pitching to the public and commercial interests, but also to governments right around the globe. Our combined efforts saw us designing and selling high-end bespoke items to the then booming Kingdom of Saudi Arabia, to Marshal Tito's communist Yugoslavia. One client turned out to be an agent for the last Shah of Iran. He came calling in 1972, keen to secure a host of phone and room recording equipment and body-worn devices. Such was the scale of the order, we felt it was right that he and his colleagues should be able to see a variety of samples at their own offices.

I remember I had grown a beard a year or so before, a decision I never reversed, and considered it might be a good look in Iran. I bought sunglasses too and donned a lightweight suit before flying out to Tehran to meet the buyers. And I remember landing in freezing temperatures as a snowstorm took hold. The first thing I did was buy a heavy coat and fur hat and scold myself for my assumptions.

The clients were from Savak, Iran's CIA-backed secret police, who dealt with domestic security and intelligence on behalf of the Shah. It was a turbulent time for the nation, evidenced seven years later when the Shah and his family were ousted in the Islamic Revolution which shook the world.

Back in London, political events were less than stable, too, with the sudden retirement in 1976 of Labour Prime Minister Harold Wilson. He wasn't long out of office when I took a call from my friendly interrogator Barrie Penrose. Barrie was giving nothing away, only to say he needed a discrete device which could record for three hours. No such device was available on the High Street, none in the trade catalogues of the time. I said I'd see what I could do. I put a call into Jim Firth.

It was an unusual thing, my friendship with Barrie. This was the man who had confronted me about working for the South Africans, who had put my name firmly in the public domain and forever linked me with various doings in the minds of the news consuming public. It was an unusual thing because I found myself not taking any of it personally nor holding any of it against him. I never clarified to him everything I did or didn't know and he was the same with me. Barrie was a pal, a valued customer and always an interesting man to be around. Maybe most of all, I had the greatest of respect for him as a first rate journalist—even if he did tend to stir pots and push envelopes from time to time. I know he understood and respected me and my work too—even if I did tend to stir pots and push envelopes from time to time.

So I sat down with Jim to discuss how best, with the technology we had, to record something in secret for three hours. Our solution, for whatever the specific job was, must not fail under any circumstances. And, also paramount, there must be no chance it could be discovered. Jim took it all on board. I left him to his thoughts.

A couple of days later and we sat down again. He had sketched out his plan. The recorder would be secreted within the upholstery of a smart leather briefcase. Two tiny, barely visible holes, one on each side, allowed miniature microphones to record. The on-switch was triggered by the handle, a grasp which could be flipped from one side to another as with many briefcases. Inside the grasp was a powerful magnet. Flipping it flat to one side caused it to trigger the mechanism and start the recording. It was a superb design, a true work of art. I called up Barrie to talk him through it. He was chuffed, commissioned its creation on the spot. The BBC, Barrie's employers for this mission, sent over a cheque and bought themselves some quality spy gear.

We wouldn't know the full details for some time to come, but in the months that followed Barrie and colleague Roger Courtier had a number of meetings with Harold Wilson. On resigning the prime minister had cited mental and physical exhaustion, but a year later he spoke publicly about his fears of a plot against him. He said he had been bugged by MI5, said there had been a 'whispering campaign' by the intelligence services who had wanted him, as a left wing figure, out of office. It wasn't until 2006 that the full story would emerge in a fascinating documentary called *The Plot Against Harold Wilson.* And it featured the recordings made by Barrie Penrose with the use of our purpose-built briefcase.

Until that time, Barrie opted to keep the extraordinary recordings hidden away. But when he finally chose to lift the lid, for whatever reason, he could reveal how Wilson talked of his fears that he was to be the target of a military coup, that MI5 was convinced he was a Soviet spy. Mr Wilson was sure that Lord Louis Mountbatten, an uncle of the Duke of Edinburgh and second cousin of the Queen, was in on it too.

His worries were not without at least some form of merit among the complex political tapestry of the times. It was a tense period, the Cold War was at its height and many in high office were looking over their shoulder. A later book, *Spycatcher*, by former MI5 agent Peter Wright, told of a security service plot to force Wilson from office, although the account has been largely debunked.

But Barrie seemed fairly convinced Wilson had got it right. Writing in the *Radio Times* in 2006, he said, *'Our establishment, from the intelli-*

gence services down to parts of Fleet Street, were all paranoid about the threat of communism. So paranoid it seems, they were willing to believe a prime minister of Britain was an active Soviet spy.'

The bugging operations we were conducting as a company through the seventies were at times controversial in themselves. By way of example, in 1971 a Conservative councillor in Kent phoned up in search of a transmitter and receiver. She wanted to monitor discussions between fellow councillors in a Bromley hotel. She feared they were planning to deselect her at a forthcoming local election. One of our agents delivered the units and ran through the instructions. The client asked if he might instead help her install the transmitter, a battery-powered unit the size of a pack of cigarettes, in the hotel room of the main suspect. He should not have done that—but unfortunately he did.

When the target reentered the bugged room, he brought along his dog. As he chatted to Bess, a local radio ham intercepted the unencrypted signal. The listener's ears pricked up when he heard the name of the dog. He knew the name. And he knew the owner. The chap passed word along that the councillor's one-way chat with his canine had been aired. The police were called and an investigation began.

Around the same time a director of a major insurance company in the City called in after a board disagreement.

John Reynolds wanted us to install a microphone in another director's office saying he suspected the man was passing leads to a competitor. I went with Reynolds to their offices and, over a weekend, we carefully hard-wired a sensitive microphone in the target's office. An ultra-thin cable secreted under the carpet led back to a recorder in a drawer in Reynolds' office.

Sure enough, in due course the dodgy dealer was caught on tape passing on information. He was confronted with the recording and fired. But that sacked director wasn't going to leave it at that. He called in the police.

The emerging problem for us was that we had no idea either case was being investigated. The first I knew was when a squad of coppers arrived at Nelson House with a warrant to search for bugging equipment and records of bugging cases. Myself, Stuart and John Franks, one of our agents, were arrested, interviewed, held for twenty-four hours and bailed.

Ian & Stuart – First trip to Old Bailey

When I showed up at the police station a few weeks later, as part of my bail conditions, John Reynolds was there. He too was accused in the case. All four of us were charged with *conspiring to evade the purposes of the Wireless Telegraphy Act*.

I had to look it up.

It turned out this obscure law had been passed by parliament as a tax-raising instrument. It allocated frequencies and imposed a licence requirement for all radio transmitters and receivers. It had not been designed with the ever-increasing use of miniature transmitters in mind. In fact it took quite a bit of twisting for the police to make it stick in the first place.

Come the court date, John Reynolds was promptly released by the powers that be. But it was a different story of us three private eyes. We were told by Bromley Magistrates Court that we would stand trial at the Central Criminal Court—London's Old Bailey, where some of the most infamous murder and treason cases in British history had been tried. I was shocked but, of course, this was the Metropolitan Police. I'd found them to be imaginative before. And in this case they had seized on a most obscure tax-raising-law and created for themselves a sinister conspiracy.

Our solicitors advised pleading guilty. A simple breach of the act carried a £50 fine yet if the court went along with the Met and considered our work a conspiracy then the penalties were unlimited.

We stood in Number One Dock, where many convicted souls before us had learned they were to be executed. But, as the judge seemed to readily agree, our crime wasn't exactly a capital offence. His Lordship was puzzled, wondering out loud why this otherwise summary taxation offence had been elevated to a dastardly conspiracy. Our counsel explained the facts and put forward our guilty pleas. The judge, in a nod of some kind to the efforts of the overzealous police, dished out short suspended sentences and a £1,000 fine.

The police were delighted. They had effectively created a new crime never before prosecuted in the UK, one never even enacted by parliament.

We left the courtroom to find a small army of press outside—photographers, journalists, television cameras. But by now we had nothing to fear from publicity. If the Met wanted to keep pushing us into the courts, we were damn sure we would come out smiling and ready to get back to work every time. Eric Levitt, our sales manager, was tasked with making hay while the glare of media attention shone on us. He was taking calls at the spy shop from an ever increasing number of interested parties.

At one point Eric was invited to demonstrate some of our numerous gadgets to the Cantonal Police in Geneva, Switzerland. They were so impressed they ordered a host of ATRs. Being a decent bunch of coppers, they presented our firm, via Eric, with a particularly striking Swiss Pen which he brought back to the office. I remember turning that pen over in my hands and thinking there was something odd about it before it dawned on me. This wasn't just any old pen, it was a gas gun—a non-lethal self-defence weapon. These sorts of things were legally sold across much of Europe and the US as self-defence devices. But in the UK such a thing was, and remains, a *prohibited weapon*. You are not supposed to have one. We decided it was best for it to stay in the office safe. I was to dispose of it. Unfortunately, I forgot.

One weekend, not long after, our offices were robbed. I can't tell you how infuriating and disheartening it was to walk through the door that Monday morning and see the place had been cleaned out. Yet although many thousands of pounds worth of equipment had been swiped, there was barely any damage done to the property, barely even a mess left behind. As I worked on taming my rage about the whole thing, I got to wondering how the sneaky gits had entered the office in the first place. There was nothing to suggest forced entry. It seemed clear, rather chillingly, that the thieves may well have obtained a key.

Some officers from the local station arrived and a glum-faced Detective Constable Noonan introduced himself. Despite the crime scene all around him and despite my obvious concern that I had just been robbed, his first significant comment was something of a joke. He said that as PIs, we should solve the case ourselves. I've no doubt DC Noonan had a wonderful sense of humour, but his comic timing was atrocious. Still, at least it made him laugh.

We got to going over what had vanished and, for some strange reason, I told him the story of the gas gun. The thieves hadn't been able to take the contents of the safe. And then, like a fool, I showed the contents of the safe to him. It was at that point that this unexceptional detective seemed to wake up. In fact, all of a sudden, it was as if he had just discovered a murder. All his attention switched from the burglary to the pen. He said I was in possession of a *prohibited weapon* and must face the consequences. I advised him that, as I had just explained to his face, I knew the situation with the pen. He didn't care. Nothing was more important than this. He left, returned within the hour with a summons.

Fast forward to Sutton Magistrates and (yet another) court date. With the help of our solicitors Stanley Smith & Co, the case was thrown out sharpish. DC Noonan and his crack team had, in their rush to have me prosecuted, quoted the wrong section number on the summons. They were sunk by a technicality. Costs were granted to our solicitor.

Amazingly, the very next day DC Noonan turned up at the office again with another summons. And this one quoted the correct section. Back to court I went, pleaded guilty and was given a complete discharge.

As for the burglary, DC Noonan never took it any further. No Scenes of Crime technicians ever showed up, no fingerprints were ever taken, no witness statements were ever requested. The only thing the Metropolitan Police did as a result of it all was issue a press release about me having been brought to court. The press loved it. The spy they liked to write about had been charged with having a *prohibited weapon*.

And still I just couldn't shake that familiar feeling that the Met did not like me or my business very much at all...

As to who broke into the offices, who knows? Perhaps duplicates of our keys had been loaned to a bad apple or two along the way? Perhaps something more sinister had taken place involving shadowy forces along the intelligence food chain?

Or perhaps, most concerning of all, the ghost of Admiral Nelson popped back to Lady Hamilton's boudoir that night via the secret door and looted some treasures.

NINE

The Statuette and the Shot Shoe (1970)

A SPRINGTIME call from the manager of the May Fair Hotel, one of the most exclusive in London. I could never have imagined where this incoming request would lead.

'We have some American guests,' the manager said. 'They need the services of a private security firm. Can you help?'

I knew the May Fair, although not as a guest in its sumptuous five-star rooms. My experience of the Stratton Street hotel centred around its theatre, casino and, most of all, The Beachcomber—its extraordinary subterranean Polynesian-style bar. To access it, punters made their way down a narrow staircase into the fantastical venue below. It featured streams and hotlamps where baby alligators lazed around to the delight of the clientele. Every now and then a tropical rain shower would be unleashed onto the creatures, the extravagance bolstered with thunder cracks and lightning flashes to make the reptiles feel right at home. To keep the humans amused, live bands played tropical music while lithe waitresses in revealing sarongs glided around delivering huge rum cocktails.

I told the manager I would help. Whatever happened, I was pretty sure I'd make time to pop into The Beachcomber for the complete change of scenery (and weather) it delivered so well.

The next day Stuart and I met a large, fast-talking American called Saul Kay and his associates Kent Olsen, John Wilson and Paul Burnham. They needed a valuable piece of art escorted from London to a Scottish university for appraisal. The piece in question was a small, erotic sculpture called *Nymph and Satyr* by Benvenuto Cellini, a 16th Cenutry Italian sculptor. It was being used as security for a £10,000 loan from a Fleet Street Barclays Bank manager called Michael Fry. He was the diligent

Dinner at May Fair Hotel with one of the Americans

type and wanted the sculpture sent to an expert in Edinburgh for detailed verification. No problem.

We arranged for an armoured van to collect the statuette from Barclays and take it north. Saul Kay paid up front, handing me a cheque for $1,200 drawn on a bank in Atlanta, Georgia, USA. There was no issue in terms of depositing a dollar cheque into a UK account, but it would take a few weeks to clear. Things were going to take some time in Edinburgh too. The expert in question was in demand and had intensive investigations to carry out on the piece.

In the meantime, we all got to know each other and got to talking business. The Americans invited Stuart, myself and others to The Beachcomber for dinner and drinks more than once over the next couple of weeks. The guys had myriad interests which, we were sure, were not all above board. But when they offered us some further legitimate work, we were happy to take it on. That boiled down to tracking a few folks who had failed to honour contracts with them. It was simple stuff. We solved their problems by day and, when we dropped off the bill in the evenings, Saul would produce a wad of cash and pay us over a cocktail.

Everything was good for those weeks—right up until the moment I took a call from Michael Fry, the bank manager who had been storing the sculpture.

Asking for complete discretion, he said, 'I have some concerns.'

Part of the security for the £10,000 loan they were seeking from him was in the form of certificates left with the bank. These were Silver Delivery Contracts issued by Universal Mining Corporation. On the face of it, they guaranteed future ownership of 100,000 troy ounces of silver—about three tonnes or so. Fry had his suspicions and asked us to verify their authenticity. And, of course, we were interested to know the answer ourselves. Saul Kay's $1,200 cheque was already in the bank. We had been allowed to draw against that while it cleared. If there was something fishy going on and the cheque bounced, we'd be out of pocket.

I called the Atlanta bank which was due to honour the cheque. When I got into the details of the account, the call was transferred to the fraud manager. I was advised that Saul Kay was a fraudster being actively sought by US police. He had pulled that same cheque scam a few times. I came off that call knowing we had a short time until our own bank got word we had been tricked into depositing a dud.

Next up, I needed to be sure of the score with the certificates. I called the Securities Exchange Commission in Texas. They confirmed what we had guessed. The documents were worthless. Legal action was already underway to prosecute the company that issued them.

I reported the bad news back to Fry. Fortunately he had not yet completed the loan. He had so far advanced just £750 to the scumbags. He put in a call to the May Fair to spill the beans on their crooked guests. It turned out the Americans had run up a hotel bill of over £7,000, which was no small beer in the seventies.

A couple of days later and I took a call from the manager of the May Fair. He asked Stuart and I over for a meeting.

'They've gone,' he said. 'They just upped and went. We're not sure when.'

He said that the May Fair does not suffer scammers and that he wanted them caught. Could we track them down and help recover the debt? Gladly.

I was passed an envelope. It held all the bills run up by Kay, Wilson, Olsen and Burnham and a £1,000 cheque as downpayment for our services. The bills listed phone numbers dialled from each room. And a search turned up discarded letters advising of possible addresses and other details of interest in respect of Kay and Wilson. I had enough to make a start and booked the first of many flights to the magnificent US of A.

I feel compelled to say that I was thrilled with America from the moment I set foot in New York, maybe even before as I viewed the city shining below me from the sky. I quickly became fascinated too with Americans and that warm passion they so often display for their most welcoming nation and its hard-won liberty. I was kitted out in my conservative suit and British regimental tie as I began my wide-eyed journey from the bustling Big Apple into the laid back heart of the US in search of fraudsters. I remember feeling like something of an oddity as I travelled, yet it was that difference, the fresh, easy and generous newness I found there, which would draw me ever closer to the United States and its extraordinary people in the years to come.

The information I had didn't prove overly valuable in itself, those phone numbers and addresses bringing me no nearer to the men I sought. But it did take me to Texas where I was certain I could close in firstly on John Wilson. It was all moving slowly but fortunately I did have a good number for Saul Kay in Atlanta, Georgia. And, to the best of my knowledge, he didn't know I was onto him. I called up and he said he was delighted to hear from me. He wondered when I might be returning the statuette to him and I advised that things were moving along. At my request, he passed on a number for John Wilson in Dallas.

I spoke with Wilson's sister on the phone, left my details and explained it was important. He clearly thought so too and arrived later at my hotel room with another man. And he wasn't in the mood to shake hands.

'What are you doing here?' he said in a less than jovial tone.

'You forgot to pay your hotel bill,' I said, 'and the cheque you guys gave me bounced.'

His face remained blank before he said none of that had anything to do with him. 'I was invited to London by Saul Kay,' he told me. 'I haven't been refunded any of my own expenses, not my airfare, nothing.'

Yet it was his Silver Certificates being used to secure the loan from Barclays?

'Did you know they're fraudulent?' I asked him.

It was then he lost whatever cool he was hanging on to. He advised me loudly that I would not leave Dallas if I was standing over that claim and I was sure that was getting close to a death threat. I remember being a little shocked at the escalation because, of the four men I had met, he had always seemed the most level-headed.

He fumed, 'Those certificates have a future value. That's what they are—promises to deliver in the future.'

I told him the issuing corporation said they had no value and never would. He told me to back off and left it at that. But I knew he knew the score.

His sister came looking for me the next day, said John had got himself mixed up in some dodgy business, that she had been surprised to learn from me that he had been in England. His loved ones were very worried about him, she said. I pressed her just to get him to pay his hotel bill, saying that would be enough to get me off his case. That same night he arrived at my room alone. But he wasn't offering any money. Instead he was holding a revolver.

He pushed his way in and began ranting away like a man on the edge. He was saying, 'I'm not afraid to use this. Don't call me again, leave my family out of this.'

I calmed him down and got him to put the gun away. I told him his share of the total $14,200 bill from the May Fair was $3,550, that it was hardly worth shooting me over. He sat down and explained he had been seeking to make a legitimate, promising investment in a patented Dexter mini-sewing machine which was proving to be a great success in America. Saul Kay, a former business associate, had come on board by vowing to come up with the cash by using the statuette as collateral. The statuette, he said, was worth in the region of $100,000. Kay had managed to borrow it for a while and was making hay while he could. Ahead of setting off for the UK where the Dexter was set to hit the market, Kay pressed Wilson to come up with some security of his own. He had got his hands on these authentic-looking certificates. A large batch had been produced by a chap called Garland Lincecum as a way to raise cash from people needing to come up with collateral. But the whole thing was a scam. They were ultimately worthless. Wilson had lost everything.

He left around 3 am after pouring his heart out. I felt sorry for him, yet I still wanted to do right by my client. I called him the next day to see if we could work something out. His sister told me he was gone, that he had cleared out saying he was off on a business trip and that she knew no more. I knew then I wouldn't get a penny from Wilson.

Kay, the ringleader, was the only other man I had located. But perhaps he was the only guy I needed in terms of fixing this thing. I went to Atlanta, called him up. He said he was disappointed I didn't have the statuette with me. I told him it was safe in London and that he would really need to think about paying his debts. He wasn't particularly interested in that line of conversation. Instead, he said we should get out on the town and enjoy ourselves as we had done quite a few times in London, that he would put me up at his place for the night. And, already knowing that he was an engaging man to be with, a blunt, gruff bloke, charismatic in his own way, I went for it. I thoroughly enjoyed those hours knocking back drinks in various bars, including the Peachtree Plaza overlooking the city. He talked about the USA, about the civil war, about crime and criminals in Atlanta and of how his wife was a professional singer. He was clearly proud of her.

Indeed he took me to see his wife on stage later on. She was a quite beautiful woman who sang in breathy, jazzy, bluesy tones before joining us at our table as we sank yet more drinks. I remember how she was cat-called a few times by a group of men at a table nearby, and that Kay was not at all pleased. As we left the club in the early hours, she got into her own car and headed towards the home she shared with her husband. I was getting into the other car with Kay, who was pretty smashed, when he spotted one of the men who had been shouting to her on the stage. Kay said it looked as if the man, who had just got into his own car, was tailing his wife. And a moment later he was convinced of it. He started the engine, revved a few times and floored it. Within seconds I was in a car chase as the letch ahead, who was as sozzled as both Kay and myself, swerved all over the place to get away from this aggressive driver behind.

Seatbelts were not yet compulsory in the UK and had just become so in the USA. I'd never used one before but, in line with the law, this seemed like a good time to start. I clicked myself in as we slalomed fast in among other cars and a hard around corners.

After a while the other guy broke away and was clearly no longer behind Kay's wife, but my conman kept on his trail. And, shockingly, as the man slowed down, Kay put the pedal to the metal and rammed right into the back of his car. We were both jolted forward. I sat back, composed myself, hoped that would be it. But nope. The bloke ahead of us, presumably terrified, hit the accelerator and sped away. Kay followed, this time even faster. I was clinging to the handgrip above the door for dear life as we continued, screeching around corners like something out of *Starsky & Hutch*. A few more minutes and Kay's quarry swung into a cul-de-sac and our car was aimed right at him. The man spun his wheels, got out of the way just in time but his exit was blocked. Kay jammed on the brakes, brought us to halt almost alongside him. His hand reached across me, flipped open the glove box and he pulled out a revolver.

Christ.

I really had to speak up now.

'Saul,' I said, loud and clear, 'what the hell are you doing?'

He didn't answer. He was winding his window down. He put his arm out and pointed the gun right at the bloke. The guy ducked down out of sight. I wasn't sure Kay would fire, couldn't believe a man would be so reckless—and then a shot rang out. Then another. And another. He blasted all six, bullets slamming into glass and metal as the man crouched down fearing for his life. I thought at first that he might fire back, that Kay's life and my own could be on the line too. But luckily no. I could just make out the passenger side door opening after the gunfire and, on hands and knees, that man crawled away as far and as fast as he could. I couldn't know if he had been hit but I felt it was likely. My heart was pounding, ears ringing. This guy hosting me for the night wasn't just a fraudster, he was a maniac.

Kay turned my way and growled, 'That'll teach the son of a bitch.'

We drove in silence to his home. I went straight to bed, ready to get up and out of there sharpish in the morning. I must say sleep didn't come easy. At about 2 am, more drama—screams from within the property. Kay and his wife were getting stuck into a domestic that sounded like a small war. Then more screams, shrill shrieks of terror telling me for sure that she might well be fearing for her safety.

I'd had enough. I threw off the covers, pulled on some clothes and walked into the lounge. Kay was thrusting the gun at his wife, his face tensed up just as it had been earlier when he pulled that same trigger six times.

'Saul,' I said, 'put it down, mate. Put the gun down. Let's talk it over.'

He turned to me, tears in his eyes, held the weapon right where it was. I didn't know whether he had reloaded it or not, but I couldn't take the chance.

'Saul,' I said, my palms held up and open, moving towards him, 'think about this. Calm down, calm down.'

'That whore,' he slurred, jabbing the gun towards his wife once more, 'was gonna cheat on me.'

She yelled, 'You're crazy. Saul, you're crazy! No way. You're fucking crazy!'

I was a couple of feet from him now, his right forearm still pointing that weapon. As she shouted I saw his muscles tense. It wasn't looking good. I lunged at him, threw all my weight onto that arm, forcing it down. He resisted and a second later that weapon thundered. A bullet slammed into the lounge carpet right by my foot. Saul dropped the gun, staggered backwards and plopped himself, dizzy, drunk, distressed, into an armchair. His wife stood in silence, frozen with fear. Then a burning smell rising up from where I stood. I looked down, saw that the bullet had nicked the end of my shoe before thumping into the carpet. Part of the rubber crepe-style sole had been melted by the heat of the projectile.

Kay began sobbing as his wife collected herself as I pondered, shoe smoking, how close I had come to losing a toe. She straightened herself up, came back to life and went off to make coffee. After that, with the gun stashed in a safe place, we made it alive back to our rooms.

I was up again at 5 am, this time with two uniformed police officers by my bed, weapons engaged, ordering me to wake, demanding I raise my hands. I was cuffed as they searched my luggage, emptying it out on

Ian Withers in USA

the bed. I explained who I was and why I was there and after a while they unlocked me. Along the hallway, Kay was arrested for the attempted murder not of his wife but of the poor bloke who had been chased through the streets of Atlanta hours earlier. Fortunately that man had not been shot. It was all one hell of a mess and it took a while, with the help of the British Embassy, to get my part of it cleaned up and get myself back to London.

My report to the client at the May Fair confirmed I had located Wilson and Kay but failed to collect money from either. What I had learned, among other things, was that Kay was chiefly known for cashing stolen travellers cheques and had lived well on the proceeds. In the end he was jailed for more than seventy years for his various misdeeds.

That extraordinary trip opened my eyes to a lot of things, but most usefully to what I knew was fertile ground for new business possibilities. I came away knowing that me and my smouldering footwear wanted a foothold in what seemed like an exciting place to be. It led to me searching out and buying fifty percent of a PI agency, *Maryland Investigations Inc*, from owner Terry McGill. And once I got myself a licence to work as an investigator on that side of the Atlantic, I got trained up and licenced to carry a concealed weapon.

In that brief first visit to the good old US of A I'd had guns aimed at me, had guns fired close to me and had been shot through my shoe. It had been nothing less than an edge-of-the-seat introduction. But, all things considered, I felt that if there were going to be guns around in future then I wanted to make sure I was at the right end of them.

TEN

London's Underworld and The Emperor of Porn (1970)

THE nature of our work would routinely take us to the fringes of the underworld, and very often right to the heart of it. London, in the sixties and seventies, was a constantly expanding, teeming world city and, along with everything else, its underworld was thriving. That underworld was perhaps personified by figures like The Krays, the infamous East End gangster twins who controlled chunks of the capital via organised crime.

Another fearsome name of the time was Jimmy Humphreys, a charismatic club owner, major pornographer and general gangster. Humphreys smoothed his own path with a game he played regularly with the police. It's said they would come to his Soho sex shops, use obscenity laws to seize all the goodies and take them away. Humphreys would duly pop along to the station, bung a wedge of cash into the right person's hand and get them all back. In doing so, he got to know a great many dodgy coppers and many ended up on his payroll.

Humphreys, who apparently revelled in the grand moniker 'The Emperor of Porn,' came into our lives in 1970. His wife, Rusty Gaynor, a former stipper at one of his various clubs, called seeking our help. She was convinced her husband was cheating. She wanted to get enough evidence to launch a divorce. We said we were the right guys for the job.

'His name is Jimmy Humphreys,' she said.

'Ah,' I said, and knew things could get interesting.

The divorce law had been reworked not long before meaning the courts no longer required direct evidence of infidelity to grant the decree. Instead they needed material to suggest an irretrievable breakdown. And thank heavens for that. Jimmy Humphreys was the sort of man who would unleash the hounds on a bloke who burst into his bedroom while he was getting his jollies, and probably never call them back.

I asked Rusty to put her request to us via her solicitor, as was good practice, and set about following the notorious Jimmy in his luxury cars around the West End. His colourful daily duties took him to many pubs, various strip clubs and a host of backstreet dirty book shops. One day we watched him pull over in Piccadilly before a middle-aged man walked over. The pair had a chat at the window before forty-year-old Jimmy passed him an envelope. The man tucked it into his inside pocket. It was interesting and told a story of some kind, but it did nothing to support the notion he was having an affair. Yet instinct told me to include photographs of the event in our report all the same.

It took a few weeks of day and night surveillance but we managed to gather up quite a few images of Jimmy close and cosy with various young women, mostly strippers, at a number of clubs and restaurants. Rusty's solicitor was satisfied it was enough to secure the divorce. The file was closed.

A while later, Rusty called again. She wanted to meet me in a bar in Soho. I didn't know what it was about but, even though she had a sharp temper, I liked the lady and she paid her bills. I went along. We chatted for a few moments before she led me to a booth. And there sat the gangster whose hard face I knew so well—Jimmy Humphreys.

She said to him, 'This is Ian, the private investigator who was following you.'

It occured to me, as Jimmy and I looked at each other, that agreeing to meet Rusty that day may have been a mistake. But there was nothing else for it. I stood my ground.

'Ian,' he said, nodding.

'Jimmy,' I said.

He asked me to sit. My first impressions were that he was not troubled by the fact I'd been shadowing him for weeks. Yet there really was something menacing in his character and I hoped to learn no more about it.

Thankfully, Jimmy's only interest in me was professional. He asked if I could mount surveillance at a strip club to count the patrons entering between 9 pm and 2 am over seven days. He felt that the manager was under-reporting the numbers and pocketing the difference.

It sounded straightforward enough. Stuart and I took on the job. But, as we would learn in the days ahead, it wasn't plain sailing. Hanging around outside a strip club for hours on end gets you noticed by various parties, not least my old friends in the police. We had to hurriedly get a simple, workable pretext in order when they wandered over on one occasion. We said we were PIs on a domestic surveillance assignment and, after checking our IDs, they left us alone.

On the last evening we had secured a good spot to park allowing full view of the doors. As we tallied up the numbers, a knock on the window. A young man from the little cafe next to the club. He handed us two coffees in plastic cups. We thanked him for his thoughtful gesture before he asked, 'Are you the Bill?'

I said, 'No, we're not police.'

'That's fine. If you want another coffee just come over.'

'Thanks. We will.'

About 11 pm and we noticed him waving us over. I left Stuart in the car to keep counting and went to see the young man. He nodded towards a customer.

'He wants a word,' he told me.

Curious, I walked to the man's table. A very average looking guy reached out his hand, beamed generously as if he knew me. He said everything was fine, just that the boss of 'next door' wanted a word. I could only assume he meant the strip club, and the boss he was talking about was Jimmy.

I followed him out and down an alleyway alongside. We entered the club through a double door fire escape. Once inside, the fire doors closed and he stopped. So I stopped. The pair of us stood in dim light among the muffled sound of the entertainments further inside.

'Are you working for Jimmy?' he said, turning my way, the wide smile gone.

'Who wants to know?' I said, sizing the guy up just in case this was going to get ugly. He didn't concern me.

An internal door opened. A giant of a man appeared and growled,

'I do.' He walked towards me, a crowbar in his hands, his eyes on mine.

My blood ran cold. I was trapped. He was closing in. I remember stepping backwards, eyes dropping to that crowbar. I reached the wall, could go no further. My palms pressed cold brick, my brain tumbling with crazy ideas about finding a secret latch, about a secret door opening.

My fingertip touched the edge of something—a fire extinguisher on a rack. I had no choice. There was no time. I grabbed it at the top, pulled it from its mount. The heavy extinguisher slipped, dropped, the release button on its base striking the floor as I grabbed it again. A powerful jet of foam shot towards the ogre heading my way. I got control of it, aimed the nozzle right at his face, hit him with a jet of compressed chemicals. He was forced back, shouted something as it filled his features. The bar dropped with a welcome clang and, adrenalin surging, I made for the door. I dashed past the other guy, who didn't even try to stop me, and slammed the panic bar on the exit. Thankfully the doors flew open and I was out of there, racing out onto the street, checking behind me all the way. I wasn't being chased and, after a few seconds, stopped running. I doubled back, pulled open the door of the car where Stuart was duly counting away.

'We have to go,' I gasped, my dad's *cesspits and roses* observation on my mind.

I later gave the details to Jimmy and I only know that the manager was later replaced.

Over the years that followed he employed us many times to keep tabs on people who were usually trying to make a few quid from one or other of his businesses. He went on to buy Southend Dog Track and had us install alarms and CCTV there. The last time I met him, he asked me to hook up covert recording devices in various offices used by the owners, trainers and betting operators at the track. He said it was to 'prevent fraud,' but I had my suspicions.

Then, in February 1972, everything changed for Jimmy.

The Sunday People's headline shouted it out:

"Police Chief and the Porn King."

The story told how Detective Chief Superintendent Kenneth Drury, the head of the Met's organised crime-busting Flying Squad, had been on a lavish holiday with a gangster. The most unlikely quartet of Drury,

Jimmy Humphreys and their wives had travelled to Cyprus and Beirut for a fortnight's break.

Amazingly Drury had signed into a hotel in Famagusta under his name, with his rank, and gave his address as Scotland Yard. Humphreys had paid for the Drury's holiday. Drury claimed it was all above board, that Humphreys was a paid informant assisting in the search for Ronnie Biggs, known for his part in the Great Train Robbery of 1963. That was quite the claim. Humphreys held a press conference. He said he was no grass, or informant, and that Drury was a liar.

I remember when a couple of senior detectives from the Met's Complaints Unit called at our office. They asked if I had worked on a case for Rusty Humphreys. I said I had. They had with them all the pictures we'd taken during the surveillance of Jimmy Humphreys, everything we had given to Rusty. They drew my attention to the images in which Jimmy had passed an envelope to a man who approached his car.

'Did you witness this event,' I was asked.

The man at the car was Drury who by then had been suspended while under investigation for corruption. The detectives asked if we would make witness statements. It was clear as light that a once mutually beneficial relationship between the cop and the crook had turned seriously sour. I agreed to testify. Jimmy himself had agreed to do the same.

The case became the biggest post-war corruption scandal to hit the Metropolitan Police. Twelve detectives, all of whom had pocketed money from Jimmy, were jailed. In turn, Jimmy won a royal pardon from an eight-year sentence for arranging the brutal assault of one of Rusty's former boyfriends.

Jimmy disappeared after all that. It turned out he moved to Co Limerick in Ireland where he ran a greyhound track. From there, after apparently learning a police raid was coming his way, he went to Mexico.

In 1988 he and Rusty returned to London, still married, and set up a number of brothels. That venture ended with them both being prosecuted. Jimmy was sent down for a year while Rusty was sentenced to eight months.

In 1999 the couple were in talks with Film4 Productions about a movie on the story of their lives. It was to be called *Rusty*. I think it's a shame it never happened. Jimmy Humphreys died in 2003.

ELEVEN

Two Abducted Girls (1972)

I KILLED a rat in France. The thing had scuttled out from behind the bar in a restaurant, stopped and looked around. A dozen or so journalists from the UK looked back. One shrieked in terror, clambered onto her chair.

A waitress close to me stood still, also observing developments, a heavy silver tray in her hand. I took it, flung it like a frisbee. It landed well, cracked our most unwelcome guest on the head. It was killed, or at least stunned. It rolled onto its side and its little legs shuddered. I went over, picked it up by the tail and walloped it against the wall just in case. I dumped it in the bin, retrieved the tray, washed my hands.

A writer with the *Evening Standard* reported on it in the *Londoner's Diary* column, turned it into a tale derring-do by a private detective while British media dined. It was the kind of account that stuck in a reader's head, that helped yet more with the profile of our agency. It would go on to play a part in creating the impression that if you needed something difficult done, you should call on Ian Withers and *Nationwide Investigations*, or any of the other names which our company would adopt. I take my hat off to that rat. He did me a favour yet got the raw end of the deal.

It was 1972 and the agency's reputation was already that mixed bag of notorious, mysterious and effective. In terms of profile at least, there was little to match us in the UK. The range of work we were involved with was constantly broadening, the significance of the end goals forever increasing. My skills were sharp, my confidence high and I didn't like to turn down anything that would test my limits. People who needed to get *Mission Impossible* done and dusted would very often turn to our firm first because they had heard we got results.

Myself and a chunk of Fleet Street were in France because of an emerging and complex new phenomenon—parental abduction. Increased international travel had sparked a rise in marriages between people from different countries. And in cases where those marriages had broken down, it was common for the parents to battle over where any offspring should live. Those battles, given what was at stake, could escalate fast.

The law in this area was slow and muddled and, as time went on, more and more parents would take matters into their own hands. In some cases they had legal clearance to access their children and, during visits, would remove them from the country. In other cases they would approach them without sanction, take them from houses or schools or elsewhere and spirit them beyond the borders.

These became known as *Tug of Love* cases in the press, the term coined by a quite brilliant journalist called Shelley Rohde at the *Manchester Daily Mail*. She had broken the first high-profile British story of its kind at the time. And I became involved when I was hired to help track down the father who had taken his baby daughter to France.

As a result of that first assignment, and with an honourable mention for the rat, a series of engagements on abduction cases would follow. Indeed they came to define a significant part of my career. Each one was different not just in terms of the adults, children and overall dynamics involved, but different too because of the range of countries and cultures that would play host to these difficult situations. One of the key complicating factors was that, of course, the law in one place can be very different to the law in another place. But, as a rule, I was engaged when custody was granted by a court to one party wherever they may be. From there I sought to ensure the child was returned to the legally sanctioned, rightful mum or dad, from anywhere in the world.

All of us are subject to legal decisions yet all of us know that such things seek to make black or white from grey, to make clear things that are often smudged and opaque. The abduction cases in which I would become involved were all intensely personal issues for those impacted, matters of unassailable importance, matters of the deepest parts of the heart. The recovery of a child from a parent who will do all in their power to prevent it takes considerable resolve. Before the decade was out,

I would know that only too well. The weapons used in the fight to secure custody would be far beyond those employed by the legal profession.

That first case in France involved Caroline, the baby daughter of Manchester woman Linda Desramault. The child, eight-months-old, had been spirited over the English Channel by her father, René Desramault. Ahead of that he had applied to an English Magistrates Court for joint custody and access to the baby. In a rash move, it had been granted with immediate effect. Within hours, Mr Desramault had left the UK with the child in his arms. His wife had been about to make the court aware of an intention to appeal when she learned they were gone.

The UK news coverage was massive. It was the first known international case of its kind with British involvement. The issue was raised in parliament. Appeals were made to the Prime Minister. High level diplomatic exchanges took place. And all the while a distraught mother in England had been plunged into the living hell of losing access to her daughter. She didn't even know where she was.

It was the *London Evening Standard,* guided by Linda Desramault's lawyer Harry Mincoff, which called me in. Obviously, they said, this was a high profile case. In exchange for a reduced fee and publicity, would I help locate the errant Mr Desramault?

'I'd be happy to,' I said.

The girl's mum had gone ahead with her appeal and, successful, a fresh order demanded the child be returned to the UK. Locating Mr Desramault meant related applications could be made to relevant local courts. Yet if the father could not be found, the law was not much use.

Harry Mincoff hammered home the point in the British press that his client had been badly let down by the courts, that a most cold and cavalier attitude had deprived a mother of her baby. The public was inclined to agree.

As a small army of print and broadcast reporters had already done, I made my way to Mr Desramault's home city of Béthune in northern France. It was a less than impressive place, easily forgettable other than the enormous Hotel de France in the centre which would become our base. I teamed up with the *Standard's* reporter and photographer and we kept ourselves and our insights tight. The competition for a fresh line on the story was fierce and, given we had quality access to Harry Mincoff, there were many attempts to lure us into spilling a few beans. The woman at the centre of the drama, Linda Desramault, who arrived a day or so after me, had signed her own deal with *The Sun* and as such was out of my immediate reach.

As I began my digging, making whatever connections I could to locate the vanished Mr Desramault, I fell in with a reporter for *The Guardian*. Serge Nabokov was Russian, a pleasant, elderly gentleman, fluent in a number of languages including French. That was fortunate because I wasn't exactly flying along with my *merci, oui,* non and *parlez vous anglais?* He welcomed the company of myself and my journalist colleagues in part because he found himself a little shunned by the younger, go-getting hacks willing to tear each other to shreds to get the story.

He happily drove us around in his rented car where we checked out every address we could—old friends, former neighbours, distant relatives. Using the pretext that Serge was a sympathetic French journalist seeking Mr Desramault's side of the story, we found out where he was. Aware the aggressive British media were on his case, he had taken little Caroline and slipped into Belgium where he was holed up with an aunt.

Sweet-talking Serge persuaded his source to phone the aunt and, when he got her on the line, managed to get her to put Mr Desramault on the phone. He agreed to meet our new Russian friend the following day.

Myself, the *Standard* reporter and Serge drove to the village in question, found the aunt's house, and began our surveillance. I used the phone in a little B&B to call back to the *Standard's* photographer in Béthune who was keeping tabs on Linda and her entourage from *The Sun*. He passed on word that we had located the father of her child, but it seemed Linda and the hacks had gone out to dinner. She would be driven over in the morning, we were told.

I found that annoying, and a little surprising too. I'd been on this tiring case for over a week and, right when we had tracked the man himself, I was basically advised to sit in the car while everyone else finished wining and dining and got themselves a good kip. Static surveillance overnight, a cold car, complete darkness—great.

Serge checked in at the B&B and myself and the reporter got as comfortable as we could. We talked for a while, kept our eyes trained on the house and Mr Desramault's car. And we waited. And waited. And I remember my eyelids growing heavy… I woke and his car was gone. I was furious with myself. Beside me, the *Standard's* reporter—out cold, snoring loudly.

Thankfully Serge, after a good rest, was ready for action. He called the aunt once more who said her nephew René, fearing the baby may be taken from him, had cleared off early. After some gentle prodding she said he had mentioned going to a friend's address in Switzerland. He had been planning to call Serge from there.

Linda and *The Sun* arrived a little after that. They were too late. Her lawyer was not pleased but said there was a positive to be had. The court order they were to serve would not have been enforceable in Belgium. The father could have just ignored it and driven away. The lawyer said the Swiss would be far more cooperative and opened talks that day with his counterparts there. We should, he said, return to England.

In time, the Swiss were able to locate Mr Desramault and agreed to enforce the UK ruling. Linda returned to Manchester with Caroline in her arms.

A press report of the time said: *"Linda subsequently divorced René— and some years later remarried—this time very happily.*

"René, a bitter and vindictive man who used a helpless little girl as a pawn to punish her Mother for daring to leave him, died some years later."

It ended well. The publicity, even about the rat, worked out. But what I took from it was the value of working directly with a client instead of via a lawyer. Abduction cases are complex, intricate and emotive. They take time, there are legal implications with every move and the stakes are high. I knew from that point that, if I were to work on more, I would want to have the full attention of the anguished parent when I needed it, not to be a guy waiting around for her to finish dinner.

In 1974, after a number of successful abduction cases, we were accompanied on an assignment to Mallorca by a TV crew from Southampton-based Southern Television. The documentary which followed, *For The Love of Helen*, saw cameraman Roy Page awarded First Prize in the News Films Regional Category of the Royal Television Society—British News Film of the Year.

I had been contacted by Marion Serra, nee Astridge. Her marriage to Jaime Pastor Serra, a tour bus operator, was over. Their only child, Helen, had been taken to Mallorca by her father, contrary to an English court order.

Marion, twenty-two, had arrived in the office with her parents Fred and Joyce Astridge and a researcher from Southern Television. Over two hours we learned Helen had been living with her mother and grandparents at the family home in Letchworth, England. Jaime's initial application to an English court for access had been denied. The court had agreed with an assertion from Marion that he might abduct Helen. If the three-year-old was to end up in Mallorca, Marion would have no parental rights and there was no extradition treaty.

Yet he had persisted and eventually the court granted him access to Helen for two days a month. It was on the first of the access visits that he, and the child, disappeared. As the mother had feared, he took her straight to Mallorca. A court order was posted to him insisting he return the child but, surprise, surprise, he ignored it. As did the Spanish government when pressed on the issue. Again, questions were raised in parliament amid major media interest.

It would be unprecedented for us to have a TV crew with us during a case, but after talking it through with Stuart and our agents, we agreed. One agent would go out a week in advance of our arrival, confirm the whereabouts of Helen and keep watch. We would follow, plan and execute the recovery and reunite the child with mum.

At the forefront of my mind was spreading the risk. I engaged agents from a number of agencies to reduce the commercial exposure in case of some unforeseen disaster. One of those was Terry Platt from a Reading-based agency. He was a fit and strong ex-army type, larger than life, plenty of tattoos and a few scars too, including those from a pet panther he loved to wrestle with. Beyond all that, Terry was a master of disguise.

Terry flew over to find the target and get a good sense of what the man did with himself each day. He got back to us after a couple of days. Helen, he said, was not being looked after by her dad but was instead living with her grandparents. Her father was living with his girlfriend some distance away. Her grandfather, Terry reported, usually drove her to a nursery school at 8 am daily and collected her in the late afternoon.

Myself, Marion, an agent called Brian Gunn, TV director Mike O'Connor and Roy Page made our way to Barcelona. From there we took the ferry to Palma de Mallorca, the capital and principal city of the Balearic Islands. On arrival, anxious Marion donned a wig and heavy sunglasses just in case.

Terry had rented us a four-bedroom, first-floor apartment and three local cars. One of the vehicles was solely for the drive from the school after the recovery. It was to be left at the airport suggesting Marion and Helen had left. A second car was for the change-over after recovery. Marion and Helen would switch vehicles and be driven back to the apartment. The third car was for general doings in the meantime, for going out, dry runs and shopping.

We launched into the surveillance, checking the comings and goings at the school and the grandparents' home. As we began perfecting our plan, Marion became more and more anxious about it all. She was already in a constant despair and, understandably, this new proximity to her daughter was hurting hard. We agreed she must stay in the apartment while we put the basics together, that we needed to be calm, clear and focused.

Three days into the operation, on a Saturday, we took her out. There was little we could do with the school closed so we booked a day at a communal barbeque to try and relax her. We picked a venue at the other end of the island and far from any risk of being spotted by Jaime or his family or friends. The location turned out to be a busy car park packed with tourist coaches from the many hotels. We kept our heads down and enjoyed the weather, grub and local vino knowing what lay ahead on Monday.

The crew filmed as we strolled back to our car. Marion was walking ahead when she turned to me. It was a look of horror. It took me a moment to realise. Jaime, a tour bus operator, stood just a couple of coaches away. He was chatting to a crowd he had just dropped off and could turn towards us any second.

Terry and Brian clocked the danger. They moved in fast, pulled all his attention towards them. They pretended they were drunk, loudly insisted he was their driver. They ramped up the tension, turned heads and an argument broke out. Meanwhile, I got Marion out of there. We made our way to the perimeter and then carefully back to the car. A close call. It seemed as if it took her the rest of the weekend to get her breath back.

We were up at daybreak on Monday. Terry was wearing glasses, his hair dyed blond. He dressed to appear ten years older. His job was to walk just behind Marion as she went into the school, to be the support in case of any problems, to make sure the child was removed come what may. Marion was to approach her little girl and explain to any inquisitors that she had just arranged a doctor's appointment and would drop the child back later instead. I was at the school gate, parked up in the rented escape car. The film crew was right behind me. Brian, in our third car, was parked a half mile away. His role was to drive the escape car to the airport right after the changeover.

Right on time, grandad dropped off the three-year-old. I watched as he lingered for a few minutes and drove off. Marion began walking in after the child right away, duly followed by Terry, to catch up with the little girl.

Marion was more nervous than ever. She had barely slept, was in a fragile emotional state. Yet as the child's mother, she was absolutely the best person for this job. I had my concerns as she entered the school building. It was a long minute.

Then she was back, carrying her beloved daughter towards the school gates, Terry by her side. They walked to the escape car, got in and I pulled slowly away.

As planned, I drove the half mile to the second rental, switched cars and Brian went off to the airport. He parked it up, left a copy of the UK court order inside as planned, checked in and flew home. The rest of us went back to the apartment. Everything was going great. Marion was beside herself with emotion. Little Helen was thrilled to see her mum. And then, about half past four, the shit hit the fan.

Helen had been reported missing. Police had moved in fast, large numbers of officers were actively searching. TV news was leading on the case. The escape car had been found. But we were ready.

As instructed, Marion's family had already sent pre-prepared tele-grams to the Palma police, Helen's school and to the grandmother. Each read simply, *"Sorry, this was the only way—Helen is now back in England."*

We figured it might take a week for things to ease up, but it took just a couple of days. The police patrols wound down and the search was abandoned. Terry, now out of his disguise, kept tabs on the grandparents' and father's addresses but Jaime was nowhere to be seen. News broke later that he had been arrested entering the UK. And that was our cue to get out of Mallorca earlier than planned.

We returned to the ferry port en route back to Barcelona. Helen was not named on her mother's passport, but that was not going to be a prob-lem. My passport did name both my son Andrew and daughter Debbie and neither needed to be pictured on such a document at the time. We passed easily as a family of three. Southern Television flew ahead to meet us on arrival at Heathrow. When we touched down, it became clear Brit-ish Airways ground staff had spotted us, that they knew the case from press reports. They came on-board to take us off the plane ahead of the other passengers. Amid tearful reunions and TV interviews in Heathrow, I had Helen perched on my shoulders for the photographers. Just a cou-ple of days later Marion and I were guests on TV's *The David Frost Show*.

In October 1976, Jaime Serra arrived at Marion's family home in Letchworth. Inside were Marion, her father Fred and daughter Helen. Denied access, Serra turned to Plan B. He had secured for himself some explosive material which he then forced through the letterbox. Seeing this coming through, and not realising what it was, Marion tried to push it back out. It detonated, seriously injuring her hand.

The door blown apart, Jaime entered. When challenged by Fred, he pulled out a handgun. He shot the older man twice in the chest and once in his head before barricading himself in. Somehow, I am glad to say, the mighty Fred survived.

Armed police arrived, surrounded the property. After three hours of negotiation, Jaime was arrested. He appeared in court on November 1st, 1976, charged with attempted murder and was sentenced to life impris-onment. He was released after serving seven years and deported to Spain.

A few phone calls followed that violent drama. Those from the press were not pretty.

'Are you satisfied with the result of what you've done?' I was asked. *'You've almost had someone killed, a woman is seriously injured, a child's father is doing jail time, are you happy that you wrecked a family?'*

I'd come to know that was par for the course for a PI.

But it was a much later phone call, one from a woman in her thirties in the year 2010, that I remember most clearly. I took it as I lay in a hospital bed recovering from heart surgery.

'Hi Ian,' she said, 'this is Helen. I called to see how you are?'

I told her I was doing just fine.

TWELVE

The Prime Minister's Bad Bet (1971)

WE did what we did as well as we could.

We set up what we called a *Pretext Room*. We would play tape recordings as background noise when we made or took calls. We would say we were from a bank and the person would hear tellers talking and coins clinking. We'd say we were from the press and the person would hear typewriters and phones ringing.

We adopted a host of trading names, taking on an idea pioneered by American agencies in search of more business. We were *London Investigation Bureau, Detectives London, Nationwide Investigations* and numerous others. The idea was that, like fishing, the more rods you have in the pond the more bites you get—and the more chance you'll get that big bite too.

And in terms of securing new addresses for vanished debtors, to ensure bills got paid or assets were recovered, we fine-tuned my four-level Automatic Tracing System which made our searching as efficient and cost effective as could be.

Step One: Files—Check the new instructions against existing files. On many occasions, the same debtor-names appeared again and again. This included checking the names against local newspaper archives for deaths, arrests and prison sentences which could help fill in the gaps. About ten percent were resolved at this stage.

Step Two: Write—Send letters to the debtor, their neighbours, any referees supplied at the time of the application and the given employers. In terms of getting that new address, around twenty percent of the time it worked.

Step Three: Pretext calls—Identify ourselves as the person we were seeking or as official interested parties, and contact those who might have the details. We would target banks, building societies and any other places where records were held. We could establish on occasions not just fresh addresses, but also if the debtor's account was in credit, if they had a criminal record. The success rate here was around forty percent.

Step Four: Footslogging—Get onto the streets, knock previous addresses, ask questions, approach neighbours, shopkeepers, landlords. Very often we assigned sub-agents from other firms for this work if the location was close to them. And about fifty percent of the time, footslogging was successful.

All in all, our hit rate was around eighty to eighty-five percent. And if we didn't find the errant man or woman, we stood by our promise to charge only a nominal fee. Our customers came back to us again and again and again.

At the time there was nothing like the UK's *Data Protection Act* of today. The law was unclear and rather unconcerned with the security of personal information. Statutory bodies very often readily gave over details which would be considered startling today. Outside of our trade and one or two others, such information was rarely even considered a particularly valuable resource.

As such, we were harvesting names and numbers, collecting the dots and joining them, from everyone and everywhere that we could. We were certainly playing the system, cutting corners here and there and we were aware that some of this was a little shady. But we never thought we were the bad guys. We were the guys chasing the bad guys. Our advertisements were in commercial magazines, in legal journals, on mailshots to solicitors. Our mission statement boiled down to being able to right wrongs. We were, as we saw it, conducting almost a form of private policing, doing work the police would not do. We were the guys on the trail of the bad guys. We were the good guys.

One day a meeting took place between Prime Minister Edward Heath and Alastair Hetherington, the editor of *The Guardian* newspaper. They were old pals and enjoyed the odd lunch together. There had been some publicity about the security of information held by government departments like the Inland Revenue, emerging questions about access to National Insurance data or medical records. Mr Heath himself had told parliament that this was effectively a non-issue, that the security of such information was beyond question. Mr Hetherington wasn't so sure. He told the prime minister he could prove otherwise. The men placed a bet.

In early 1971 I was invited to lunch with Hetherington. He told me of the friendly wager. He said he would give me four names and I was to find out as much information as I could about each. He assured me there was no funny business at play, that all the individuals he would name knew what was going on, that I had the all-clear to look into people who had done no wrong.

We got stuck in. We researched and pretexted, gathered as much as we could fairly easily. In due course, we presented our detailed results and sent over the invoice.

A few days later the front page of *The Guardian* told the story. *"Personal information in the hands of government departments is not safe,"* it warned. Almost anybody can get it via *"confidence tricks,"* it said. And it went on to relate the case of the four volunteers, employees of *The Guardian*, although it did not and would not name the source of it all—myself and my colleagues.

The issue exploded in parliament. Questions from Conservative and Labour alike were fired at the prime minister who, without a doubt, had lost his bet. The embarrassed Mr Heath said he would be directing the Commissioner of the Metropolitan Police to mount an immediate inquiry. The country must shut down on all of this caper, he said, and it would start by finding out who did the digging for *The Guardian*.

The Met gave the job to Detective Chief Superintendent John Hemsley—known in the force as Ginger. He was a tough nut yet a colourful old school Welsh copper known for his bright bow ties. The first thing he did, in a dramatic opening salvo, was have the offices of *The Guardian* raided. But he didn't get what he needed. So from there he launched raids on PI agencies right across London to flush out the evildoers. Amusingly, he did it via the classified phone directory and started with firms whose name began with A, before moving on to B. We were listed under a number of titles, including C. And so when the Met was done with B, it came calling at the offices of *Christopher Robert and Co.*

But, partly due to the less than cryptic investigative pattern, word had been getting around. An anonymous phone call to me in July of 1971 warned of trouble in the early hours of the next morning, a Saturday. The tipster said 'CO' were paying a visit to our new offices in Kilburn, north London, and I should make sure my 'house is clean.' CO, or Commissioner's Office, was slang for New Scotland Yard.

Funny thing was those early hours were when I was supposed to be crossing the channel with Phyl. She was by now my steady girlfriend, the pair of us living a few floors above Stuart and Helen in an apartment building in Wallington. Phyl and I had planned to get away via ferry to Dieppe, to drive to Switzerland to surprise her sister who was married to a local man.

We met up to discuss the phone call and agreed Phyl and I should go ahead and clear off fast.

'Go to Switzerland,' said Stuart. 'If there's any truth in it, I'll deal with the police.'

Phyl and I headed off, took an earlier ferry en route for the beautiful city of Lausanne. We met with friends and family, had a few drinks and all was well. I put a call in to London on Saturday. Stuart said nothing had happened. It must have been a prank. I called him again on Sunday, just to check in, and there was nothing to report. The fact that he didn't answer my Monday call to the office sent a shiver down my spine. It would emerge that our tipster had been right about the raid, but wrong about the date.

DCS Ginger Hemsley, with around twenty officers and two police dog units, had arrived at Stuart's apartment. He was in bed at the time. Helen answered and demanded to see a warrant, which Ginger shoved into her face. It said they were searching for explosives. The squad had already visited my penthouse apartment a few floors up, used a sledgehammer to smash through their way in, before banging on Stuart's door. Stuart and Helen were arrested, cuffed, taken away in separate police cars.

It had been an aggressive, over the top and shameful raid. In order to get the warrant, it turned out they had lied about what they were searching for. The police knew that citing explosives as a reason was a guaranteed way to get legal consent. They had ripped up carpets, smashed cupboard doors and drawers, thrown everything onto the floors. And not content with that, they went on to arrest our company secretary, Patricia Barker, at her home.

During questioning, the police accused them of illegally gathering confidential information from various banks, building societies, government offices and police stations. They warned them of 'years' in jail if they didn't speak up, told scary stories about criminal records which would ruin their lives.

Stuart was driven to Kilburn, to the new offices we had taken on since leaving Nelson House. The secretary's desk there had a switchboard with two incoming phone lines, and six extensions. Of those six, two were for agents, another two for a second office where Stuart and I worked, and one for accounts. The sixth extension ran to the third-floor *Pretext Room*—the additional office we had rented which was accessed through a separate front door. It had three outside ex-directory lines used to make or take calls. And all the open or recently closed cases files were in there too.

But Ginger and his sidekick detective Bernie Davies didn't know about it. They strode around our main office muttering sarcastically, having a go at the amateurish nature of our organisation. But they could not find the files they expected to find. Stuart told me how Ginger wandered to the reception desk.

'You have six extensions, Stuart,' he said, 'but I see only five desks with phones.'

Stuart said, 'You forgot about the receptionist's phone,' pointing to the desk where Ginger stood.

'Ah,' said the policeman.

He called to his colleague searching the inner office used by Stuart and I.

'Find anything, Bernie?'

'I've got something in the cupboard, sir,' said the sidekick.

As Ginger wandered over, a noxious stink filled the room. Stuart said it was like some kind of peppery tear gas, foul and pungent. The two coppers started spluttering and Stuart looked on in total confusion.

Bernie called out, 'It's a gas gun, sir!'

What on earth…?

The Met officers coughed and pointed the finger at my brother, glared at him as if to say they had found enough to cause him major problems.

Bernie held up what looked like a fountain pen—the offending weapon he had just discharged. It was just like the one I had handed over after the robbery at Nelson House. He chucked it at Stuart, said, 'Explain this?'

It was a fit up. There was no gas gun in that office. There never had been. The only gas gun in our possession had been the one I volunteered to show the police at our previous office at Nelson House, which they had then seized. The device presented to Stuart was very similar, if not the same. That whole issue with the first device had ended up in court in what was, as the court agreed, a waste of everyone's time. We had no other gas gun. As I said, this was a fit-up, something they had thought through before arrival. And Stuart told them so.

'You've staged this,' he said.

Ginger kicked off, raised his voice, said that was 'an insinuation' his team was crooked. He marched over, took him by the arm saying, 'I am re-arresting you for possession of a prohibited weapon.'

It took a day before I could get any feedback on what the hell was going on. Eventually I put a call into Scotland Yard, asked to speak with Detective Sergeant Bernard Davis. He was as insincere as could be, told me to make sure I enjoyed my break, to let him know when I got back. Phyl and I, both anxious, annoyed, feeling as if things were out of control, headed straight home.

We arrived in Newhaven at 5 pm on Monday, July 12th, 1971. As we identified ourselves going through Immigration Control, the next surprise—cops and officials surrounded us, slapped on the cuffs, sped us to Kensington Police Station, put us in cells overnight. In the morning I was taken to an interview room to meet Bernie Davis.

'Why did you have us arrested?' I asked, making it clear there was no need for the theatrics, that I had told him I would be in touch when I got back.

His words were unforgettable. He said, 'It's our way of dealing with people—like you.'

We looked at each other for a while as I thought of the things I would like to call this overblown buffoon in front of me.

He said, 'When the Detective Chief Superintendent comes in, you make sure you stand to attention. He is a very important Senior Officer in charge of the Murder Squad.'

'I see,' I said. 'So have I been accused of murder?'

'Not yet.'

More thoughts rolled around in my head. Who on earth do they think I might have murdered? Are they going to fit me up with something as high level as that? It all felt completely possible in those tense minutes.

And in walked chubby Ginger in the comedy bowtie. His sidekick and the uniformed officers stood to attention. Ginger slammed his clenched fist hard onto the desk. The ashtray and papers jumped. So did I. He put his face point blank into mine and that voice boomed.

'I am Detective Chief Superintendent Hemsley. I am in charge of the Murder Squad at New Scotland Yard. You are my prisoner and you are accused of serious criminal offences.'

He stepped back, let himself calm down. He said, 'You and I, Mr Withers, have many things in common. We're both investigators, professional investigators, and we are both liars, professional liars. In fact, the only difference between you and I, is that you are a prisoner and I am a Detective Chief Superintendent in charge of the Murder Squad.'

He sounded nuts. I wanted to say so but thought better of it. The golden rule in such situations, as I had been advised many times, is to say just one thing.

'I want my solicitor,' I said.

Amazingly, despite the threats and rhetoric, we were all bailed the next day. We went back to the offices to clean up. It was then we realised that every file they could get their hands on was gone, that they had stripped the place bare. We cautiously made our way to the *Pretext Room*, concerned they might just have been too thorough for comfort. But no— they missed it. The place was untouched.

As the TV news reported the story, as tipped-off journalists played their footage of boxes of our admin files being removed from the offices, we got back to work. And the wonderful little phrase proved itself right once more.

There's no such thing as bad publicity.

New orders came in from new clients; old clients got in touch with more instructions; fresh enquiries came pouring down the phone lines.

In due course, Stuart, Helen, Phyl and I, were charged with having *conspired to effect a public mischief,* contrary to common law. Another almost unheard of charge, another rule twisted to suit the needs of the police hellbent on getting some kind of result. This *public mischief* conspiracy charge had been used successfully before, in very rare circumstances, against other PIs. Yet, despite being clear as mud, it had never been properly challenged.

We asked for advice and were told what was happening to us was effectively an attempt by police to manufacture law to suit their own needs. The idea was that lying, while dishonest, is not a crime in itself. So their view was that our pretexting was an illegal form of lying as it was likely to amount to a mischief of detriment to the public-at-large. We really didn't think so. We had to fight.

At the first hearing, at a Magistrates Court, we tried to get it thrown out saying there was no such offence known in law. But the court just avoided hassle by kicking it all along, sending us for trial at the Central Criminal Court. We were back at the Old Bailey, our second visit to the infamous Number One Dock on another messy, invented charge.

Four PIs accused of telling lies to get the information creditors needed to execute their court judgments against debtors?

Goodness me… Prepare the guillotine!!

It was interesting to us to wonder why so much money was being spent on this. If we were to be convicted, a legal precedent around private information would be established via Case Law. Such a thing would enable control to be applied through the courts, situation by situation, bringing private investigators and others to heel. And that would happen without a need to enact high-profile and costly legislation which ushered in sweeping, controversial change. The state itself would be able to pick and choose the cases it wanted to fight. Indeed it was the state itself and its myriad arms and agencies which was the largest user of private information. With this case it was, to my mind, setting out not to protect its citizens' information but, via the courts, to declare itself the exclusive owner and controller of the resource.

As the theories were mulled over by many, it did not escape us that blood was being shed in the gangland London of the time, that the crimes of terrorism, prostitution, drug dealing, robbery and extortion were on the rise. Yet here we were, four private investigators being nailed by the top ranks of the Met. We knew from our own contacts that the rank and file thought the case against us stank.

The two week *conspiracy* trial eventually opened on Monday, January 22nd, 1973. Stuart and I were represented by the late Lord Jeremy Hutchinson QC, who later became a High Court Judge. Helen and Phyl, who was now my wife, were represented by Gerald Owen QC. We were not on Legal Aid, which meant we had to pay for the lot. Company money was tied up with wages, investments and loans yet there we were in court and not running our business. Whatever liquid cash there was began to dwindle fast.

Prosecutors alleged we had accessed criminal records via a bureau at New Scotland Yard. We did that by calling in and asking questions using telephone numbers we should not have had. Ginger Hemsley, in his sworn evidence-in-chief, made quite the show of saying how these numbers were secret, not for public use, and that anyone calling them was assumed to be a police officer. We had, he said, obtained them illegally. Crown lawyers produced a book as an exhibit. Ginger identified it as the book which held the secret numbers. It had been found, he gravely told a silent court, during the search of our office.

Jeremy Hutchinson QC checked with me later.

'Is that correct?' he asked. 'The book was in your office?'

'Yes,' I said. 'It's the *Police Almanac*. It's sold in WH Smith.'

'I beg your pardon?'

For the sum of £10, we bought ourselves another *Police Almanac* that same lunch time. Our QC placed it out of sight near his desk. He had questions for Ginger. The numbers in the book, he asked, 'are confidential numbers known only to the police, and only used by the police?'

Ginger nodded, 'Yes, that is what I stated.'

Mr Hutchinson presented the book, said it was on general sale, added, 'It rather makes a hole in your idea that this is a confidential document for police use only.'

Ginger said he had 'no idea' the book was on 'general sale.'

The lawyer said, 'If I or anyone having bought this book telephoned the listed number and spoke to someone and asked "Could you get the criminal record of John Bowman born on such and such day." And being that the call was on the confidential line, he said, "Yes, of course, I can", believing that just because it's on the confidential line?'

Ginger, a little flustered, said, 'He's supposed to ask you who you are and what your number is.'

'But what if he didn't?'

At which point the judge intervened. 'I don't think there would be any offence,' he said wisely. 'I mean if somebody asked you for something, you don't have to tell them. But if you do tell them, why would it be a criminal offence to have asked it? It seems ridiculous.'

It's not easy to state just how much we enjoyed all of this. It was a joy to see Ginger get tangled up in the confused mess of his own making. As for the gas gun that mysteriously appeared in our office, the judge wasn't particularly interested. He ordered that the charge be 'left on the books.'

But as for that costly, high-profile conspiracy trial, as it moved towards its conclusion we ran out of money. Our QC applied for Legal Aid to get things wrapped up. In making the application, which he did verbally to the judge in open court, he inadvertently told everyone we wouldn't be able to pay any fines in the event of a guilty verdict. In which case, if we were to be found guilty, the judge would automatically be left with just one option—sending us to jail.

The jury rose to decide our fate. Several hours later we were called back in. Their verdict on the charge of *conspiracy to affect public mischief? Guilty.*

We were shocked, winded by the conviction, left struggling to understand how a jury had gone along with this farce. In effect, a new law with vast, untold potential had just been created.

The judge, Mr Justice Caulfield, glared over before speaking.

'Will the prisoners stand.'

A bad bet by the British prime minister was about to send the four of us to jail.

THIRTEEN

HMP Brixton and the Old Bailey Bomb (1973)

'IAN Douglas Withers,' he said. I held my breath.

'Twelve months imprisonment.'

Christ.

'Stuart Robert Withers,' he said, 'nine months imprisonment.

'Phyllis Withers and Helen Gearing, six months imprisonment—suspended.'

It was like someone had pressed a pause button on my life. The silence was immense. I could barely believe it. I don't think I blinked, forgot to breathe back out. Was this real?

A jab in the back told me it was. A prison officer forcing me back to reality, directing me to the guilty man's exit. Phyl and Helen, ashen faced, were directed to walk out the other way, into the body of the court. They were free to go, but their shock was no less than ours.

Stuart and I were led down a narrow, stone stairway to a holding cell beneath the courtroom. The officer directed us to a concrete bench, said to wait. We could hear others in this underground jail—muffled voices, shouts, rage. Not a word passed between us brothers. We knew each other well enough to know we needed time to get our heads around what had just happened.

Our counsel, Jeremy Hutchinson QC, appeared at the door, wig still on, black gown flowing behind.

'I'm making an immediate application for bail, pending appeal,' he said. 'This needs to be challenged.'

He seemed confident he would succeed. It gave us a little hope. But in the meantime, he advised, it was likely we would be taken to the remand prison in Brixton, south London. It was, he said, a 'gentler' prison, a place where most inmates were pending trial.

'You'll be there over the weekend,' he said. 'As long as I can get to a judge, I expect to get you both bailed on Monday.'

He left and moments later a prison officer arrived, slapped on the cuffs and told us to follow the other cuffed men. We were all led to the vans for the short journey to Jebb Avenue and the grim, grey walls of Her Majesty's Prison Brixton.

There we were escorted to the euphemistically-named 'reception' area, still having said barely a word.

The orders came thick and fast, barked at us by no-nonsense men who had barked them a thousand times before.

'Undress. Everything off. I mean everything.'

A group of us stood stark naked and shivering in the cold shower area as everything was bagged and tagged. We were hosed down with cold water, sprayed with disinfectant and told to stand under a communal shower. We were handed prison garb, ordered to dress and led through the wings, the shouts of other inmates audible all the way. Stuart and I were allocated a cell in 'C' Wing. We both sat and looked at each other. At least we were still together. I had a feeling that, as an ex-cop whose face was all over the national press that very day, things could get uncomfortable.

Sleep didn't come easy on that first night. Prison sounds are a cacophony of sobbing, groaning, joyless yells. It goes on and on and, for the newly arrived, it's hard to tune out and switch off, especially when your mattress feels like a Brillo Pad. We maybe dozed a little, woke to the clanging of tin plates and mugs, the clunking and sliding, grinding and slamming of steel gates and cell doors.

Day one was Saturday. The prison governor wanted to see us. He was a pleasant enough man. He said he knew the case and expected us to secure an appeal pretty soon.

'As an ex police officer,' he asked me, 'do you feel you need to go into a secure unit? It would minimise risk of attack from other inmates.'

'I'll take my chances,' I said, thanking him for the thought.

The system swung into gear. We were allocated jobs to begin in two days—Monday, February 12th, 1973. As our lawyer sought to secure the appeal, we were given two minutes training by our two co-workers in how to staff the canteen. It was basically a glorified tuck shop within a converted double cell on the ground floor of 'C' Wing. It stocked all kinds of confectionery, tobacco and miscellaneous bits and bobs from shaving kits to decks of cards. Remand prisoners, those still on trial, could access a limited amount of their own money and visit twice a day. Given most inmates were on remand, the place got busy. And given we were still making the headlines on TV and in the press, most already knew who we were.

'Are you investigating here then, mate?'

Yeah, yeah. We must have heard that one twenty times.

And let's not forget the notice we found fixed to our cell door.

"Private Eyes—advice by appointment."

We just had to roll our eyes. In fact, it turned out that notice had been the work of the screws.

I called our solicitor on that Monday. He said the application was scheduled to be heard within hours. The judge would be Mr Justice Mars Jones, known as Mars Bars. He had a difficult reputation, was said to be stickler, an awkward man, but there was nothing we could do about that.

Later on—a phone call. My heart skipped a beat. But the news was a belly blow. Jeremy Hutchinson QC's bail application had failed. Mars Bars wanted to see a transcript of the entire court case on his desk before reaching a decision. That meant ten days of detailed court proceedings needed typed up. We were told it would take at least a week.

It was depressing. We felt as if our spirits were being crushed, and all for no good reason. We knew we would soldier on as best we could but it wasn't easy. We felt cold inside, our hearts heavy, our moods bleak. We were stuck in there with people who may very well have been on one or two of our lists, some people who saw us as the enemy. I was thirty-one, normally bursting with energy, typically hard at work. In recent days and weeks I had been out sailing, had been driving my top of the range car, had been looking into buying up PI agencies around the country, had been loaded with ambition, fully alive, sleeping deeply and loving happily in my top floor apartment. It was much the same for Stuart. And now the pair of us were crammed into stinking cells in what was ultimately an attempt by the state to make an example of us.

But Stuart and I were strong together. That was the best thing about it. We had been through a few scrapes and we laughed that this was just one more for the memoir. We were fortunate that the incarcerated community did not turn on us. That was the case, at least in part, because we made it clear in our actions that if someone brought trouble to one of us they brought it to both of us. It helped too when we had a visit from our dad. He showed up with Phyl and Helen, said he had got the impression we were 'feeling down.' Such a thing was of no use to a plain-speaking man like that.

He said, 'You got yourselves in here so toughen up. Hold your heads high. No matter how down-in-the-mouth you may feel, complaining won't help. Right will always win out in the long run. And you all have each other for support. *Cesspits and roses, cesspits and roses.*'

It was blunt, potent and bloody excellent to hear. He wasn't talking about just getting through the long days, he was talking about doing it with pride, with the sure knowledge that we were wronged men not men who had done wrong, that we would stand tall and smell of roses soon enough. It was a boot in the backside—just what we needed. So we got to it.

Each morning we joined the two lags already working in the canteen and got down to running a business in jail. Stuart and I had a desk each in the double-sized cell, shelves and cupboards all round. We'd kick off the day by stocking shelves with everything you might find in a local corner shop, minus the booze. Then we would load up the trollies to make deliveries to inmates who were unable to come to us. We would walk the whole prison—A, B and D Wings, then to the sickbay. After that it was on to the inmates in isolation, the Rule 43 prisoners—the paedophiles, known as nonces, other sex offenders, the informants or grasses and, like me, the former policemen. Then it was breakfast.

The grub, served by inmates, was not only bland, but there was hardly any of it. Yet, soon enough, that would not be a problem. It didn't take long for us to work out how the system was being played by others and, in turn, how to play it ourselves.

It became clear early on that once the servers knew we were from the canteen, the portions they gave us became more generous. We got the message. So when the faces we knew from the kitchen showed up at the shop, they would find themselves getting a little extra tobacco and a few free sweets here and there.

As week two rolled into week three, and still no word on the transcripts being completed, we found ourselves barely even having to queue. The kitchen staff would encourage us to come up the line, straight to the service point. What with the ever-growing meals, the chocolates, boiled sweets, tinned goodies and the lazing around smoking cigarettes and cigars, Stuart and I really started to put on the beef.

In terms of ensuring the shop was being run correctly on paper, we were advised to take a note of each item we took for ourselves for whatever purpose. At the end of the week a sales total was put together for what was basically missing stock. But how were we to account for it? Our two colleagues explained. There was, they said, a register of remand prisoners which was updated every week. Each remand inmate had monetary credit based upon their own cash plus the allowance of forty-seven pence per day. As they bought goods from us, their accounts were debited accordingly. However when they went to court, some were bailed or released and did not return. Yet their forty-seven pence daily allowance continued to be credited to their prison ledgers for a time. So, we learned, all we had to do was debit the extra stuff we had taken from those accounts.

What was particularly handy was one of our co-workers in the canteen had been a Barclays bank manager who had been fiddling the books. What better man for the job? He could make our totals balance like the scales of justice themselves.

The whole scam slid along especially easily given two screws, Prison Officers Bell and Wills, were tasked with ensuring there was no funny business. Because they were in on it too. And, to top it all, they looked the other way when we used the canteen phone to make personal calls to whoever we liked.

It was via this phone that we arranged board meetings for our companies, that we called our wives and friends and contacts. Indeed it was from there that we made calls to other inmates' wives, that we made legal inquiries on their behalf, that we made business calls for them. As word got around, we had inmates lining up to ask us to help out with some aspect of their past, even to help trace errant witnesses or to investigate an issue they figured we could resolve. They even asked in some cases if we could organise surveillance on rivals, on enemies, even on girlfriends they suspected might not be waiting for them as wholesomely as they should.

Given we were regularly in touch with our wives, we hatched an idea with them too. We arranged for both to be listed as legal clerks on the visitors' register to ease their access to the jail. And in all the days we were there, not a single soul queried the number of visits we were getting or the number of calls we were making. The best part of it was that no one even supervised what was going on when we had private meetings with our, er, legal clerks in the solicitors' room.

Yet on the outside things did not run so smoothly. Despite our best efforts, our business was tanking, our client base slipping from our grasp. Everything we had built was beginning to fail while we were still waiting for the bloody transcripts to get typed up.

It took a month. A call came to advise the papers would soon be ready for dispatch from the Transcription Room of the Old Bailey, bound for the judge's desk. Another few days passed and another step forward. A hearing had been lined up for the next afternoon, March 8, 1973. The end, we hoped, was in sight.

On that morning we were packed with excitement. We could very well be back in our suits and ties and walking free from prison in a matter of hours. After lunch we both laid down in our cell, minds swirling with the sweet promise of freedom. As we waited for the call, we became aware of something truly unexpected happening.

Urgent faces, whispered rumours. Talk of something terrible happening in central London. Suggestions there had been a bomb, no two, maybe more... stories of mass slaughter on the streets...

We couldn't make sense of it. We dashed to the canteen, got the news on the radio. The Provisional IRA had struck for the first time in England. There had been, we learned, two bombings in central London. Two hundred people had been injured. One blast went off outside the Ministry of Agriculture in Whitehall. The other, we learned, had exploded right outside the Old Bailey.

Naturally we understood when our solicitor called to say the bail hearing had been shelved. Stuart and I counted ourselves lucky we had not been there, had not been arriving or leaving when the car bomb detonated. There had been a belated warning and police were evacuating the area when the thing went off. The days that followed brought the nation sad news of one death by heart attack as a result of one of the blasts. And it told of two further IRA bombs which had thankfully been defused. There was also news of a number of arrests.

And then, it must be said, there was the intensely bloody annoying news for us personally. The Old Bailey bomb went off right outside the Transcription Room. The entire office had been totalled. As for our transcription, the one that had been ready for delivery that very day?

Gone. Wiped out.

Fuck!

FOURTEEN

The IRA Arrive (1973)

WHAT happened in 1973 was a rude awakening for many in Britain to the escalating violence in Northern Ireland. Trouble had flared up between pro-united Ireland nationalists, who were mostly of Catholic background, and the unionist supporters of Northern Ireland's position within the UK, mostly of Protestant background. In 1969, British troops had been brought in to help quell the disorder but there was no sign of things easing up.

While I knew of the situation, and few could have escaped the grim news in 1972 of *Bloody Sunday* and *Bloody Friday*, I had learned a good deal more of its awful realities from Phyl. Seven members of her family were in the Royal Ulster Constabularly, the local police service whose officers were routinely targeted for murder by the emerging Provisional IRA. Each one of them was at risk of attack, of being shot, of finding a bomb under their car or, worse, not finding it.

I had become to some extent familiar with Belfast in Northern Ireland and with Dublin in the Irish Republic, had often travelled to both for breaks and for business. Indeed we had made connections there, had struck deals with other agencies to give us a foothold in both cities as part of our expansion. I loved Belfast and Dublin, had loved Ireland since that first visit when I tracked down the young bloke who had been so rudely dumped by Jeremy Thorpe.

Yet while I was aware of the complexities and bloodshed, like many I had viewed that as a facet of life peculiar to the six counties of Northern Ireland. I knew for sure that the vast majority of people on either side of the region's political faultline did not support violence and played no part in it. Yet enough people did support it to allow that violence to create a chain reaction of its own. Shootings, bombings, rage and vengeance led only to more shootings, bombings, rage and vengeance. In 1972 alone, 479 people died as a result of the Troubles in Northern Ireland, including 130 British soldiers. The figures are striking. Perhaps, deep down, we all suspected the Troubles would hit mainland UK sooner or later.

It would take another handful of weeks to get the court report transcribed once again. We were going to have to wait. Our business would just have to keep on sinking. Yet despite the fact all our creations were going south, the legacy of some previous cases was never far away.

In one case, in the company of two prison escorts, I was driven to Birmingham to give evidence in-camera at a disputed County Court divorce hearing. Phyl met me with the case file and we chanced our arm at having lunch. One of the prison officers said, 'If we don't put you in handcuffs, will you promise you won't do a runner?' I gave my word that I wouldn't.

They sat at the next table as we dined on first class pub grub. Phyl paid the bill for all four. She and I walked hand-in-hand back to court. I gave my evidence and, heading out, could not see my escorts. The exit was right there, people and traffic and normal life just beyond the glass doors. I stood for a moment to let temptation play its game, but it would have been crazy. I spotted the escorts and my wife all having a mug of tea in the canteen. It wasn't easy saying goodbye to her after relishing every minute of that day together, but it was better to have had it than not at all. I appreciated the trust of the officers on that trip.

Rather than drive back to London, they dropped me at nearby HMP Winston Green for the night. And, compared to Brixton, what a dump. I had to go through the same malarkey as if I was a new inmate—strip, shower, uniform, cell allocated. I could see the dread on the faces of the new admissions, their spirits deflated within minutes. The place had lots of Indian and Pakistani inmates who had special dispensation to prepare their own food. It was packed and hot and sweaty and especially gloomy after a day in the fresh air, but those rich aromas really gave me a boost. I'd arrived somewhere akin to a street lined with curry houses. It was heavenly. An hour later, after making a few friends, I was stuffed with great food for the second time that day. I slept like a log.

Next morning I was all ready to head back to Brixton, but nope—a glitch in the system. Instead I was taken to another south London lockup,

HMP Wandsworth. And, yet again, a change of atmosphere. The place was infamous for housing some of the most dangerous inmates in Britain and was managed with military discipline. It echoed to the roars of screws yelling orders and, sadly, there wasn't a curry to be had. Fortunately, the next morning I was returned to my own more homely jail.

I got back to work at the canteen, back into the routine. A few days past and then an unusual event. Rumours flew once more as screws started to clear out the cells in 'A' Wing, the next block along. This was because, we were told, it was becoming a 'high-security' section of the jail. The IRA bombers arrested after the two blasts were moving in. They'd been nabbed at Heathrow Airport and, after being charged, were now due for a stay on remand at Her Majesty's pleasure. A heavily-armed convoy arrived, police and military entering the jail. The new arrivals, male and female, were marched in handcuffs to 'A' Wing, the doors were slammed and the keys turned.

In time, the lockdown loosened. Although under constant watch, they were allowed to mingle in their wing to some extent. Their names were passed to us in the canteen as part of the process to allow them to make use of it. I read through the list: William Armstrong, Martin Brady, Hugh Feeney, Paul Holmes, Gerry Kelly, William McLarnon, Roisin McNearney, Dolores Price, Marian Price, Robert Walsh.

Eight of the aforementioned would be jailed for life. And among that number some went on to make their mark in other ways. Gerry Kelly became a leading figure in Sinn Fein, the political wing of the IRA. He became an MLA (Member of the Legislative Assembly) at Stormont in Belfast after the Good Friday Agreement of 1998 largely ended the Troubles. The Price sisters ultimately took a different path with both opposing that agreement and objecting to Sinn Fein's overall strategy.

Our new customers could not leave 'A' Wing but we were able to wheel the trollies, laden with goodies, to their doors. And we had no problem doing that. The ethos in the jail was one of equality among inmates, an atmosphere that helped keep tensions at a minimum. The security was ramped up of course and we were searched daily on entry, but everyone understood.

Gerry Kelly was perhaps the most friendly of the bunch, at least towards us. We spoke a few times and it seemed clear he was the man in charge. Our exchanges were pleasant enough but, as an ex-soldier, it was hard to avoid the idea he was part of an organisation which murdered troops whenever it could. And neither Stuart nor I could bring ourselves to forgive him for blowing up the damn Transcript Room and, as a direct result, adding to our time behind bars. I never did get to bring that up as, beyond the most minor of conversations, we were not allowed to speak with them. In order to get access to the high security wing in the first place we had to give our word not to discuss anything at all with the inmates there. And we were watched every step of the way.

The Price sisters were a different kettle of fish. We found them curt, angry, constantly unsettled. Their mood didn't exactly make it easy for any of us, least of all themselves, as we all tried to get on with our respective incarcerations. They would spit on the floor when approached by a screw and couldn't find it in their hearts to show much grace at all to anyone. It seems to have been something that stayed with them through the years.

A few more weeks passed and then, lo and behold—good news. The transcription had been completed. Again. After more than three months in jail our application was to be dealt with. We weren't there for the hearing but sat, breath baited, waiting for an update in the canteen office. It was infuriating to hear that the judge, this time around, didn't even want to look at the transcripts. His mind was already made up. The case, he declared, was a matter of public interest. We should be fighting it as free men. My brother and I should not be behind bars. We should be released immediately.

Yes!

We cleared our cells, the accumulated photos, letters, sketches and, in my case, even a poem written to bring something out from inside about those strange days. Our wives and our dad were waiting outside the gates of HMP Brixton. It was a wonderful moment—a farewell to a testing battle and a big hello to loved ones.

PRISON

By Ian Withers—H.M.P. Brixton—March 31, 1973

Reveille

Tinkle of—approaching key
Starting—yet another day
Blankets warm—stone floor cold
Breaking day—takes slowly hold
Cleaning teeth—wash and shave.
Thoughts do dwell—freedom crave.
Shouted orders—re-echo through
Breakfast—landings one and two
Plastic bowl—plate and tray
Wishing, wishing—time away
Porridge, bread—lazy beans
Minutes to hours—so it seems.
Within our secure—society
Inmates dream—liberty

Morning

Breakfast over—banging up.
Luke-warm tea—mug, not cup
Open windows—make good the bed.
Leftover scraps—pigeons fed.
Looking out—bars and fence.
Concrete walls—high and dense
Barrier—to the outside world
Behind these walls—offenders hurled.
Dreaming—those we care about
Cell door open—slopping out.
Praying—earliest release date
Sentence served—out main gate.
Within our secure—society
Inmates dream—liberty

Afternoon

Applications—twelve-thirty
Bath or shower—you're dirty.
Exercise hour—ten minutes yard
Screws and dog—standing guard
Scrub floors—stairs and peters
Menial tasks—societies' cheaters
Prisoners paid—recompense.
Weekly wage—thirty pence
Sick Parade 3 pm—doctor mumbles
Three days of—Salty gargles
Welfare, social, probation—call by.
Vicar, good Father—Mullah, Rabbi
Within our secure—society
Inmates dream—liberty

Nightfall

Dinner over—back to cell
All to soon—lights out bell
Darkness falls—screws last round.
Clang of keys—counting sound
Coarse blanket—still the chill
Sleep alludes—despite the will.
Cold silence—circulates.
Snores, murmurs—irritates.
Screams, yells—wanting out.
Shut up, quiet—responding shout
Slam of doors—clink of locks
Still, stuffy—smelly socks
Within our secure—society
Inmates dream—liberty

FIFTEEN

Appreciating, Restarting, Winning (1973/74)

Liberty is a terrible thing to lose, even for a few months. It wasn't exactly Colditz in terms of how we were treated, but incarceration does focus the mind on the immense value of being able to make one's own decisions about day-to-day life.

It was truly precious to be back together with my wife, the woman whose visits had kept me going while waiting for justice to come my way. The strong bond between Phyl and I predated that jail spell, but it was being locked away which demonstrated so clearly that our connection lacked nothing. We were lucky to have each other. But I was the luckiest one.

Phyllis (Clarke) Withers 1966 – Daily Mirror

I'd met her in 1966 while still married to Rita. I'd been on an assignment in Northern Ireland, tasked with repossessing an Austin A55 saloon. We had a sub-agent in Belfast at the time called Thomas Marshall Orr of *New Ireland Yard Detective Agency*. He was a fine PI and, as such, had earned himself the nickname Tom Marshall Law. He provided all the usual services plus security guards and dogs. One of his interests was retail security involving store detectives.

I'd had some requests in London about this line of work. Department stores were expanding and, as is the way of things, so were the incidents of organised shoplifting, pickpocketing and opportunist thieving. Tom agreed I could 'steal' his best shop floor detective and, in London, Phyl went on to land contracts with a number of major outlets quite quickly.

She and I built a bigger team to ultimately service a host of clients in the retail heartlands of Oxford Street, Kingston and, our primary area, Chelsea's King's Road. Between 1968 and 1974 she was running operations with a team of twelve. Each day they nabbed a dozen or more light-fingered visitors, mostly first timers tempted by open displays.

One Saturday in late 1968, Phyl and I were strolling along the King's Road when she spotted a group of twenty-somethings. She recognised a few faces, knew instinctively something was afoot. I was intrigued. The pair of us casually moved closer. Three suited and booted young men and three attractive girls in full-length fur coats. All spoke with Australian accents. Phyl said the girls had been wandering around a few of our outlets earlier, that their behaviour had triggered her interest. We stayed put, kept tabs on the gang. And, soon enough, they split up, the young ladies in fur heading off into one of our client stores.

As they entered, us following behind, Phyl turned to me, whispered, 'They're naked underneath the coats.'

'Pardon?'

'You heard,' she said.

The gang's MO was to choose items from the displays, take them into the changing room and get dressed. They would walk out, put some items back on the stands and leave.

I took up position at the door in case of any runners. We had a member of staff dial the police. This was a professional gang who had likely

Phyl, store detective in Chelsea pre-black-eye! – Northcliffe Newspapers

been challenged before. We had every reason to suspect they would be ready and willing to do what they could to get away.

Sure enough, the three young women emerged from the changing cubicles. Phyl attempted to stop them as they crossed the threshold and out of the store. One belted off. I grabbed one furry arm while Phyl held the other. But I was shoved hard in the back and wasn't ready for it. I stumbled forward, lost my balance. That arm slipped from my grasp. My captive dashed off towards Sloane Square. Phyl was hanging on to the third girl. And, from nowhere, one of the men strode right up—and punched her hard in the face. Phyl fell back. He had knocked her out. The man and woman were away in a split second, racing up the street.

Phyl was rushed to the old St George's Hospital at Hyde Park Corner. The police arrived and soon after the press became involved as well. There were, of course, plenty of salacious headlines about *"naked beauties"* raiding frilly panties from upmarket King's Road stores.

Phyl recovered okay, but was sporting a sizable shiner and thick lip after a night in hospital. The press asked her about the gang as she walked out. She said it was a professional shoplifting gang of Australians. Now maybe it was her Belfast accent or maybe the fat lip, or a mix of both, but the following press report identified the thieves as the *"Strine Gang."* For years to come, store security staff were on the lookout for the *"Strine Gang."* Groups of Aussies, we would learn, were suspected for long after as being part of a partly-nude, violent group of organised thieves.

My relationship with Rita had been slowly depreciating since I left the police house and got buried deep into the PI work. Although we lived in the same new property in Ham, in the Richmond area, we had been living almost separate lives for a while. After Phyl came on the scene, well things happened and Rita and I agreed to separate and later divorce.

On December 2, 1972, Phyl and I wed at Caxton Hall, Westminster. I had reserved the wedding breakfast at a place I knew well—the very fine May Fair Hotel where my exploits with the American fraudsters had begun. Since then, the manager had always welcomed me in. On that day, to my surprise and delight, that same manager laid on a function room, food and champagne. He said in a short speech that the hotel had been 'most grateful' for the assistance with the conmen a year before.

In early 1974 my gorgeous wife gave birth to our gorgeous boy John, known as Johnnie, and in the spring of 1977 she brought our second gorgeous lad, Jamie, into the world. She went on to be a wonderful mother, to become my most trusted aide, my closest companion in work, in life, in love, in all that lay ahead. While Stuart and I were banged up in Brixton, she and Helen did what they could to keep our business afloat. Both went out and got jobs in pubs, worked long hours to bring in the money to keep the lights on, to keep something coming in ahead of us being released on some future day. Phyl visited me when she could, lifted my heart many times and I don't know what I would have done without her.

But, despite best efforts all around, the business was in bits when we left jail. Our clients felt as if they'd been left in the lurch. Some that

December 2, 1972 – married to Phyl at Caxton Hall

owed us money hadn't paid and, given we were banged up, decided they wouldn't bother.

At the same time, those people to whom we owed money had been giving Phyl and Helen plenty of grief about it. Ironically enough, some equipment suppliers had even been to our offices to repossess goods. Everything was grinding to a halt. We were frustrated, angry, skint and getting hit with bills, legal and otherwise, all the time. And with no immediate prospect of any cash coming our way, Stuart and I both went to the unemployment office in Croydon.

Stuart asked a bored-looking clerk, 'What jobs have you got?'

'What do you do?' he said.

I said I was most recently a company chairman and managing director. Stuart said he was company director and company secretary.

At least it brought a smile to the clerk's face.

'So sorry,' he said, 'but we have no jobs for company directors, chairmen or company secretaries.'

What we had hoped to suggest was that we knew how to run a business, that he might just have some positions where our skills would be a good fit.

I was about to speak, and then—

'But,' he said, picking up a pen, 'I do have a possible position for you both with a large public company.'

He wrote down details and handed the note to us in an envelope.

'Go and talk to them,' he said. 'And good luck.'

So off we went to Tate & Lyle, the sugar suppliers, and furnished the HR manager with our details.

'You have just been released from prison and are pending an appeal?' he queried.

'That's correct.'

'I can't help with a director's job but there are a couple of positions going.'

'Oh?' I said, curious.

'You would be unloading bags of sugar from lorries and putting them in the store. And you'd be tipping the contents of damaged bags into large bins in the warehouse.'

I looked at Stuart and Stuart looked at me. Let's just say we had been hoping for something a little more challenging.

We trudged back to the job shop.

'I'm really sorry,' said our bored clerk, 'but if you don't accept these jobs you can't get unemployment benefit.'

So be it. If we were going to get ourselves physically exhausted every day, there was hardly any hope of us having the energy to launch back into what we did best. There had to be another way. Stuart told the clerk where he could stick his rules.

A couple of years earlier we had bought an end terrace property at Boundaries Road in Balham. Our dad had converted it into two flats and, since then, we'd used the address for office purposes. It was there that a meeting took place with our wives. And, over coffee and bacon sandwiches, we managed to lift ourselves up, to remind ourselves of how far we had come. We had no money, no credit, no work—but we still had our pride. We came away from the table knowing that the coming weeks would be tough, but there was nothing else for it but to fight.

I got on the phone to old clients and was hit fast and hard with rejection, with the clear sense that many did not want to know us. But so what? I was used to difficult calls. I kept on dialling. And, bit by bit, the conversations started and, bit by bit, the work came in again. Yet we really were flat broke. In order to get our business running we had bills to pay, needed petrol, sustenance, essentials. Phyl and Helen took on more shifts at the pub, started working seven days a week to help keep things moving along. And slowly but surely, we began to rise once more. But a significant obstacle loomed.

On Friday, October 19, 1973, we took our seats at the Court of Appeal at The Strand in central London. We were confident and positive, ready for some good news. But none came. We were stunned to hear the judges, in their wisdom, conclude we had been correctly convicted. Our appeal was dismissed. The custodial sentences were too, but we took little joy from it.

As we left court that day we agreed we would not give up. We had fire back in our bellies and we were going to fight. I remember the sun shining as we stood on The Strand and talked of how resolved we were to get it sorted. And then, as if from nowhere, two men marched right up. I knew one of those faces well. Detective Sergeant Bernie Davies and a Detective Constable Ben Dwan. Both CID, both worked for Ginger *bloody* Hemsley. Behind them, a cluster of journalists and a TV crew filming the action. We were shocked.

'Gents,' said Davies, ensuring every lens was on him, 'I have extradition warrants for your arrests. You failed to attend court in Co Cavan in the Republic of Ireland in February.'

Phyl and Helen protested as we were cuffed on the spot, put into two fast-arriving, siren-blaring police cars and sped away with the blue lights flashing. The cameras got it all.

We were raced to HMP Pentonville and banged up for the weekend. On Monday morning, Davies said, we'd be flown to Ireland. Our solicitor looked into it all, came back with the bad news that we were snookered. Everything was in order, legally speaking. That Saturday and Sunday ticked by with excruciating slowness.

About a year before we had taken on a case involving a client whose ex-wife had abducted their son contrary to a High Court order. Our job had been to locate the pair of them. The seven-year-old lad had been spirited away from Southall to, it was suspected, somewhere close to the mother's family home in Co Cavan, Ireland. In terms of our business, it had been a fairly standard mission.

We had tracked them to a house just outside Cavan town. Together with the child's dad, we arrived with copies of the court order to serve on the mother. If, and only if, our client saw his son in the house he would collect him and we would drive away.

I knocked on the front door and a woman appeared. I recognised her as the lad's mum and handed over the court order. Out-of-the-blue our client barged past me and into the house. Stuart joined me as I went in, assuming the father had spotted his boy. A man came bounding down the stairs swinging a bat. I stood my ground.

'Who the hell are you?' I said.

'Garda,' he said.

I asked for ID. He tucked the bat, actually a long truncheon, under his arm and pulled his warrant card. Fair enough. I explained we were here to serve a legal order.

And then it became clear something else was going on. Other men emerged from within the house, at least six in all. And all were police officers. There was a scuffle up ahead, some shouting from our client. We had been set up. We had walked right into a trap. But why?

Our client was arrested, cuffed, driven off in an arriving police car. We were not arrested but agreed to follow the cars back to Cavan Garda Station. I spelled out the details over tea and, a few phone calls later, we were let go and advised they would be in touch. We had little choice but to head home.

It turned out our client had conveniently forgotten to mention he was wanted in Ireland for questioning about an arson attack at the home of his estranged wife's parents a year before. Stuart and I were asked to return a few months later and did so. As with our client, we were formally charged with attempted child abduction. The court date was set. Unfortunately at the time of the hearing I was locked up in HMP Brixton.

So, back to our arrest outside the court in London. At 6 am on Monday, October 22, 1973, Stuart and I were woken in HMP Pentonville and taken to a police car. Inside was our friend Bernie Davies and another officer. We sat in the back, cuffed, were driven to Heathrow and put in a cell at the airport cop shop. We didn't even get as much as a cup of tea from them.

Around midday Davies arrived with two men—both officers we had dealt with in Cavan. One was Detective Sergeant Michael Walsh. He greeted us warmly and said he didn't think we needed to be cuffed or held in a cell.

Bernie said he didn't mind, but asked his Irish colleague only that he didn't 'send them back.' He was only half joking.

Off we flew to Dublin. I must say that, as we made our way, it was the only time I have been in police custody and been offered, by the police officer concerned, some whiskey. All of us had a double or two on that short flight.

We were driven to Bailieborough in Co Cavan. The Garda Station was a converted stable. It still had the split stable door and the two cells were constructed from the original horse stalls, vertical iron bars floor to ceiling. Superintendent McMahon's wife made us tea and sandwiches and, as we talked things over, he walked off to take a message. He returned to ask if I had a brother-in-law called George? I did. He said George was with both our wives, Phyl and Helen, who had checked in a hotel just down the road. We had been invited for dinner there.

The copper said, 'If I let you two lads out will you promise to be back afterwards?'

Amazed at the offer, we gave him our promise. And off we went for a slap-up meal and a few pints of stout. We arrived back at the station soon after midnight, tiptoed into the open cell and closed the bars behind us like good prisoners. In the morning we woke to the scent of a first class fry up, courtesy of Mrs McMahon. The whole experience, given how we'd felt so crunched and crushed up by the system, was slightly surreal.

Into the Irish court to hear the usher call, 'The State against Withers and Withers.'

The State Prosecutor stood to address the judge.

'The state will not be offering any evidence in this case,' he said.

My eyes popped wide open. The court fell silent. Our solicitor looked confused. He stood, asked what on earth was going on given we had just been extradited from the UK? The prosecutor apologised, said he had received the instructions from the Attorney General's office just that morning.

The judge looked across at Stuart and I and asked if we had anything to say.

I stood, said, 'May we apply for costs to cover our return trip to London?'

He looked at me, narrowed his eyes, said, 'Absolutely not. Count yourselves lucky with what has happened here today.'

My solicitor tugged my arm, said, 'Time to go.'

We heard later that our former client had admitted arson and been jailed from the same court. His London solicitor did eventually pay our bill.

But back to the ongoing English case, back before we were so rudely interrupted once again by Bernie Davies. We had been sunk again and made an application to get our case reviewed once more, this time at the Court of Appeal. But the judges said it was not a public interest case and it should go no further.

We fought on.

Our lawyers leapfrogged the system and petitioned directly to the House of Lords Appellate Committee. And, finally, some traction. On Wednesday, June 5, 1974, some eighteen months after being found guilty of *conspiring to effect a public mischief*, Phyl, Stuart, Helen and I, made the journey from our homes, now in Sussex, to the Houses of Parliament in Westminster. And there was not a single journalist in sight, seemingly no interest at all in the case of *DPP v. Withers and Others*.

House of Lords – hearing notice

Over the next six days the case was laid out. The judges heard that to do our business, we made inquiries, usually by telephone to banks, building societies, government departments and local authorities and, to induce the officials or public servants to disclose confidential information, at times pretended to be acting in an official capacity.

It was alleged in Count One that we had unlawfully obtained private and confidential information from banks and building societies. It was alleged in Count Two that we had secured information from public officers of the government or local authority departments. The seven law lords were told that if we had agreed to do deceitful acts which would cause injury to the community as a whole, we would be guilty of *conspiracy to effect a public mischief*—the charge we faced.

All four of us were now represented by Gerald Owen QC, who kindly agreed to give his services completely free. He was diminutive in stature, spoke with an East End accent and was, without doubt, treated shabbily by some lawyers and even a number of judges as a result. There, in the country's highest court, he was cut off sometimes, overlooked, even ignored by some. It was disgraceful.

Yet he soldiered on, made clear and concise points, and was very much across his brief at all times. He knocked back the Crown's arguments again and again, day after day. His research brought him back to obscure precedents in law, even as far back as the Star Chamber of centuries ago. He had found precedents relating to public mischief from the sixteenth century to back up his argument. And all the while, in his own masterful way, he made it plain that just because the state disapproves of something that does not make it criminal.

On November 20th, 1974 the seven law lords delivered their judgement.

'There is,' they said, 'no such offence known in English law as a conspiracy to effect public mischief.' They said that 'on no occasion' should such a prosecution be made again.

We had committed no crime. We had lost almost all of our business, spent over three months in jail, spent every penny we had on legal costs, but we had committed no crime. We were awarded £15,000, which didn't even cover the legal fees, but it was something. *Cesspits and roses,* and all that.

Ultimately what we did was right a wrong, which was the essence of our business in the first place. And, in this case, the wrong was done by an aggressive persecution from a self-important Metropolitan Police officer and his sidekicks. We left court and, once again, no press, no TV cameras, no one wanting to hear our story. The Lords unanimously determined there was no such offence known to the English Law, and not a single newspaper showed any interest.

I'm proud to say the case of *DPP v. Withers and Others* became the law of the land. This legal precedent is, to this day, often cited in conspiracy cases in British and overseas courts.

I want to get on the record my complete disgust at the way the Metropolitan Police irrationally drove forward this ultimately ludicrous case. During their inquiries my wife was threatened with 'prison for life.' My employee Sheila Pattenden was at one point told her family life could be turned upside-down. Indeed, in her witness statement, she stated that

Bernie Davies said to her, 'If you don't sleep with me honey, I'll have your kids put into care because you are a witness. And as you are a participant, you will end up in court with them.'

Sheila, I'm glad to say, told him to piss off.

Ginger's squad did everything it could to nail us, the Withers brothers and our wives, because they didn't like our reach, our success. It is our belief that they felt they were on something of a long leash given that the British prime minister himself wanted results. They ran wild as far as they could. They tried to crush us using illegitimate law, spitefully tried to pull our reputation apart. I absolutely assert that the gas gun was planted and that perjury was committed by some among those men. We complained a number of times about it all but it was a case of the Met investigating the Met so, funnily enough, nothing ever happened.

Yet we did manage to get ourselves a little revenge. As we had been found not guilty we were entitled to have our criminal records destroyed in our presence. The disposal method was by fire. We demanded it. One winter morning we made our way by agreement to the yard at the disused Wandsworth Police Station where this burning was to take place in front of our eyes.

DS Davies himself operated the blackened incinerator at the back of the derelict building. The four of us stood in the cold with our solicitor as Bernie and colleagues showed the bundles of files on us before torching the lot. Afterwards, Davies whispered to me, 'We have lots of copies.'

DS Davis was later promoted to a Detective Chief Inspector and put in charge of Wimbledon Police Station. And as for Ginger, it was only after everything was done and dusted that our Counsel Jeremy Hutchinson QC spilled the beans. He said he had prosecuted him in the past, but that he couldn't mention it earlier due to conflict of interest. It turned out Ginger Hemsley, when a superintendent in the Flying Squad, led a raid at a house after a bank robbery. Some £30,000 was recovered. Yet the robber, and the bank, said he had made off with £50,000. Ginger had been charged with the theft of £20,000. He was found not guilty. The cash was never recovered.

SIXTEEN

Rebuilding Case by Case (1973/74)

A PRISONER at HMP Brixton asked if we might get in touch with his friend. The friend's wife had accused him of having a fling and thrown him out of their apartment. Just before the split, the bloke had bought furniture on a finance deal. He said he was fed up paying for it given she had been a less than honourable wife.

'How do you mean?' I asked.

'It's complicated,' he said. 'But she's having an affair.'

'I see,' I said.

'It won't take long to prove it,' he told me. 'The man has been visiting her at home.'

Stuart and I, keen to take any PI work we could get, packed the cameras and drove to Surrey. And sure enough, within a day or so questions began to arise. A police car rolled up in the evening, right outside the apartment. The driver got out, opened the rear door for an obviously more senior officer. The passenger alighted, went swiftly to the apartment in question, went inside. The police car pulled away.

We sat until after midnight. He didn't reappear. We broke away for a rest and returned before 6 am. Around 8 am, once again, a police car pulled up. The senior officer left the apartment and was driven off.

We took the news to our client. He said his suspicions had been confirmed. He explained he had been falsely accused of an offence by this very officer, a chief inspector, and remanded for a month pending trial. It was, as had been suggested, a messy situation.

We needed stronger proof of an affair. An idea struck me. The finance company's contract said it had a right to request inspection of the goods in the buyer's property given it owned the furniture until everything had been paid.

Back we went to the apartment for another long wait. The following evening the police car pulled up. The same officer went inside. We sat through until after 7 am, then went to the door. Our pretext was that we were from the furniture finance company. We needed to inspect the goods. The lady answered the door in a light dressing gown and very little else. She was taken aback by our story, but that was understandable.

'Come in and have a look,' she said, a little baffled.

Our policeman wasn't visible. We took our time. The kettle was already boiling. We hoped he might pop down for a cuppa. And indeed he did. Footsteps came our way as we looked at the chairs and sofa, pretending to care. The chief inspector, full of the joys of his fling, walked merrily into the living room. He wasn't wearing any trousers. He froze, looked at us, looked at the ironing board on which lay his unpressed trousers. Without a word, he turned and went back upstairs. All of this, it was clear, very much suggested the married lady was having an affair.

We thanked her for her time, confirmed that the furniture was in good order and left with the image of a trouserless chief inspector held fast in our memories. As we waited outside, his car duly arrived. He emerged, fully dressed, and was whisked away. We duly informed the client and his solicitor. The police officer concerned was later cited as the co-respondent in a divorce case. The prosecution in the criminal case against our client offered no evidence when it came to court.

There are, of course, bent coppers. The Met has had its own investigations to root out those rotten apples, not least after the fallout of the Jimmy Humphreys case. Indeed, the stories of corrupt cops are legion, yet the truth can be a hard thing to pin down. The tragedy of Daniel Morgan, a London PI who was murdered in 1987, is a case in point. He was thirty-seven when he was fatally struck in the head with an axe and left, the murder weapon buried into his skull, in a Croydon pub car park. Mr Morgan had apparently been exposing police corruption. It has been alleged his horrific killing was part of a police conspiracy and that suggestion persists. After numerous inquiries, this most disturbing murder remains unsolved at the time of writing.

Despite my concerns, beliefs and lived experience of police corruption, I know well that the vast majority of police officers are perfectly professional people who do a difficult job well. And, if I may say so, the same goes for me. I have, across my career, been as professional as I could be. At all times I have wanted to get the job done right, to bring things to a satisfactory conclusion for my clients. If you had hired me, you would know my word is good.

However there are times when I may have gone about things the wrong way. I am a determined man. I am not easily fooled, intimidated or otherwise pushed off course. And, during my career, the more successful I was at getting what I wanted to get, the more success I continued to seek. Perhaps I pushed a little hard in some places at some times, but I never did so for any other reason than a strong desire to do the right thing. What I brought to my role, I am sure, were the qualities any good PI should have. I have found myself disdainful at times of those in other positions, particularly police officers, who have been more cavalier in terms of their duty to their clients—the public at large.

So, with another example of a dodgy copper on our files, we were back in business. Despite all the legal bills and myriad other payments, the fresh money we were earning was beginning to show on our accounts. We took the decision to move out of London and take our business to the less hectic arena of Brighton, Sussex, on the south coast. We took premises on Middle Street to serve as our new head office and both Stuart and I moved to new build homes in nearby Shoreham. We had done some downsizing in London and maintained a single office in Kilburn under the control of a manager who operated the day to day caseload. We had many concerns about moving from the bustling capital to the coast but it seemed there was always a demand for what we supplied.

A client walked into the Middle Street office one afternoon. His wife, he said, had left him and the children. She had taken herself to the Spanish town of Benidorm, he said, and it was from there that she informed him she wanted to split. The client was being asked to send money each month to support her in Spain. Yet, he said, he was sure she was with another man which would make her guilty of a betrayal of the marriage vows. As such, of course, a divorce would loom and the matters of his payments to her would be settled.

Stuart and I flew to Alicante, drove to Benidorm. At the time the town was little more than a fishing village, which is quite the contrast to what it is today—a sprawling tourist mecca packed with British holiday-makers. We made our way to the address the client had provided only to discover it was a post office box. We found a phone and our man was baffled. He had been posting letters from him and the kids, including travellers cheques, to his wife at that address. In fact he had posted an item just a day or two before. We wondered if it had been collected yet. It had not.

We waited. And waited. After two days in the blazing sunshine, we watched as a small, elderly lady slowly shuffled her way towards the post office box in question. We watched as she gently inserted a key, carefully turned the lock. She removed the letter and took it to a counter. Stuart and I were already one hundred percent certain this frail yet elegant pensioner could not be our client's wife. But who on earth was she?

I wandered over, discreetly looked at what she was doing. She was readdressing the letter to the Caribbean island of Curacao. And she had used the pen to change the surname of the recipient. The plot, one might say, thickened.

'Hello,' I said, and she smiled. I told her I was the brother of the missing wife. She seemed to know what I was talking about. I took out a small wad of pesetas, placed it down. She looked at it, picked it up. We understood each other.

It seemed she was a landlady, that our client's wife had stayed with her for a time. The wife, she said, had a lover who visited each weekend. One day the client advised the lady that she and her gentleman friend were moving to Curacao where he had a job. For an agreed fee, the elderly lady had agreed to collect and forward mail.

We discussed matters with our client, packed once again and off we flew, via Madrid and Caracas, to the beautiful, sun-kissed Dutch Caribbean island of Curacao off the Venezuelan coast. The object of our errant wife's affections, we discovered, was working as a chef at a hotel there. It took no time at all to find him. He was living with her in staff accommodation at the beachside resort. In terms of gathering evidence of adultery, this location was one of the most enjoyable. By day we sat beside the pool, lounged at the bar and wandered around in the sun taking the occasional photograph. And by night we did exactly the same thing. Evidence gathered and tanning complete, we flew home with everything our client needed to allow him to begin divorce proceedings. Our bill was settled on the spot. At last, some money in the bank. But it's true that our ladies were browned off at being left alone for some ten days. We were just brown.

As Stuart and I worked hard to rebuild our business, we were always open to anything that might help promote our name. And, just when we needed it most, a golden opportunity landed when the documentary team behind *For The Love Of Helen* got back in touch. The director we had worked with, Mike O'Connor, wanted to make a film about a PI agency. We could barely say 'Yes please' fast enough. He said he would shoot footage over three months and track us as we worked on some of the more interesting new cases.

A few months later and Southern TV aired *The Rise and Rise of Withers and Withers*, and the feedback was first class. It was a bold documentary, opened with music just like that from the movie *Jaws*. To give it some context, it's important to remember that Brighton was booming in the mid-seventies. Increasing numbers of people were moving to the town, many escaping the costs and crush of London some fifty miles away. Moving our business there hadn't just been a good idea in terms of escaping the metropolis and its Metropolitan Police, but also because local solicitors were coming under pressure with the soaring demand for their services. In turn, they were seeking ours.

One young up-and-coming solicitor, David Barling at law firm Weeks, Legg and Dean became a long-term client. The firm had cornered a small but buoyant market involving squatters. In line with Brighton moving forward, some felt they had the right to break into any unoccupied property they liked, bar the doors, refuse to leave and pay nothing. It seemed as if there was a political philosophy right across the country at the time, and certainly on many university campuses, which said that while there were homeless people, empty properties were fair game. Unsurprisingly, the landlords who bought the buildings, paid the rates and hoped to rent them out didn't entirely follow that line of thinking.

In legal terms, once announced as squatters, they could only be forced out with an Eviction Notice. That could take months, even years to obtain. My firm developed a way to resolve the issue by doing something similar. We would wait until the house was empty, move in, dump the previous residents' stuff on the pavement and bar the doors. It was, after all, unoccupied. We had the same rights as the squatters did. I always found it amusing that very often the squatters called the police.

Southern TV were intrigued by all of this given it was an emerging social issue. Mike O'Connor wanted an example and tracked us as we recovered a house from a group. The cameraman followed on as, when the residents went en masse to sign on for benefits, we moved in to secure the property. We had to check, of course, it was empty first. I took a walk up the stairs, the camera in tow, and heard a noise from one of the rooms. I pushed the door open to see a young woman on a mattress in her underwear. She was sweating profusely and I could sense all was not well.

'Are you all right, love?' I asked.

No response. I went over. She seemed almost unconscious. Her forehead was searing. We called an ambulance and she was taken in for a week to recover from a very nasty infection.

In the meantime, our squatters returned to find all their stuff stacked neatly on the pavement. They checked the door and windows, but there was no way in. As expected, they called for the law. The Old Bill arrived and told them to clear their stuff from the pavement.

The sixty minute doco also featured a blackmail case involving a married man who had a gay fling. Brighton, then as now, was extremely liberal and a signifcant gay scene was developing in the seafront town. But the man had been put in a terrible situation where his one night stand was demanding £1,000 or else his wife would be shown some damning photographs. The client said he would not be paying up, that he would not be going to the police and that he would not be telling his wife. Could we help? Of course we could.

A top tip for dealing with blackmail without wanting to involve police? Reverse the threat. To get that done, we needed evidence of the demand in the first place. It had been verbal, unrecorded, and that wasn't enough. I fitted our client with a tiny transmitter in his shirt pocket. Its range was about 150 yards, so we needed to be pretty close to pick up and record the conversation. Our client duly arranged to meet the blackmailer at a coffee stand on Dyke Road Avenue.

Stuart and I sat in one car, the cameraman in the back, and waited. Mike, the director, was in a separate Southern TV car nearby. We all sipped coffee as our client arrived. The reception was excellent. We could hear him breathing nervously as he sat waiting for the blackmailer. About ten minutes later, a blue Ford Cortina pulled up. A man, about thirty, got out and walked to our client. The voices were crystal clear.

'Have you got it?'

'No. I need more time to get that much without the wife knowing.'

'If you don't sort it out, I mean it—I will send the photos to her.'

Bingo.

The cameraman following, Stuart and I got out and paced over to the blackmailer. Mike, who was a good six foot tall, joined us.

The suspect freaked out, bellowed at our client, 'You stitched me up —I will ruin you!'

He bolted for his car, locked the doors and spun off almost bowling us over as he went. We gave chase, sped along the narrow roads of the South Downs, the Southern TV car following. I came alongside him at a junction, pulled in front and slammed on the brakes, forcing him to stop. He leapt out and legged it but our client, who pulled up in his own car, sprinted right at him. He smashed him to the ground in a fantastic rugby tackle. I went over, took the dazed suspect by the arm and advised his words were on tape, that in the eyes of the law he had demanded money with menaces. I said we would go to his home, be allowed to collect all the relevant material and we would leave it at that. Or else the police would be called. I added that if he ever contacted our client again, likewise—the police would be called. In front of a TV camera, the man apologised. That would be the end of it, he said.

The final case filmed was one of fraud. It centred around a farmer's daughter who had got herself a new boyfriend. The lad had taken a job in her family business. He fitted in well, had earned some trust and, after a while, had taken on management of the farm's accounts. But the farmer had realised over time that the bank balance was a lot less than it should be.

The crew filmed as I arrived at the business and began a little digging. I saw quite quickly that counterfoils had not been filled in on the cheque books and, cross referencing, that many of these cheques had been cashed. One of the crew came along to film from a car as I went, miked up, to doorstep the offender.

I said who I was and, as is often best, went in bluntly. I said I'd reason to believe he had stolen money, said he was liable for arrest and prosecution, that I could arrest him myself for theft under the common law. He almost collapsed.

'I am so sorry,' he said, sobbing. 'I meant to replace it but haven't got round to it yet.'

'Do you wish to make a statement under caution?'

He agreed. Across six pages, as he talked, I wrote down his confession and explanation. He had cashed over five grand in cheques.

I arrested him, citizen on citizen under common law, and told him to come with me to the nearest police station. He asked in the car what he was likely to get in terms of a sentence. I asked if he had any previous convictions, and he didn't. I said a suspended sentence was most probable, as well as an order to repay. When the film aired, that conversation was carried in full and the narrator clarified that last part. I'll admit, to my surprise. I had got it wrong.

The narrator said, *'Despite the PI suggesting a suspended sentence, the court sentenced him to four years for this gross breach of trust.'*

All in all, it was a powerful documentary, a great insight into our activities that was talked about far and wide. Our workload, as a direct result, rocketed. We took on four office staff and relaunched our drive to open new relationships with clients and agencies across the UK and Ireland.

And it played a part in helping something else I had been working on—building a mutually-respectful relationship with the Sussex Police in Brighton. In time, an ex-Detective Sergeant by the name of Brian Lewis from the local force would become the office manager. The Met would not be missed. Despite their best efforts, the brothers Withers were back in business.

SEVENTEEN

Mission to Saigon: Finding Patti (1974)

PART of the legacy of the Vietnam War is found in the children fathered by American soldiers. More than two and half million US troops served in the Asian nation between 1965 and 1975, often meeting young women in bars which popped up around the sprawling US bases. Inevitably some fell pregnant and, inevitably, not all the men remained by their lovers' sides.

Around the time I'd been invited over to Hong Kong by my old contact Jim Raper, the USA was extracting itself from what was a truly horrific conflict. What had been an ideological battle, with north Vietnam backed by the USSR and the south backed by America, had become an almighty, bloody mess. For the first time, the unified USA had lost a war. It was beating retreat and the whole thing was the biggest story in the world.

My role across the South China Sea in Hong Kong had been to monitor the meeting of some corrupt businessmen. As Stuart and I had discovered, they had been plotting to murder my client. But while in the city for a number of weeks, Jim kept me busy with other matters too. He had a vast array of interests and, working together, he, Stuart and I bugged a number of locations where he felt he would be able to gather useful intelligence. What I'm referring to here is corporate espionage or, if you like, industrial espionage. Jim might call me at a moment's notice, ask me to rush to an office or hotel and install a recording device before one of his many meetings. I would, on most occasions, use a briefcase equipped with a unit able to collect up to two hours worth of sound in the room in question. Jim would begin the meeting, lay on a few drinks and relax the attendees. A while later, he would make his excuses and leave them for a time. Very often the participants' conversation would turn to the subject of price, terms and their overall position as regards the deal they were seeking to make. When the issue at hand involves enormous sums of money, this kind of insight was clearly intelligence of a very high value.

I was enjoying my time there. I was gathering great information for my wealthy client, living in luxury at the fantastic Mandarin Hotel and every expense was covered. All in all, as a builder's boy from London, I was somewhat spellbound by the culture, diversity and sheer pace and force of life in Britain's far flung colony.

One morning Jim asked me to attend a meeting in Kowloon, a short ride from the island on the Star Ferry. The destination was the world-famous Peninsula Hotel, said by some to be one of the finest in Asia and beyond. I was in great form as I walked briskly from the dock to Tsim Sha Tsui rail terminal, from where the Orient Express leaves for Europe, and towards the hotel. At its entrance a row of Rolls Royce limos gleamed in the sunshine, all polished and ready to meet the needs of guests. Inside, I took a seat in the large lobby and admired the extraordinary antique decor as the Hong Kong social elite enjoyed English High Tea.

Jim walked in with a beautiful, well-dressed woman of around twenty-five. She smiled warmly as she was introduced to me as Patti. He told me she was from Saigon in Vietnam, that she worked for Gatco, his company in Central, an area of Hong Kong.

Patti's hometown, I knew, was a vast metropolis and a key prize for either side during the war in her nation. This was 1974 and that awful conflict was coming to a close, Saigon on the cusp of falling to the communists and soon to be renamed Ho Chi Minh City. Patti had fallen in love with an American GI, given birth to his daughter and, as with many young women in similar circumstances, sought to escape to a new life in the USA. In her case, Peter, the soldier, very much wanted her to do the same. He had formally registered his baby with American authorities and had even secured a permit to bring them both over to begin a new family life. The couple wanted to marry.

Unfortunately, Jim explained, Patti did not have a Vietnamese passport. The Vitnamese government had collapsed and there was no hope of organising any official documentation. In desperation, she had left her child with her mother and made her way to Hong Kong. She had joined a group who, at great risk to their lives, made their way across that treacherous South China Sea. In raging storms and with basic rations, their small and rickety fishing boat had just made it to Hong Kong. The authorities had scooped them up at the shore. She and the other travelers were detained at an overcrowded refugee camp for months, a place where thousands of other fleeing Vietnamese nationals were being housed. Patti was one of what was becoming known the world over as the Vietnamese Boat People.

Patti was prepared from the start. She was a driven young woman, absolutely set on securing her passage to America, on arranging to be reunited with her now two-year-old daughter and her GI once more. Before setting out for the high seas, she had carefully secreted all her paperwork in a money belt. This included her national ID card, an application to go to the USA and copies of letters documenting her relationship with her fiancé.

In time, Patti had negotiated her way out of the camp and into employment in Hong Kong. She had made contact with Peter and he was working hard to clear her official path. All the while, Patti had been writing to her mother and had been receiving updates on her child. However in the past few weeks Patti was receiving nothing in return. It had become clear that in Saigon, as pockets of conflict raged, many families were being split up and moved around. Patti had been told her mother, father and daughter had been moved to a place of safety yet she had no idea where. She was not just emotionally distraught, she was stuck too. She had forwarded visa application forms to her mother, as the child's legal guardian, and needed them back to facilitate travel. But she had heard nothing.

Jim paused his story there. He looked at me before turning to the woman.

'Patti,' he said, 'If anyone can get into Saigon, find them, get the documents signed and get them back to you, it's Ian Withers.'

He looked back at me once more.

'They could be anywhere in Saigon, Ian,' he said. 'And I should tell you that attacks are ongoing. And there's a 10 pm curfew after which people can get shot on sight.'

I nodded, mused out loud, 'Somewhere in Saigon…'

'Yes,' he said. 'I'll cover all expenses.'

I could see the hope in his face, the tears in Patti's eyes. I nodded, said, 'I'll do it.'

I would be on my own. Stuart's daughter Caroline was due anytime and his priorities, of course, were to be found in England, not in the dangerous streets of Saigon. I took a direct Air Vietnam flight from Hong Kong.

On arrival, things were not what I expected. It was all much worse. Either side of the runway featured bashed up American military planes, some having made emergency or crash landings. Some, pounded with heavy fire in the sky, had thumped down ablaze on the landing strip, the wreckage still smouldering as my flight pulled in. I disembarked into a corrugated shed in the centre of what was basically a military base. My passport was stamped quickly and off I went into the unknown.

Outside it was surreal as dozens of eager cab drivers, rickshaws and tourist guides, their lives and businesses in tatters, fought for my attention. I picked a driver who spoke English and, along the way, arranged that he might ask a few questions for me if I needed it. He would speak, we agreed, as a local and not bring me into any of what might follow.

The journey was perilous. All the rules of the road seemed to have been scrapped, cars and vehicles of all kinds racing around, trying to get somewhere before the curfew fell. I was sweating hard by the time we arrived at the Hotel Caravelle, a grand, five-star Air France-managed establishment close to the famous opera house in the heart of the city.

Inside and the contrast was amazing. The place was an oasis of tranquillity, the French flag flying overhead, a glorious rooftop bar and swimming pool favoured by foreign press. As I took in the view, I could hear sporadic gunfire from out there across that battered concrete jungle. I knew I would need to be as sharp as I'd ever been if I was going to get this job done right.

We set off in the morning, navigated our way through the battlescarred streets, past bombed-out buildings and wrecked cars as we made our way to Patti's family home. But it was gone. The whole block and the buildings around it had been flattened. We sat for a moment as I wrote down the mother's name and passed the note to my driver.

'I need to find this woman,' I said. 'She lived here.'

He read it, nodded, and we set off for a local bar. He dropped me off, told me to wait. I trusted him, knew he was aware a handsome payment was coming his way. I went inside. The bar was full of off-duty US soldiers and a variety of local ladies. I got chatting to some of the GI's and recall how surprised I was at how young they looked. Most seemed relaxed, were friendly, drinking Bud, playing pool and listening to the jukebox. I joined in, found it strange how easy it was to forget a ferocious war had been raging for close to a decade in this country. The young soldiers were clear about it all being nearly over, that they knew for sure the Viet Cong 'are at the edge of Saigon.' They said they knew they would be shipping out soon.

It took three hours for the driver to return. He told me he had a good lead on the whereabouts of Patti's mum. Off we went again, wheels juddering over the smashed highways and cratered lanes, making our way through unsigned streets and muddy tracks, past children playing among bullet-holed buildings. The light was fading as we reached the edge of the city, the countdown to the curfew underway.

The location was a city of tin huts, some three, four, five storeys high, stacked on top of one another right at the river's edge. Bamboo poles were sunk into the wet earth to act as uprights. Square holes had been cut into the corrugated metal to serve as windows. Each storey was built on one of the decks, each with a vertical ladder fixed against the wall, the way to the dwelling above. They had done what they could to build these homes, displaced victims of war fighting back among the destruction and extreme poverty that none of them deserved. It was a vast, rat-infested, tragic riverside shantytown and it stank of raw sewage to the point where I could barely take a breath.

My diligent driver went from home to home, knocking doors and asking questions, getting directions from person to person to person in the hunt for Patti's mother and daughter, also called Patti. After some time, maybe an hour or more, he called out to me in the darkness.

'Come,' he said.

I walked his way, heart racing, hoping there could be some good news among all this misery. He pointed upwards to the fifth floor of one of the shanties at the river's edge.

'I have found her,' he said.

Distant gunshots as we climbed a wet ladder from floor to floor, the final ladder on the rear and directly above the vile stew of the river. At the top, a landing area and a door ahead covered by a curtain. The driver called out, and an older lady appeared. The woman looked my way. She said in broken English that somehow she knew someone would be coming.

Patti's mother had been living there with her husband and their granddaughter for some weeks as a result of the carnage that destroyed her home. What really stood out to me was just how tidy, cosy and remarkably comfortable it all was inside, despite the view from the outside. I felt as if I was on a ship, the whole construction swaying slightly, although I knew a ship would have been more secure. There were two rooms, a kitchen of sorts on a little balcony and a living area complete with TV, fan and a couple of small armchairs. In the corner was a table with four dining chairs. The electricity was via a somewhat dicey looking, heavy-duty cable through the window that had been hooked to a meter-box fixed on the wall. Wires ran to the appliances and to a centre light and into the bedroom.

I gave her an envelope from Patti. Inside was a letter, the forms to be signed, and about $200 in small notes. She was shocked to see the money. I showed her photographs of Patti looking smart and professional in Hong Kong. She held them tight, lovingly, as if feeling a physical connection to her own daughter.

The lady said the child was sleeping and offered us green tea boiling on a paraffin stove. The driver translated as we discussed Patti's situation. As he spoke, she began to break down. Through her tears she told of losing Patti, perhaps forever, from her life. And now, she said, she was going to lose that much-loved little girl too.

Patti's father emerged from the bedroom. He had barely featured in what Jim had told me. He seemed exhausted, sad, as if afflicted by the same gathering loss. He sat in a chair and I watched as he and his wife both wept at what had become of their lives. Turning to the bedroom, I saw the tiny little two-year-old Patti sitting up in the corner, quietly observing, looking quite puzzled about it all. As I looked at her, and back to her grandparents, I too could feel that tears may not be far away.

I told them that whatever was going to happen, it was not going to happen right away. I said their daughter may well arrange for them to visit the US at some point, that I was sure she would find a way to meet them again. They said they knew they could only be custodians of tiny Patti, that they would have to one day hand her back to her mother. They said they would do all they could to ensure the right thing was done. They signed the forms.

It was a success but it didn't feel like it. I came away after about two hours feeling emotionally drained. My driver felt the same way and we drove swiftly in a kind of sad silence. The 10 pm curfew was closing in and, we both knew, there was no time to waste. No street lights were working and very little was illuminated at all beyond the headlights of homeward-bound cars.

I rewarded my magnificent driver appropriately and hit the hotel bar for a strong gin and tonic or two to collect my thoughts. Half an hour later I called Jim from my room. He was, as ever, not at all emotional as he congratulated me in his quiet, matter-of-fact voice.

'Well done Ian,' he said, 'that was fast. Now get back to Hong Kong. We have new challenges, a lot more to do here.'

Unfortunately it wasn't that simple. Flights were becoming less and less frequent, the exodus was growing by the day as the city's slow fall continued. The only flight I could get was to Singapore, but it would be at the end of the week and I had days to kill.

On a stroll around the area I remember the fearsome scars on the children maimed by the obscene napalm bombs dropped on the small villages of Vietnam. They had been brought to the city for treatment and remained there with nothing. They were spending their days seeking dollars. I gave one to a small child and, within seconds, another was by my side seeking the same. Within a minute or two I was surrounded by children bearing awful injuries, battle scars on young limbs and faces from a battle in which their only role was to be wounded for life. And more and more kept appearing from every alley way, almost as if from nowhere among the city's maze of streets.

Hands were outstretched all around me and I began to feel worried, concerned that this was somehow taking a turn for the worse. They began tugging at my pockets, trying to take what they could and I needed to stop them without causing any pain, without injuring one of these innocent victims. I could barely even walk at pace for fear of treading on a bare foot, of knocking over a child of seven, six or five.

I made it back to the hotel and the concierge clocked the issue. He moved in, shooed them away, ushered me inside and closed the doors. The children stayed put, crowded the main entrance for the rest of the day hoping I would go out to them once again. It was, the concierge told me, a regular occurrence.

On Saturday, the day I was to fly to Singapore, two suited men approached me just outside the hotel. They asked for my ID and I asked for theirs. One flashed a police card. The other had a handgun in a shoulder holster. The only ID I had on me was my hotel key card. I took it out of my wallet and…

I hadn't seen it coming. One shoved me against the wall and grabbed my wallet. He pulled the cash from it and they both stepped into the crowd and vanished. I was about to chase but sense kicked in. Instead, I retrieved the wallet from the pavement. I had nothing left. Fortunately, I had prepaid the hotel on arrival. I told them what had happened and they paid for a cab to the airport, no problem.

I boarded what was to be the last flight out of Vietnam to Singapore for some time. It turned out there were many more prospective passengers than seats. Fortunately for me, I held a confirmed ticket and most were hoping to board were on standby. At the exit I was asked for the departure tax—$100. I told the gentleman my story and he took me to one side.

'If you cannot pay, you cannot leave,' he said.

I approached an airline official who said the same thing. I was, I knew, stuffed. But not for long. A well-dressed American man who had overheard the exchange came over and said, 'It's okay, I'll pay for him.' He wouldn't hear of it when I tried to get his details to arrange repayment. Whoever he was, I'm still grateful.

I found out only on landing that luggage had been offloaded before we took to the air in order to manage the excess human weight. I was already skint and now without so much as a pair of pants or a toothbrush.

I picked out a hotel from the phone book, the Goodwood Park Hotel, and explained my predicament. I said my brother would be flying over from England to get some cash to me and that I was still a guest at Hong Kong's Mandarin Hotel.

A cab was sent for me, took me to the hotel and I was led to a stunning executive style room with a view over the gardens, full of multi-coloured tropical vegetation and fruits. A note from the manager said I had a hotel credit limit of SGD$500 plus a cash advance of SGD$250. I was able to buy some clothes and arranged for Stuart to fly from London before we both went back to Hong Kong. Sometimes things just have a way or working out.

Two years later, an envelope arrived at our office addressed to me. Inside was a picture of Patti, her American husband and their beautiful daughter all having winter fun in the USA.

A note said, 'Thank you. Patti.'

EIGHTEEN

The Dentist's Son and
The Scientist's Daughter (1975/76)

It was never an easy decision to take on an abduction case. People who approached seeking resolution were often on the edge, most certainly at an extreme point in their lives. I had to discern the full facts from among, very often, a confusion of claim and blame and rage.

Sometimes I could not assist due to logistics, the far flung location of the child in question, the complications and costs involved. And I said 'no thank you' also to those cases where the legal paperwork was not in order, where things may not have been quite as they were being presented. Under no circumstances could I allow myself to be involved in the retrieving of a child without a court order endorsing such an action. I acted only as enforcer, never abductor. The distinction is critical.

But when I was sure things were in order, that a legitimate court had reached a decision, that the funds were in place and the child was within reach, myself and my team would come on board with nothing less than a steely determination to get the job done right.

In 1975 we were approached in person by Dr Zygmund Bejnarowitz, a Polish dentist based in Chicago. He had made his way to England after securing an order from the Cook County Courthouse. It demanded that his ex-wife, the mother of his five-year-old son, return the youngster to his care. The boy had been taken four years ago and was believed to be somewhere in London. His wife had grown up in England before moving to the USA. Dr Bejnarowitz knew we would want to check the details before making a decision. He had arrived with a file of newspaper cuttings about the case which, very clearly, had been a significant story in the American media. Over the past four years Dr Bejnarowitz had tried to reach his ex but without success. He said she was hiding out with the boy and that, 'I don't know if he is alive or dead.'

The boy, Wojciech, had been abducted, aged one. I was told that his mother's London connections were mainly in the west of the city and her Polish parents still lived there. He asked that myself and the team locate her, retrieve the boy and ensure he and his son made it safely back to Chicago.

Our first port of call was her parents' home. We launched into a week long surveillance operation to establish who was coming and going, but it was not easy. They were a wealthy family, their property secure and relatively secluded. We talked this over with the client and he was very clear. He said whatever resources we needed, we would have. We said it may be wise to secure a surveillance van to allow us to spend longer at the location, to raise us up a little and maximise our field of view. He returned to Chicago advising us to get one, saying he would pay for it.

Stuart and I sourced a large left-hand drive Ford Transit van which had previously been used as on-the-road accommodation by a motorcycle racing duo. There was space for two mighty bikes and two hammocks as well as all the gear the guys had needed, including cooking facilities and a chemical toilet.

Each day we parked in a different spot and, splitting shifts among surveillance operatives, covered the property for 14 of every 24 hours through one way glass. The surveillance team began to take notes on a large woman who, very infrequently, left the house with a small child of about five by her side. She would wander with the youngster to local shops and return. This happened perhaps once every few days, so it seemed clear they were living at the address. Yet the child, as far as our people could tell, was female.

They took pictures on a number of occasions, secured the clearest images they could of both. I spent a while looking at them before becoming fairly sure these were the right people. In which case, I knew, the mother must have taken to dressing the boy as a girl. I mailed the images to Chicago. Dr Bejnarowitz called me. He said this was his ex wife and son.

He returned to London the next day. I took him to the van. He sat glued to the back window in the hope of seeing the child. I carefully talked him through the plan should the boy appear. We agreed it would be vital to avoid any trauma for the little lad who had not seen his father's face in four years or more, who knew nothing of him. The idea was that his father would approach the mother and boy. He would of course be recognised by her. He would speak first to the boy in Polish, tell him who he was in the hope that might reassure him. He would lift the child and, as the van pulled up to the kerb, get in the sliding side doors. I would drive the van away, turn right into the next street where the escape car was waiting. Its driver would take father and son to a prearranged safe house, the home of a previous client, and rest for a couple of days. After that they would go to the US Consulate, get a passport for Wojciech and fly home.

It was not going to be easy. This was an incredibly blunt and intense operation we were planning. We could factor in complications for as long as we liked, but the live response of a mother and child in such a scenario was something we could never know in advance. It would take a certain drive to get it done, to dramatically change the circumstances in order to meet the demands of both client and law. But, as I say, we were a single-minded squad.

It was likely the police would be called before we could call them to explain what had taken place. If so, they would be looking for the van and we would already have vacated it. Yet if they did find us, we could prove with paperwork that our client was the legal custodial parent. In any case, we would, as was our MO, leave a copy of the court order in the van for the Met to discover.

The plan in place, Stuart, myself, the client and a third agent settled into the van, parked around one hundred yards from the house in the leafy suburban street. We were going over the details once again when our assisting agent, peering through binoculars, turned to us.

'They're coming down the road,' he said.

Sure enough, the mother, the boy dressed as a girl, and a second sizable woman, the mother's sister, was there too. Dr Bejnarowitz was agitated, stared out of the window, watched intently as they meandered slowly towards our location.

Right out of the blue, he yanked open the sliding door. I called to him as he leapt out and dashed up the street. His wife and her sister saw him coming right away. They froze then both began yelling.

'Wojciech! Wojciech!'

The little boy was ahead of them and watching as this man was belting towards him. As our client closed in, he reached out to grab the child. At the same time, the women drove forward and reached out to grab the man and, like something from a wrestling match, flung him onto the ground. One lady dropped down hard onto his legs and the other sat on his chest. Both started screaming for help. Dr Bejnarowitz was going nowhere.

'Help! Police! Police!'

People appeared, began making their way to this unusual scene. I got out, began heading towards the drama as if I was a bystander. I strolled purposefully right into the middle of it all and grabbed our client by one of his flailing arms.

'You're coming with me,' I said, as baffled little Wojciech looked on.

Both women stood and, as I pulled him to his feet, the swelling crowd parted. I walked him a couple of steps, then released my grip. He was right beside his son. And he understood the tactic. Dr Bejnarowitz reached for the boy, picked him up and ran for the van, leapt in through the sliding door. I jumped into the front and our agent went to pull away. But people had followed. They came right to my door, assuming it was the driver's door, and tried to pull it open. But the wheel was on the other side. I jammed on the lock and, avoiding someone who had come onto the road, the agent drove off. He floored the vehicle towards the end of the street, turned right and stopped. I jumped out, Dr Bejnarowitz and his son followed, and we switched vehicles as the van sped off. I indicated, pulled away and drove calmly onto the main road and into the shelter of thickening traffic. The left-hand drive van was left, as discussed, at a car park in Hammersmith, a copy of the court order on the seat.

I drove to the safe house and put in a call to the police. We spelled out the details and they seemed almost completely uninterested. If we wanted to file a report, they said, someone should come to the station.

After the child's mother had filed a report, the police went looking for the van. They called me, as the registered owner, to establish the details. I went through it all again. We had been acting, I said, under a court order valid in both England and the United States. They said everything seemed to be in place. The case, as far as they were concerned, was closed.

Now we just had to get the boy and his father across the Atlantic. There was work to be done in terms of getting a passport for Wojciech. That issue was complicated to an extent when we learned that the client's ex-wife had appointed some London solicitors. Anticipating problems, we made our way to Dover a few days later. Myself and the client used our own passports to board a ferry to France. My passport was also valid for my son Johnnie. As I say, we did what we had to do in order to get the job done. We made our way to the US Embassy in Paris and an emergency passport was issued for Wojciech. Both flew to Chicago from there.

A few days later, with the story making TV and newspaper headlines in America, I flew over to meet the client once more. I was asked also to attend Cook County Court to file a sworn statement outlining the facts and was happy to do so.

About a year later, Wojciech's mum returned to Chicago. She was quickly arrested for the breach of the court order and was jailed for contempt. She appealed and, to genuinely massive surprise, the custody decision was reversed. The court said that, on reflection, the child had only known his mother and should have been allowed to stay with her.

That led to a whole new legal battle opening up during which Wojciech was taken to an unknown place with his father for a time. And given I'd worked so closely with Bejnarowitz, the press reported I was suspected of hiding them. In turn, I became the focus of attention and for a time surveillance was carried out on my home. British police, US officials and American embassy staff were all involved in tracking my movements to see if I might lead them to him. They weren't subtle about it either and took to calling at my door to ask me what I knew. I knew nothing.

Eventually, via mediation, a custody deal was reached in the US and that particular trans-Atlantic tug-of-love was, in as much as it could be, resolved.

Such was the fraught nature of the child recovery work that I always anticipated complications. That included, of course, being arrested myself. Indeed, given past experience, I generally felt that I would be prosecuted for something or other soon enough. The case which did it was, as with the Chicago dentist, a UK-US tug-of-love. The circumstances were familiar. A mother had illegally taken her little girl to England from America. Yet the outcome would be completely different.

The King family lived in the Washington DC area. The mum in question was the daughter of British embassy employee from London. She had fallen in love with Robert King, a high-level scientist in America's powerful Food and Drug Administration, the FDA. The marriage turned sour and, by agreement, Mrs King took their daughter Lara to the UK so everyone could get a break. Unfortunately, she did not return and Mr King was plunged into deep distress.

He had been unable to reach his in-laws in the Southampton area and, suspecting things were not going to get any better, called in a lawyer. Strong letters followed and the mother replied to say she was still in England, the marriage was over, that she had a Spanish boyfriend and planned to move to Spain. The two-year-old girl, she said, would be going as well.

Mr King went to court in Washington DC. An order was issued granting him custody of Lara and calling on Mrs King to bring her back to the USA immediately. She did not respond when the order was served by mail. The father flew to England and applied to the High Court for an order banning the mother from taking the girl to Spain. The court's response was to issue a wardship order, making the child a ward of the court. She could not be removed from the court's jurisdiction without its consent.

Yet Mr King had been unable to locate his wife and child when in Britain. She had been reachable by mail at her parents' address but they were keeping schtum about her whereabouts. He engaged us, said she may be staying at a relative's house, asked us to confirm where she was and make sure she did not flee the UK. We agreed to do what we could and he flew back to the States.

We confirmed that the mother and toddler were staying at her sister's house in Hampshire. We set up surveillance to make sure she met her legal obligation not to leave the country. I lined up three agents and three vehicles so the house was covered around the clock. A few days later Mr King arrived. I was surprised when he told me he had cancelled the wardship order. It seemed like a strange thing to do, but he said he saw no use in it. I double checked that with the High Court in London who said there was no record of that order. I could only assume that, as the client had said, it had been scrapped.

Mr King turned to me, in the next surprise, asked if I would help him recover his daughter. I said it would be best to operate via his lawyers given the complex legal picture. He said he was sure that if she got wind of him being in England with lawyers on the case, she would make the break for Spain. And the ward order was no longer in place to stop her. It was becoming clear that he was planning to remove Lara from the jurisdiction himself, which he was legally entitled to do.

I took him to where his wife was now staying. As we closed in, he spotted her pushing the child in a buggy. He asked me to slow down so he could get a closer look. In a heartbeat he had the door open and was dashing towards them. He shoved Mrs King out of the way as he lunged for the child, pulled her from the pushchair and came racing back. It was a moment of madness on his part. And perhaps on mine too as, although shocked, I drove away. Two of my surveillance agents had witnessed the whole thing. They got out to help the mother back to her feet. They too were stunned at how things had unfolded. Mr King asked me to drive him to a hotel in west London and within a few days he flew home with Lara.

One evening, a gin and tonic in my hand, I was at home in Shoreham, Sussex, when the door knocked. A police constable, a man I knew to an extent, was on the doorstep. I invited him in. I was sure it was something to do with parking tickets.

'Sorry Ian,' he said, 'couple of Hampshire officers to see you.'

Two plain clothes detectives emerged from behind. They confirmed my name and arrested me for 'child stealing.'

'Come again?'

The suspected offence, they said, related to the King case. The Director of Public Prosecutions in London had decided that myself and three agents who worked on the recovery would face court for *child stealing*. This was not the first time I had been arrested for a crime with a name that seemed to have been made up on the spot. My solicitor was quick to question it given I had been working for the child's parent, the legally recognised custodial parent. But that absolutely key fact seemed to cut no ice.

I pleaded not guilty at the trial. I said I was assisting in the recovery of a parentally abducted child. My counsel petitioned the court to say there was no case to answer. In doing so, he did not submit a specific defence in terms of the King case. The strategy backfired. I was duly pronounced guilty as charged. My client, the child's father, escaped prosecution given he was out of reach in the USA.

I was fined £250 and immediately gave notice of appeal, but I did not succeed. After that, I gave up. I wasn't about to launch headlong into another hugely expensive court battle with a legal system that showed no interest in exploring the facts.

As I left the Court of Appeal that day, fuming at the poor legal strategy, I took a few moments to myself. My solicitor would be joining me at the front of the building in a few minutes. It was while I was waiting, deep in thought, that a man walked towards me. He came quite close and introduced himself as an officer with the Metropolitan Police. I knew his face, recognised him as having been sat in the gallery of the court during the proceedings. I asked him what his interest was in the case. He said only that he had been 'an observer.' He seemed pleasant enough. And then a smile that somehow did not seem pleasant.

'Ian,' he said, 'a friendly word in your ear. We don't want you in London. Do yourself a favour, move somewhere else and take your business with you.'

I think my mouth fell open. I was absolutely stunned. Who the hell did he think he was?

And then I was raging.

I said, 'What the fuck has it got to do with you?'

His response?

'Heed my words.'

And with that, he walked sharply away. I stood in a kind of furious trance just as my solicitor arrived at my side.

NINETEEN

Escape from Sweden: Recovering Denise and Lief (1976)

SWEDISH-born Anne-Marie Hill had become desperately homesick. She had married Bob Hill and moved to his native California to raise their two children, but life there had been getting her down. Her husband was a rugged bloke, a gun-toting all-American guy who had been in the US military for a number of years. They had met in Germany, fallen in love, got hitched and brought little Denise and Leif into the world.

Bob wanted nothing more than to settle down in his home state. At first Anne-Marie was keen, but her mind changed. The cracks began to show. Fearing the worst, Bob had secured an order from a San Jose court forbidding his wife from taking the children, aged nine and seven, out of the jurisdiction. That brought him some comfort, but it would not be enough. When it all became too much, Anne-Marie gathered the children and, in secret, left the family home. She returned, of course, to Sweden.

A year passed by and Bob found himself frustrated at how slowly and uncertainly the legal wheels were turning. He was the custodial parent yet was getting nowhere. One evening he saw me on television discussing a tug-of-love case and wondered if I might be able to help. A phone call followed and from there we agreed on a contract to locate his family. If necessary, I would go to Sweden to assist in recovering his kids and getting them safely back to America.

We worked with a PI in Sweden who traced the missing mother and children to a small town called Linköping. Before putting a plan together, I sent one of our agents, Lee Fieldsend, off to confirm what we had been told and to report back on relevant details. He advised that Denise and Lief attended the only school in the area. In fact, he had met with the principal on the pretext that he might send his own children there. He told the principal he had noticed two American pupils were already at the school and was advised they had been there for about a year.

Lee told me, 'The whole place is quite friendly and most of the locals speak good English.'

'Thanks,' I said, 'that's good to know.'

'There have been some very heavy snowfalls. It's bloody cold here.'

Again, good to know. I said I would act accordingly.

I called Bob in California and he booked his flight to London right away. We met for the first time at Gatwick Airport, and I'll never forget it. He was tall and well-built with long hair, bound by a ribbon, almost to his waist. On his head, a large cowboy hat and, on his feet, a pair of magnificent, unmissable cowboy boots. He knew my face from television and I felt I knew his from a John Wayne film. All jangling silver buckles and blue jeans, he strode my way.

It wasn't long after our big handshake and getting to hear his loud, drawling voice that I politely suggested he might need to tone down the look if he was to go undercover in a little Swedish town. I said he may need to become more 'European' looking, albeit temporarily.

Bob did not like that idea one bit. He was offended at my words, seemed to think I had something against the men who tamed the west. I assured him I did not and went on to explain he would soon find that, in rural Scandinavia, he was literally the only cowboy in town. If he wanted his children back, he would need to be more discreet. I put it to him that he had the rest of his life to dress however he liked.

Bob came around to that way of thinking. Indeed the ladies in the office liked the idea of creating a new Bob. With, eventually, his consent, they de-cowboyed him, cut off most of the ponytail and, all in all, toned him down. And then it was time to go.

Myself, Bob, Lee Fieldsend and another agent, Tim Austin, took the ferry to France. We picked up a few bottles of duty-free whisky before driving through Belgium, Holland, Germany, Denmark and into Sweden. And Lee wasn't joking. The snow was deep, the temperatures deeper, my Ford Granada losing grip the further north we climbed. We pulled into Linköping and checked into the small hotel where Lee had stayed before. Strangely, the hotel owner approached me to enquire about our luggage. He had noticed the whiskey. Stranger still, he said we could have two nights' accommodation for the price of one, free breakfast and dinner, and as much beer as we could drink in exchange for three bottles of whisky. It seemed like one hell of a deal—so we took it. I can only tell you that the food was excellent. And we drank a lot of beer.

We surveyed the area over the next couple of days, decided on the best routes out of town and what to do if it all went belly up. I practiced a little driving too, just to ensure I was confident with terrain much more slippery and sloshy than I was used to.

We said our goodbyes to our friendly hotelier, shook hands, and promised more whiskey if we ever returned. We loaded up and drove to the school. I parked outside and waited in the driving seat. Before long Denise and Lief arrived, walking unaccompanied. With Lee and Tim waiting nearby, Bob strode into the school to approach their teacher. He said there was a dental appointment. Moments later, he appeared with a child holding each hand. They all seemed happy, were chatting and laughing as they walked towards the car. It was great to see. They all got in and I drove off as introductions were made.

The school phoned Anne-Marie. Not unexpectedly, she exploded and immediately called the police. We had an hour's head start. By that time we had taken the long bridge into Denmark and were en route for the German border. At passport control, as the children slept, we were told to pull over. The Swedish authorities had been in touch. Bob had a copy of the court order and I was ready to explain in detail everything they needed to know. One key problem was that I had been counting on my passport, which listed two children, to get the kids over the border.

Phone calls went back and forward and, after four hours, we were given the all-clear to continue. The passport issue, fortunately, was not an issue. And they did not even ask to see the court order in the end. What they did was establish if there was any court order in Sweden preventing the children being removed from the country and there was not. Their father could take his kids wherever he liked.

Back in England, Bob went to the US Embassy and arranged for travel documents. He collected them, as well as his hat and boots, and I flew with him and the children to San Francisco and onto San Jose. The US media was out in force at the airport for an upbeat *Welcome Home* story. We gave interviews, posed for pictures and, over the next few days, made the necessary legal statements and signed the necessary forms. All seemed to be well. The children were thrilled to be home, to meet with their friends once more, to reunite with their grandparents.

About a year later I was on holiday in Las Vegas with Phyl and our then three-year-old son John. I had liked Bob, respected his style, liked the way he was very much his own man. I thought it over and, given we were in that part of the USA, gave him a call to see how things were going. He was delighted to hear from me, said he had moved to Reno, Nevada, and invited us over. He told me, best of all, that he and his wife had reconciled. The family was back together. It was wonderful news.

Off we went to Reno where we stayed for a week with what was a truly happy family. We explored Carson City and Lake Tahoe and celebrated as Denise turned ten while we were there. I was back again about five years later at a time when Bob had become a crop dusting pilot. He donned his boots and invited me on board for a spin in his biplane. I'll never forget swooping through the long narrow valley towards his parents' home. His mother waved as he zoomed, at about 300ft, over the house, banked around and landed in the not-so-long garden. We all had what you might call a local lunch—lots of refried beans and chili—before we took off again. And given the garden was too short to act as a runway, Bob pulled off a terrifying manoeuvre involving a rope wrapped around a sturdy tree and looped around the tailwheel of the plane. Full power applied, our bones shaking with the vibrations, we shot into the sky like a bullet. I've had a few adrenaline rushes in my time, but that one was something else.

To this day I'm in touch with the family. They are, I'm delighted to say, as close as ever.

TWENTY

The Primodos Scandal (1977)

IN August, 2020, Sky Documentaries broadcast a film called *Bitter Pill*. It covered the Primodos pregnancy test drug scandal in the UK back in the seventies. I was interviewed on camera. The issue it covered is nothing short of shameful. In terms of its victims and its extent, the Primodos case is one of the most disturbing I came across in my career.

My involvement came as a result of a connection in the legal world. I had many friends who practiced law. When I wasn't working for solicitors, I had them working for me in one way or another. When I wasn't enforcing legal orders, I was quite often standing in the dock for one reason or another.

One such friend in Brighton was David Barling. He had been my client and I had been his many times. We had come to trust each other's judgement. He called me to his office one morning in June, 1977. He said he had a client who needed help with a highly confidential matter. I was introduced to an Eddie Cruickshank-Robb, the Chairman of the local Conservative Party Constituency Association.

David excused himself and Eddie came closer. He was, he said, a senior executive with Schering Pharmaceuticals, one of the biggest drug makers and distributors in the world. He had become concerned about a prescription-only product he was involved in marketing which went by the trade name Primodos. It was a pregnancy test drug which could, he said, potentially cause harm to the unborn foetus. The echoes of Thalidomide, which had maimed as many as 20,000 babies up until the early sixties, were inescapable.

His company, he went on, was in possession of both internal and external professional warnings about the high risk posed by Primodos.

Yet due to the massive investment in developing the drug, Scherings had opted not to act on the word of its own experts but to defer the matter for the UK regulators to manage. The company was neither withdrawing the drug for now, nor indeed was it highlighting any concerns at all. The British government had, in 1975, issued a half-hearted warning in some circles about a 'possible association' between the drug and 'an increased incidence of congenital abnormalities,' but the pill remained on the market. Eddie said he had which documents revealed beyond doubt that there was a much more unsettling truth.

He wanted to get the story into the press. He asked if I would assist and represent him in doing so. He wanted, he said, £10,000 to reveal all and to remain anonymous at the same time. I was surprised. Ten grand was quite the ask. He explained it was possible he would be identified as the source of the leak and if so it was likely he would be booted out and lose his company pension. The money was essential, he said, if he was going to put his career on the line. At the time there was nothing at all to protect whistleblowers and he was taking a sizable risk.

I believed him when he said he had not wanted to get involved in such a mess in the first place, and certainly not one that would shut down his income, but that he felt that he had to make a stand. His was ultimately a moral, not financial, decision. I said I would act on his behalf and protect his identity until the day he died.

He opened his briefcase to show me documents he had copied, about twenty pages or so. I flicked through, noted the Schering logo throughout. I took them away, read them all. I was left in no doubt about the veracity of what he had told me and what was at stake. Among the information was insight into a dispute between Shering's British and German executives over whether Primodos should remain on the market. It seemed the Brits wanted it removed from the shelves but a decision to the contrary in Berlin had overruled their will.

I spent the next week contacting journalists, calling up former press contacts, meeting several to discuss. I needed to be cautious about whom I trusted with what I knew, yet at the same time I had to divulge information in order to secure a deal. It was not an easy position in which to find myself.

The first paper to show interest was *The People*. I'd worked with its reporters many times before. Its journalist Fred Harrison asked if he could see the documents and I trusted him enough to let him have a look. The documents spanned several years. They made clear that Schering had known of the severe risks in all that time yet they were still churning out the drug. The linked birth defects included missing limbs, heart problems, spina bifida and potential early death. Harrison knew it was an extraordinary story, but also that I was asking for an extraordinary sum.

We had met in good faith but, I'm sorry to say, I was stitched up. He didn't arrange for any payment. Instead he ran what amounted to a hit piece on me linked to the case of a child who had been born with abnormalities. I was portrayed as the controversial private eye who had been sneakily sifting through secret company files to get money for himself. I was, he said, a 'rat' who was trying to 'cash in on a toddler's suffering'. Although he reported on the explosive issue at hand within the story, it seemed he didn't much care about it. A charming man, indeed.

Eddie was shocked to see what had happened. He was upset, became certain he would be outed as the source of the documents which, *The People* said, had been leaked to me. I calmed him down, advised him that, as I had promised, no one would get his name. In the meantime, I launched a libel action against the newspaper. I was not a happy bunny at all.

It emerged soon after that a law firm was looking into making a claim against Schering on behalf of a number of women. On Eddie's behalf, I sent the copied documents their way and I'm glad to say their case, though complex, was bolstered as a result. I was later contacted by Greg Dyke at London Weekend Television, a future Director General of the BBC, who was seeking to explore the story. I discussed that with Eddie who provided me with another set of copies which I passed to LWT.

The issue, involving huge sums of money and high-priced lawyers, has been very much something of a slow burner. There have been a number of inquiries and investigations but the legal wheels have turned at a glacial pace. There has been no proper resolution for the victims, no real recognition from the company at the time of writing. In the Sky documentary former Prime Minister Theresa May said reports into the scandal have found no solid proof of wrongdoing 'despite the fact there was obvious evidence.' She said victims have not been listened to, that they should be entitled to redress from the British government. She said that former ministers and healthcare professionals had sought to 'stop them in their tracks… saying that "you didn't really suffer".'

Eddie was never rumbled by the firm and, thankfully, was never sacked nor had his pension stripped from him. Indeed he went on to flourish as a well-known local political figure and became the Mayor of Hove. He died in 2018 and, as was my promise, I divulged his name to no one while he was alive. I have since disclosed his name and provided further information to the lawyers representing the injured parties. I can only hope that helps in the victims' fight bring an end to this sad episode.

TWENTY-ONE

Operation Unit Six (1977)

SUMMERTIME. A board meeting underway. I break off to take a call.

'My name is MA Howard the Third,' the caller announced. I was already intrigued.

He said he represented the Indian Ocean Commercial & Development Bank (IOCAD) and sought an urgent meeting to discuss a most sensitive matter. Could I visit the merchant bank's office in Mayfair to discuss? As soon as possible? But of course. I made my way to the grand old building where Mr Howard III was based.

A plummy-voiced secretary brought me to a large polished oak boardroom door. She knocked lightly and opened it to reveal Mr M A Howard lll. He was, she had said, a senior executive within the bank. I shook his hand and took a seat while admiring the various framed certificates advising how important he was. Mr Howard outlined his issue. He was, he said, responsible for looking after high-value Middle Eastern clients. Some of these clients, he went on, wanted to purchase a stake in a London casino. His role, he told me, was to determine which would be the best casino for such an investment.

'I want you to help my clients identify which has the wealthiest customers,' he said.

He would provide me with a list of six target casinos. I was to arrange for undercover agents to visit during the evenings. They were to identify the high rollers, take pictures and secure their names and other details. I was to submit results weekly. It was an unusual and potentially complex request, but then they often were. I had no problem signing an initial agreement and got straight to work.

Stuart and I arranged a roundtable with our dozen agents. We would, we decided, call it *Operation Unit Six*. It was likely to demand all our physical resources. All twelve agents applied for membership cards at all six casinos. We would operate in six teams of two. Each team would be allocated to one of the casinos and each team would move to a new casino every three days.

At the time, Stuart, Helen, Phyl and I were also working every morning on admin, and every afternoon and evening repossessing televisions all around London. When we were done, we agreed, we would also assist with *Operation Unit Six*. We would help with getting the names from the relevant punters and generally ensure things were running smoothly. We knew it was likely we would often be on the go until 4 am, but we were not afraid of a long day's work.

The client paid the promised retainer in cash and, all agents in suits and ties, we launched into what showed every sign of being a lucrative operation. As we settled into the routine and circulated the teams, it didn't take long to be able to spot the big players. The clubs had VIP tables where only the high rollers could go, very often wealthy Arabs. The problem was ordinary players couldn't get into those rooms. In reality, we had little chance of getting to hear and confirm names, almost no chance at all of getting a picture of them inside a location where cameras were banned. We did what we could but by the end of the first week we were going nowhere fast. I had to tell the client.

I remember we met on a bench in Hyde Park while Mr Howard III was on his lunchtime walk. I suggested the best method may be for us to get the car numbers, as most of the big players were driven to and from the location each evening. I said I could repurpose my agents to watch out for the high-end cars and get their numbers. I felt that was a solution given Mr Howard had already mentioned to me that his own security staff could identify owners via licence plates.

'It's a good idea,' he said, 'we will change your brief.'

From then on, over the coming weeks, our agents camped discreetly outside, took the numbers and took pictures. One of the target premises was Ladbrokes Hill Street Casino. The others were the Playboy Club, Claremont Club, Crockfords, Knightsbridge Sporting Club and The Colony Club.

Each week, after many hours of surveillance, I would meet with Mr Howard III at that park bench, deliver the details on paper—car makes, colours, licence plates, times, dates, descriptions—and he would settle up in cash. We would chat about things for a while as the world went by and I got to know a little about him. He was certainly an unusual character. He told me after a time that he was working with the betting and entertainment firm Ladbrokes which, in its three London casinos of the era, had a close to thirty percent share of the market. It was then that I realised our work at the Ladbrokes' casino on Hill Street had been a control, my Danish client's way of gauging how accurate we could be. He passed me his genuine business card which said he worked for Ladup Ltd, part of the same group. The card carried his real name—Andreas Christensen.

It all created quite some suspicion in my mind given the certificates on his office wall named Mr Howard III and not Mr Christiansen. And what about that office? I'd been in just the once and, since then, he'd ensured we met only beyond its walls. A shadowy, almost theatrical character, without a doubt. Yet many clients were, to a greater or lesser extent, in the shadows.

And then one day he didn't turn up. I called his office but there was no answer. A few days later, that same number became unobtainable. This was a man who owed me £3,000. I thought it over, reflected on our chats. And then I put a call into Ladbrokes.

'I'm seeking to speak with your employee Andreas Christensen,' I asked.

'Oh, he's just left the company, sir.'

'I see.'

The old grey cells were really starting to fizz now. Could it be that, all along, my client had been gathering commercial intelligence for his employers at Ladbrokes? Might it make sense for the casino owners to discreetly secure for themselves a fuller and deeper picture of the market and its key players in London? It seemed very possible. But I wanted my three grand. At the time of writing, that sum equals something closer to £15,000. I was damn sure someone would be paying up.

My solicitor, David Barling in Brighton, suggested I send Ladbrokes my bill and see what they do. I did precisely that. It showed each invoice for the whole assignment and the payments received. I specified Andreas Christiansen as the Ladbrokes representative.

The company replied. It acknowledged that Mr Christiansen had left and said it was unaware of this particular operation. It said it would not be paying. In doing so, it had confirmed in writing he had been an employee at the time he commissioned me for the job.

My solicitor said to press on. He put Ladbrokes on notice to say if they don't pay we will issue High Court proceedings. They said they would not be paying because they knew nothing about all this dodgy business. We went to the High Court and filed the claim.

It appeared on the court's notice board:

1977-W-No.3517 IAN DOUGLAS WITHERS,
Plaintiff V. LADUP LTD

Someone took it on themselves to tip off the national press. A headline appeared in the *Evening Standard* informing the public that a PI was suing Ladup Ltd, the owner of Ladbroke Casinos. Ladbrokes lawyers phoned my solicitors trying to get the claim withdrawn. They were in turmoil over the publicity and insisted there was no merit to this damaging story. My solicitor explained their employee had entered into a contract on their company's behalf and they were liable. And, once again, they said they would not pay. So on we went.

On the date of the High Court hearing, their Counsel conceded the claim was legitimate and agreed to pay related costs. On November 29, 1977, I received the lot. They had finally done the right thing.

A telephone call followed from the Serious Crimes Unit of Nottingham Police. They were launching an investigation into Ladbrokes in connection with the misuse of the Police National Computer on their patch. It appeared serving and ex-police officers had been employed by the company as security consultants. Some had been researching individuals on the restricted equipment.

In an interview we talked over the extreme lengths to which the mysterious Mr Howard aka Christiansen had gone to satisfy the demands of what was referred to within Ladbrokes as 'quality control.' The Dane had created the dummy Indian Ocean Commercial Bank, hired an office (possibly for just 24 hours), printed certificates, briefed a fake secretary as part of an ongoing fraudulent lifestyle both before and during his time with Ladbrokes. His mission with the betting company, via myself, had simply been to identify high-rollers, to reach out and lure them towards its casinos. Under the UK Gaming Act, this was completely illegal.

As the evidence was gathered, I was asked to be a witness in the case against corrupt former and serving police officers and a number of members of staff at Ladbrokes. It took about two years before it all came to trial in Nottingham. During that time a large number of unpleasant phone calls, all anonymous of course, were made to my office and home. In at least one, the caller even mentioned the name of the casino company I had taken to court.

He said, 'You don't really want to get involved with Ladbrokes people. Nasty things happen. People get killed. People disappear.'

My wife answered at times as well as myself, other members of staff too. They were coming at a rate of three or four a day at one point and we were able to record them. I forwarded the tapes to Nottingham Police who took the threats very seriously. They arranged for Sussex Police to install silent panic alarms in the house which, when triggered, directly alerted Shoreham Police Station.

One afternoon my wife was sitting in the kitchen with friends when one woman, clearly shocked, cried out, 'Men are climbing over the back fence!'

Moments later other blokes, already on the property, came bursting through the back door. The women were terrified. But those men were the good guys. It turned out my youngest son Jamie, aged two at the time, had found the panic button, pressed it numerous times and hidden himself under a bed.

We needed to get away at one point, the stress becoming too much. We asked our housekeeper, Lynn, to pop in each day if possible while we were over in Belfast for a couple of weeks. One week later she called to say someone had broken in, that the whole house had been flooded. I took the next flight over. The police were at the scene when I arrived. An intruder had been in, entering either by picking a lock or, even more chillingly, they had their own key. I had a large office in the house at the time and they had been in there too. They had completely emptied ten four-drawer filing cabinets, piles of paper scattered over the carpet. They had tipped the desks onto their sides, had lifted the typewriters and telex machines and carefully placed them upside-down on the floor. There was no damage, just a sort of gentle yet sincere destruction.

As I surveyed, one police officer said, 'The worst is upstairs.'

My stomach was in a knot as I went with him. We passed the kitchen on the way, its ceiling hanging down, water dripping through. My unknown visitors had left the plug in the bath and blocked the overflow. They had placed all of my suits in there, shirts and ties too, and turned on the taps.

They had moved into the study and cracked open my cigar collection, which included a few Cubans and other quality smokes I had been gathering. They had taken them from the wrappers and simply dropped them on the floor, treading on a few as they went. Yet, after a good look around, it was clear not a single thing had been stolen.

The police had little doubt this was all connected to my being a witness in the upcoming court case against Ladbrokes, although we could never know for sure who did this deed and why. Nevertheless, it was not going to put me off.

The court hearing involved the prosecution of a number of members of Ladbrokes staff, including management figures, and three serving police officers. Just one defendant pleaded guilty and was jailed as a result. The rest fought the charges and were found not guilty. All had been charged with the same conspiracy but given just the one was found guilty, there was technically no longer a conspiracy as that requires two or more. An odd legal situation. However the company had most certainly violated British casino laws.

Anyway, that seemed to be the end of the story. That is, until I took a phone call one day from the police officer who had led the case in London. He invited me to lunch. I wondered why? We met and dined well and, he explained, he simply wanted to thank me for assisting with the inquiry. I said that I hadn't even been called to give evidence in the end, but he said that he appreciated I had been ready to do so. A spread

Ladup Limited
Casino Division

 **Ladbrokes**

14-16 King Street,
Leicester LE1 6RJ
Telephone: Leicester (0533) 542700
Registered Office: Chancel House,
Neasden Lane, London NW10 2XE
Registered in England Number 816582

Our ref. GI/sg

29th November 1977

Mr. Ian D. Witlers,
Nationwide Investigation Group,
408 Upper Shoreham Road,
Shoreham by Sea,
Sussex BN4 5NE.

Dear Mr. Witlers,

I refer to your letter of the 16th November.

I have not as yet had an opportunity of discussing the matter with Mr. Christensen, but it is apparent that you were instructed by him and I enclose our cheque to dispose of the outstanding charges.

I will in due course be taking the matter up with Mr. Christensen accordingly.

Yours sincerely,

pp *G. Irvine*

G. P. J. Irvine
<u>Director</u>

Ladbrokes leisure

Chairman : C. Stein
Directors : A. R. Alexander (Managing)
J. A. Cowling, F.C.A., R. U. Gaskell,
G. P. J. Irvine, F.C.A., E. W. MacAdie, F.C.,
J. R. Morriss, M.A., F.C.A., D. J. Sate, F.C.,

179

in the *London Evening Standard* appeared around the same time. It was headlined *Operation Unit Six*, the name we had given our casino surveillance project. It carried photographs of myself and Andreas Christensen. My Danish client was, without doubt, a complex man with a complex history. I feel lucky we were both at odds with Ladbrokes rather than each other.

The publicity around the case went on to start something of a chain reaction. I began to get summonsed to attend Magistrates Courts around the country to act as a witness in cases being taken by anti-casino campaigners. People opposing bids by Ladbrokes to renew casino or betting shop licences or open up in various towns latched onto the *Operation Unit Six* story as an example of why they didn't want the firm in their area at all. On one day alone I had seventeen subpoenas to attend in different parts of the country. That couldn't be done so my solicitor prepared a standard sworn affidavit for each hearing.

It was a tough time for all involved. The honest employees at Ladbrokes were caught up in something not of their making. As for my family, it was a time of immense stress.

The good news is that all of us, including Ladbrokes, survived to take another roll of the dice…

NOTTINGHAMSHIRE CONSTABULARY

SHERWOOD LODGE, ARNOLD
NOTTINGHAM NG5 8PP
Telephone (0602) 269700 Ext.
Telex 37622

Your Ref.

Our Ref. HQ/CID/F
(PLEASE QUOTE REFERENCE WHEN REPLYING)

20 Nov 84

Dear Ian

I am sure that will remember that between 1978 and 1981 you assisted me in my enquiries into the business activities of the Ladup Casino Division Ltd.

Following both criminal and civil court hearings I am now in a position to release back into your possession all the documents which were provided by both yourself and Weekes Legge and Dean Solicitors. This follows your instructions given to Detective Chief Inspector Smith last week.

Would you please acknowledge receipt of the documents and I enclose a pre paid envelope for favour of your reply.

I know you will appreciate that this has been an extremely long and difficult series of enquiries and I wish to place on record my grateful thanks for the ready assistance which you and your staff gave to me and my Officers.

Please accept my best wishes for your future and should you be in this area at any time please do not hesitate to contact me.

Yours sincerely

John McNaught

John McNaught
Detective Chief Superintendent.

Mr I Withers
PO Box 116
Belfast
N. Ireland

181

TWENTY-TWO

Mission to Argentina: Recovering Lanny and Randy (1978)

'Your children are fine. There is no need to worry.'

That's all the card said. It was postmarked Cordoba, Argentina, suggesting that's where the two boys might be. Maybe the writer meant well, but the message did nothing to ease the anguish of the mother of those children.

Madge Gunia had requested my services after she saw me being interviewed on *Good Morning America*. I'd just wrapped up on a case that had made headlines across the USA. A father had snatched his son from his estranged wife in Switzerland. I'd found the father and son hiding out in a house in San Francisco. The house was between two railway lines, one line in one county and one in another. The case attracted interest partly because it involved police departments from three jurisdictions. When I had called at that door in California, the missing son had opened it. On seeing me, his mother and three different types of cop, he broke down.

'Why did it take you so long?' he said, tears rolling.

The following day a court ordered that he be returned to his mother's care in Switzerland, as had been the stipulation on a custody order. She and myself appeared on national TV as a result.

Madge had been listening to me talk about all this from her home near Milwaukee, Wisconsin, one hundred miles north of Chicago on the edge of America's Great Lakes. She operated a large stud farm, bred Arabian horses, and shared her home with second husband Tony, the local sheriff. She called me after the show. She said her sons Lanny and

Randy had been missing for ten years, abducted by their dad and her first husband Wayne Schultz during a legally sanctioned visit. Lanny had been three at the time. Randy was two. Schultz's girlfriend had helped spirit the boys out of the USA. The FBI and other authorities got involved, but their inquiries came to nought. The kids were on the missing list and Schultz remained a wanted man in America.

At the time myself and my Maryland partner Terry McGill had rented a small office in New York city, a place to meet clients. I flew there to meet Madge, her lawyer and her sheriff spouse. Tony, the husband, made it plain that he didn't like me very much and didn't really like PIs at all. I let him sit there, all quietly disgusted, as we muddled through that initial meeting.

I said we'd agree a handling fee and that if successful a larger fee would be payable. In most cases, locating the child or children was enough to get the job done. It meant parents could go on to enforce the custody order and begin the process to retrieve their offspring. But it was a different story with places that were both beyond the legal jurisdiction and beyond any relevant treaties. In that case, as I explained, a recovery operation might be considered. But we should not get ahead of ourselves, I said. First, I needed to find the boys.

That anonymous postcard was the only clue Madge could offer. Cordoba, Argentina. We reckoned that, on balance, it had been written by a female hand. It had arrived quite recently but why had it been sent in the first place ten years after the abduction? I considered that perhaps an ex-girlfriend of Madge's ex-husband may have posted it knowing that the mother had been in some despair for a long time. But it could only be guesswork.

I assigned researchers to determine if there were any US businesses in Cordoba. And I asked a contact in the local post office if any useful information could be extracted from the postcard. But I wasn't exactly bursting with other ideas right away. It was an unusual case in that the only pictures we had of the boys had been taken all those years before.

In round table talks with agents we decided to focus on schools. It was likely the boys were being educated somewhere. And it was reasonably likely, we thought, they would be attending an English-speaking school, or one where a sizable number of other American kids were on the register.

In those days we had no choice but to make our formal requests in writing. We wrote to the US Embassy in London, complete with a copy of the US Court Order, asking for a list of American Schools in the Cordoba region. And, having decided a little white lie might be in order, also wrote to the Argentinian Embassy in London saying we were moving out there and wanted a list of local schools. In a couple of weeks we had the names of dozens and dozens of English-speaking schools. So off to work we went.

Taking the time difference into account, from midday, across the afternoons and into the evenings, staff began making the calls. There was no long-distance direct dialling at the time, meaning every call had to go through an operator and, very often, those who answered spoke as much English as my staff spoke Spanish. It was slow progress, too slow in fact. So instead we started sending overseas telegrams to each of the schools asking that a message be passed to the boys to call our Maryland number collect. The pretext was that this was a matter of funding affecting the young brothers.

We sent out the first fifty. Each was addressed to the Principal:

Reference: Gunia Students' Funding. Message: Please call collect to USA (1) 301-627-XXXX to confirm payment.

Forty-seven schools ignored it. Two got back to say they were a little confused. And a third got in touch to say it was already receiving funding for the children in question from the Mormon Church in America of which Wayne was a member. Unfortunately, being a little suspicious, they declined to clarify which school they were calling from when we asked, but it didn't matter. It had been a collect call. We just had to ask the phone company for the number. From there we established the school was near the town of Villa Carlos Paz, some twenty-five miles west of the city of Córdoba.

We brought in a Spanish speaking colleague to call the school to ask to speak with the boys, just to confirm. I remember her excitement as she was told by staff that Lanny and Randy were outside playing football. They asked if she could call back later. I called Madge.

She almost shouted it, 'Ten years we have been trying! And you located them in a few weeks!'

I was delighted for her, but we had much more to do.

I flew to Milwaukee to get the legal papers updated. All the details had to be spot on. Argentina was not a traditionally cooperative country when it came to US court orders. And in this period it was being governed by a mercurial military junta which was no friend of the USA. I agreed with Madge that myself and Barry Trigwell would go to Cordoba, locate the school and wait for her to join us. I would then assist in the recovery and get everyone back into the USA.

The pair of us arrived as tourists in Buenos Aries before flying up to Cordoba, renting a car and scouting out the best route to and from the boarding school just outside Villa Carlos Paz. While in town a few discreet enquiries revealed where Wayne Schultz was living with his girl-friend, Maria. It seemed he was working as a missionary for the Mormons, or the Church of Jesus Christ of the Latter Day Saints. He had earlier married another local girl, Aurora, and they had not divorced. They had two daughters.

As we got familiar with our surroundings, we learned more and more about the current regime, about its suspicion of Americans, about its hostility towards any kind of opposition. Indeed there were many stories about those who had fallen foul of the government simply disappearing. We would be doing our best to keep out of its way.

Madge duly arrived in town and, after hiring two cars, off we went along winding roads towards the school. Barry led while Madge and I followed, she in the back and ready to secrete herself if necessary. She was plucky enough to just go on ahead in and speak with a member of staff, to introduce herself and get a sense of things. She met an easy-going male teacher who told her Lanny, the older boy, was boarding at the school. He said Randy was staying with a local family nearby. Both stayed with their father on weekends. Madge asked if she could speak with them. She showed her ID and some legal papers and said they had business to discuss. The teacher went to get them.

A few minutes later and they saw their mother for the first time in ten years. Randy was delighted, became overwhelmed, grabbed her and refused to let go. Conversely, Lanny took off, dashed away screaming, 'I'm calling my father!' Madge was, naturally enough, a mix of raw emotions. She told the teacher she would take Randy and return him that evening and he did not object.

We drove back to Cordoba where Madge took her youngest out shopping and to a restaurant. Speaking to her later, I said we had planned and checked our proposed escape route from Argentina but that it would no longer be a safe option if Lanny wasn't going to come willingly.

'Well no,' she said, 'but I couldn't leave with only one. It's both or it's none.'

I thought things through and advised Madge to do something difficult. It seemed to me there was a way to get in front of this. I asked her to call Wayne, to be pleasant and calm and to say she had discovered where the boys were and really wanted to see them. She should tell him she had taken Randy out to the shops and was hoping to spend time with Lanny too. So, she should suggest, what if we all met up for dinner to talk things over? She could introduce her ex to the two friends she was travelling with?

We all listened as she put in the call.

'I'm so pleased you called,' he said. 'We thought you had kidnapped him. There's no problem. Let's meet for dinner.'

He named a restaurant in Villa Carlos Paz and said he'd bring Lanny along. We drove over, Madge and Randy in the back with bags of clothes and presents.

As we approached the area, coming through a town square, Wayne pulled in front of us. He waved to our car, beckoned us to follow. We did, and a moment later he pulled in. We stopped too. Out of nowhere, armed and uniformed men surrounded the car. One police officer, pistol trained on us, marched forwards. Barry and I went to get out. We were seized, wrenched from the vehicle, thrown heavily to the ground, roared at in Spanish. As I lay there trying to process it all, Madge and Randy were, in a gentler way, taken from the car. She was cuffed and firmly shoved across the street to some kind of police or military facility. Randy, upset and crying, was taken by his father.

A policeman shouted, pointed upwards. He was ordering Barry and I to stand. We got as far as our knees before we were jabbed hard with pistol barrels. It hurt like hell, knocked us back to the ground. As we tried to recover, we were ordered once again to stand. As we moved we were stabbed again by the business end of the handguns. And again, ordered to stand. Again, more pain. Over and over. Men with their fingers on triggers were literally punching us with weapons. Sharp, agonising stabs, hard pokes repeatedly into the kidneys, ribs and the small of the back. Shouts to get up. Then the pain. Falling back. More shouts to get up. More pain. It was a truly brutal, agonising assault.

There were about twenty of them, mostly soldiers. They forced us, hands and knees, across the brick-paving, ramming blunt metal into us all the way. We were ordered up the steps of the police station, made to crawl through the front doors. Inside they emptied our pockets before pushing and dragging us towards a seven feet high, three feet wide steel-plated cell door. It slammed behind us. A key ground in the lock. We lay gasping and aching in this horrendous dark, stinking, tiny room. The ceiling must have been eighteen feet high yet the floor space was no more than four feet square. There was just a disgusting bucket in the corner, no furniture and the only light was like a torch beam through a six-inch diameter hole in the wall. Our bodies felt as if they were burning. All we could hear was shouting, screaming, the rhythmic beat of soldiers marching, the barking of orders like we were in some kind of frenzied military garrison.

'They had their fingers on the triggers all the time,' I said to Barry.

'I know,' he said.

Those pistols could have fired at any point. Those guys were nothing close to professional soldiers. We were lucky to be alive but didn't exactly feel it. Already part of me knew this was just the beginning. I didn't want to say it, but I was starting to get the sense we would be executed.

An hour passed, maybe two, the bruises spreading under our skin, our limbs, torsos and backs throbbing. The heavy door was pulled open, light streamed in. We were told to get up, eyes squinting as we were led to a large space between some offices. We sat on the floor, as instructed. And we waited. Armed soldiers were all over the place, some police too. I could see that Barry's neck had turned black. I expected mine was the same. As I took it all in, the scathing looks from the soldiers, weapons everywhere, I thought again that this really might be it. Finally into the cesspit with not a rose in sight. We were, I was sure, about to be shot dead.

Madge was brought over. She looked ghostly but at least didn't appear to have racked up any bruises. She was offered a seat and took it. As we sat on that grimy floor, watched by at least a dozen pairs of eyes, we became aware of an argument in one of the offices. We couldn't understand much of it but we had the strong sense it was about us. The looks we were getting seemed to confirm it. From what we could work out, the police and the military were at odds over what to do next. Soon enough, an army officer stomped out of the room. He glared our way as he passed by, a squad of half-arsed soldiers falling in behind.

It was only later that we'd learn the military wanted to treat us as American spies and take us to an interrogation camp. But the police were insisting we were kidnappers and should be dealt with as criminals. All I can say is thank heavens the police got their way. Perhaps a sweet smelling rose was starting to emerge?

We were ordered into the office. In slow English a police officer in plain clothes, aged about thirty, said, 'I'm sorry you all had to go through this. Tell me what this is all about.'

I told him of the US court order, detailed all that lay behind our trip to Argentina.

'I believe you,' he said, nodding. 'Where are you from?'

'My office is in Brighton in England,' I said.

His face lit up.

'My wife lived in Brighton as an au pair,' he said, a cheerful smile.

'Really?' I said, smiling back through my pain and fear of imminent death.

'Yes,' he said, 'I hear it's a lovely place with lovely people.'

'That's true,' I said.

And I really was starting to get the scent of roses.

He said police typically don't provide food or water to those in the holding cells but that he would arrange for Wayne, of all people, to bring us sustenance as matters were processed above his head. I was perplexed given it was Wayne who had led us into this nasty trap. I suppose the looks on our faces said as much. So he went on to explain that Wayne had not wanted us treated this way. He had filed a complaint that Randy had been kidnapped by Americans and the police and army had eagerly sprung into action. But he had tried to cancel the complaint after Madge called. Wayne had wanted to smooth things over with the waiting officers in the square but that's not how it worked out. In Argentina, he said, in order to curtail bribery of police officers, only a judge can withdraw a complaint.

We were sent back to the cell with literally no idea how long we might be held. A couple more hours? Until the morning?

Wrong.

Barry and I were bolted into that tiny cockroach infested hole for seven days and nights. It was hell on earth. Screams would ring out in the dark as captives were beaten, yelled at, tortured. The roaches would climb all over us, their spindly legs scuttling along our limbs. We could feel them moving in our hair. We would slap them hard and feel the sticky goo run over our skin, their vile, squashed bodies stuck to us like glue. The stench from a fat, South American cockroach is something to behold. Definitely more cesspit than rose.

The hold up in that little horror chamber was down to the military returning to insist again that we be taken in as American spies. They were fixed on the idea that we were undercover CIA operatives seeking to destablise the rotten regime there. We were pulled back into the office a few times, asked to provide statements about our business in the country. Besides our friendly copper, the only other person who could translate our words was a local prostitute who spoke English after living for a time in London. We dictated to her as she wrote and we could only hope it was a faithful conversion. She was in deep distress herself, her hands shaking as she worked. She would whisper as she was writing, guards looking on, 'These bastards, every night they all rape me.' She'd say, 'Every damn night they all rape me. All of them, evil, evil.' Our predicament was desperate, was something right at the hardest edge of our experience, yet that woman's situation was even worse.

We were offered no lawyer and knew there was no point in requesting one. We spent our days, filthy and bored, walking around in tiny circles in that tiny, boiling cell. Each evening, just once a day, Wayne arrived with water and a few basic foodstuffs for us and his ex-wife. He would come close to the door, pass a bag to a guard who spilled it out and passed the bottles of water and edibles to us. We would gulp down that water and eat as the sun set, the last light vanishing and the walls turning cold.

Madge was also being held during all this time, although she was locked up in an office and sleeping on a sofa. But none of us had ever known anything like the hunger and thirst we experienced. Safe to say we all lost a few pounds in that unforgettable week.

One morning, the light beaming in, the key scraped into the lock once more and the door opened. Barry, myself and Madge were brought to the friendly officer's office.

'I can resolve your problem,' he said, 'but you have to trust me.'

In slow, faltering English, he said we should all plead guilty at a local court hearing.

'This way the judge can sentence you to be deported,' he said, 'but you must plead guilty.'

'Plead guilty to what?' I asked, suspicious of everyone, everything. I did not want to blunder my way into a longer stretch for both of us in that pit.

He smiled, said, 'You are on tourist visas? But you are working, yes? Listen to me. The judge is my father-in-law. Just go into court, plead guilty and say you're sorry. There will be no problem.'

We had to take him at his word. What else could we do? At least it would get us into the system, perhaps allow any officials who came looking to get some insight into where we were. Our company system was always that agents abroad would be in contact with the office daily, and that if two days passed with no communication staff would alert the British Foreign and Commonwealth Office. That would have happened by that point. Unfortunately, experience told us that the FCO usually did nothing at all for about a week. But, once again, what else could we do?

It was a daunting thing to walk into a courtroom in Argentina at that time and plead guilty to a crime. There was no translation in court, no lawyers in our corner. It was a huge leap in the dark.

After words were said, the judge looked our way and, in English, said, 'Culpable or no culpable?'

We spoke in unison. 'Culpable.'

And we waited, breath baited, dead roaches and sweat on our skin, as he collected himself.

He responded in Spanish, looking at us. We had no idea what he was saying. A woman, a member of court staff, approached the dock.

'The sentence is you must leave Argentina within seven days,' she said.

I said, 'That's it?'

'Yes,' she said, smiling, detecting the all-new joy in my heart. 'Good luck.'

We were free. We walked out together, collected our car, met Wayne. We were so delighted that we thanked him for the food and water instead of, as the temptation had been, kicking him down the street for getting us arrested in the first place. He chatted for a while with Madge before she joined me and Barry. We drove back, stinking, relieved, emotional, to Cordoba. Thankfully our rooms were still being held and we each showered for something like an hour. I slept for sixteen hours straight. And it was beautiful.

We met Wayne the next day to finally get that dinner with his family. He and Madge talked of the boys returning to the US and it seemed as if he might consider such a dramatic change for both them and himself. But we all got the impression that, as he talked of how much he had spent on looking after them, he was looking for money.

I said, 'How much would you need to compensate for funding the boys this last ten years?'

He was blunt and, frankly, shameless in his response.

'I want $10,000,' he said. 'I need that to return because I've got to pay lawyers to keep me out of jail when I get there.'

Madge spoke privately with me, said, 'I don't have that much money with me.'

'Don't worry,' I said. 'He might accept a post-dated cheque from my account in Maryland.'

Wayne agreed to accept it. I post-dated it until January 1st of the following year, but had no intention at all of giving him a red cent. We agreed arrangements for him to bring the boys to Miami from Argentina at the end of the current school term. Madge and I would arrange to collect and take them home. He said 'yes' to everything and took my cheque. We left Argentina the next day.

Back in Brighton a few weeks later and I took a phone call from Wayne. He wanted me to collect the boys in Argentina but said he wouldn't be leaving the country. I checked with Madge and she agreed I should do it. And after a long journey and a long queue at Customs in Buenos Aires, some bad news.

'You cannot enter,' the official said. 'You were here before working without a visa.'

I tried to explain but it was no use. I let Madge know. It was, at least for now, no go. So I was booted out, ended up flying via Rio to New York on Pan Am. En route the flight hit a substantial air pocket, violently plunging us some distance towards the sea. Luggage bins were flung open, people flung around and hot drinks scalded skin. Some passengers were left bleeding from their injuries. My suit was stained but I wasn't hurt. At JFK we were offered disclaimer forms to promise not to sue, as well as a $1,000 voucher for signing. Indeed, after advising staff of the hassle I had already been through, they arranged for me to stay two nights at the Roosevelt Hotel in Manhattan and handed me a voucher to get the suit dry cleaned. Swings and roundabouts and all that.

Back home I contacted our friendly policeman in Argentina, told him I had been unable to get the boys. He said he would ensure everything was updated and sent a letter inviting me to Villa Carlos Paz as a guest of the police. So on my third visit to Argentina I was met like a VIP, collected from the airport in a police car, introduced to the chief of police and presented with a certificate and a flag. The next day I was given a tour, shown a beautiful lake and taken on a guided ascent of a spectacular mountain by cable car. Regardless of what I had been through there, it really is an astonishing land.

And then, on meeting Wayne, he told me he had changed his mind once more. He wanted this time to keep the boys at school there until the end of term. I tried to push him off his all new hill but he was firm. We agreed he would meet me on New Year's Eve at Miami International Airport, two months away. He kept trying to have me change the date on the cheque or make immediate payment instead, but I wouldn't do it. I said no money would get paid until the boys were back in the US. Off I went once more back to London.

Wayne, Lanny and Randy flew into Miami on December 30th and I went to meet them. He insisted on driving them all the way to Wisconsin, to drop them off and go nowhere until he got his money. And it was an awful journey with him in the car. We had a nation to cross, from south to north, and he wouldn't stop jabbering on about this and that. It drove me bonkers. When I fell asleep, instead of him motormouthing, he drove too fast and got pulled over for speeding. The hours were crawling past and we were still such a long way from Wisconsin. When we hit Cincinnati I laid it on the line. I said the boys needed to be home and safe before the year ended, that was part of the contract to allow Wayne to get his money. I said I was worried about possible problems ahead, that the journey was a long haul for them, that it would be best if they flew from Cincinnati to ensure they made it. I told him he should get a night's sleep somewhere, that I'd take the boys and I'd be in touch. Wayne agreed. Myself, Lanny and Randy flew to Chicago and, in a rented car, drove the last leg towards Milwaukee. As a matter of fact, I was pulled over for speeding myself along the way.

The boys arrived home at half past midnight, just into the last day of the year. The *Welcome Home* party was in full swing. The press were waiting, TV cameras all over the place. It was a heck of an end to a journey that had been so long in so many ways. The following morning, as agreed with my client, I cancelled the cheque. Wayne arrived the next day, after I had left, and was picked up by the police and held for abducting the boys all those years ago. He went on to launch an action to sue me for stopping the cheque, but I was never served anything by the court so it came to nothing. In fact I didn't know he had even done that until 2018, at which point I appealed a default judgement against me and won. Wayne had passed away by then.

As for Madge's family, it would only thrive. Wayne's Argentinian wife Aurora, the mother of his children Dawn and Debbie, emigrated to the US after Randy and Lanny moved back. So did a young man called Gabriel from Aurora's earlier relationship. Madge provided a home for the entire clan on her enormous ranch and they all made a happy life together. We all came to know that it had been Aurora who had penned the postcard to Madge from Cordoba which led to my involvement.

Madge Gunia wrote a book, published in 2002, called *No Place That Far* about the loss and recovery of her children and of all that followed. She kindly asked me to write the foreword for her story.

TWENTY-THREE

A Drink With Farrah Fawcett Majors (1979)

WAS one of *Charlie's Angels* doing the dirty on the *Six Million Dollar Man?* It's a question which caught the attention of many millions of people in the seventies. And I was asked to answer it.

Those TV shows were among the biggest on earth across the decade. Blonde bombshell Farah Fawcett Majors starred as former California cop Jill Munroe. She was the best-known of three high-kicking, leggy, bikini-wearing PIs assigned to cases by the mysterious disembodied Charlie. Her real life husband was handsome, steely-eyed actor Lee Majors who played enhanced hero Steve Austin, a bionic (ie:part-man, part-machine) former astronaut turned crime-cracking government agent.

Both stars' names came my way via a third all-American legend—*The National Enquirer*. It was, and remains, one of the most infamous players on the US stage. By any measure, it was the boldest, wildest mainstream publication of the time. And, in a phone call to me, an editor wanted to know if I might keep an eye on the *Angel* who was coming to town. I said I'd be happy to. But why?

Here's where another heartthrob of the time entered the drama, one Mr Ryan O'Neal, star of hit movies including *Love Story* and *What's Up Doc? The National Enquirer* had been tipped off that he and the married Mrs Fawcett-Majors were having an affair. I didn't need to be told this was a potentially enormous story for the tabloid.

The then thirty-two-year-old actress, known to be a savvy businesswoman, was starring in a film called *Saturn 3* alongside Kirk Douglas and Harvey Keitel. It was a British production, being shot at Shepperton Studios, designed to appeal to the massive global *Stars Wars* market of the time. As its space-age name suggested, it was a futuristic, science-fiction concoction which, to be honest, went on to win awards only for being absolutely appalling. Nevertheless, we were sure that *Saturn 3*, via TV's favourite poster girl, was about to put some Hollywood sparkle into our gumshoe lives.

Farrah was accommodated in an apartment on Wilton Row in well-heeled Belgravia. She was chauffeured daily to and from Shepperton in a limo laid on by Granada TV. There was always an escort car and, split between the vehicles, never less than three heavies to ensure her safety.

The National Enquirer asked if I would keep eyes on her where possible to see if she met anybody else while in London. They were thinking in particular of Ryan O'Neal. There had already been complications in her marriage to Lee Majors. It felt as if those in-the-know in the US knew that, sooner or later, something was going to give.

Initially I was contracted for several days of round-the-clock surveillance with the possibility of things going on for much longer. In central London terms, this was a big job not just in the money stakes but the manpower too. I put a team of three together, including myself, to ensure her residence would be watched non-stop. And I also tasked an excellent motorcyclist, an essential addition to any serious London watching brief, with helping out.

As we got to work, the British press was already learning the famous American actress with the signature bouncing blonde locks was in London. They did not know where she was staying and appeared from time to time at the studio in a bid to know more and snap the odd picture. We were much more discreet and tracked her for a number of days as she left Belgravia to be driven to Shepperton and vice versa. We established that her role involved her wearing a rather revealing white outfit and that on most days she wore it while being ushered back to her apartment.

As I say, we were discreet, but we were not discreet enough. We had underestimated her security detail. It became evident inside a week that they were onto us. As our guys and her guys got a sense of each other, we came to realise they were extremely professional in terms of how they managed her movements and very observant in terms of their immediate environment. We soon understood why. Reports were emerging that, while filming in Mexico recently, a gang had attempted to kidnap the actress. The men charged with her safety in London were not about to let any such thing happen on their watch.

As our car trailed their cars, her two drivers would frequently take evasive action. They made sudden turns, dodged down side streets, occasionally did two or even three laps of roundabouts before zooming off at the last second. On one occasion, as our biker tracked the car she was in, the driver suddenly floored it. He roared ahead and, as our motorcyclist twisted the throttle to keep up, the chauffeur slammed the brakes. Our man locked his wheels but it was too late. He hit the rear of the limo and tumbled onto the road. A second later, as he lay in agony, the limo revved up and sped off. Fortunately, only his pride was injured.

We regrouped, replanned and got back to work. We would switch vehicles often, change over agents, become harder to spot. But we would always be there. We increased the use of our Aircall two-way radios in the cars and on the bike to allow us to do shorter stints. The technology allowed us to peel away from behind the goons yet, via a tag-team system, reappear in different form before they got suspicious.

The general schedule saw Farrah leave her accommodation around 7.30 am daily and return around 5 pm. One Friday afternoon, when I was taking over the duty at Belgravia, I picked up my eldest son Andy en route. He was thirteen at the time and would be spending the weekend with me. I said I was keeping an eye on a movie star and he was more than happy to come along.

As expected, Farrah arrived back in her car with the escort car in tow. She got out, glowing wonderfully in white as usual, and paused. She looked towards my car parked a short distance away then went on inside. I looked down to take a note of the time.

'Dad?' said Andy.

'Hmm?'

'Two huge guys are coming over.'

I looked up. He wasn't wrong. Two man-mountains in evening dress. And it didn't look like they were approaching to ask directions. We made eye contact. They walked right up to my window. One leaned down. A large knuckle.

Tap, tap, tap.

I looked at him, my face all puzzled. I turned the handle, opened the window a few inches.

'Can I help you?' I wondered.

'Why are you following the lady?' he said, his broad face and fixed eyes too close for comfort.

'I have no idea what you're talking about.'

He smiled a fake, sarcastic sort of grin, added. 'Who are you? What do you want?'

I said nothing, turned to look forward.

'Are you Old Bill?' he said, scanning the inside of the car.

'No,' I said, looking to the child beside me, 'we're not Old Bill.'

'You have a two way radio there,' he said.

'Yes,' I said.

His hand lifted up past the side window and onto the roof. I wasn't sure what he was doing. Then I heard it. He had gripped the radio's antenna in that big fist.

'So,' he said, standing tall, 'you won't be needing this then.'

Andy and I both listened as he bent it backwards and forwards a few times before it snapped off in his hand. He chucked it onto the narrow street where he stood. His friend, just a couple of feet to his side, smiled, laughed. They looked at each other, laughed some more, walked away.

I'm a measured sort of bloke but, bloody hell—I was furious. On saying that, I'm wise enough too to know that getting the crap kicked out of me in front of my son was something to avoid. I wound the window up and talked with my boy about the twists and turns of life.

I had no antenna now and, as such, had very limited communication with the rest of the team. But I was going nowhere.

About twenty minutes later, my friend reappeared, was again heading my way, ugly as ever. What would it be this time? A wing mirror? A hub cap? He arrived at the window once more.

Tap, tap, tap.

I ignored him. I wasn't going to entertain this thug.

Tap, tap, tap.

No thanks.

Tap, tap, tap.

'Excuse me,' he said, his voice quite low, quite polite. He kept on talking—something about the lady, about talking with her? Had he just asked if...? No, that couldn't be right.

I turned to him. He certainly looked more pleasant than he had before. So I dropped the window a little.

'Say again?' I asked.

'The lady wonders if you would like to have a drink with her,' he said. 'She wants to ask what you're doing.'

An extraordinary development.

'Well,' I said, 'if the lady comes out and goes into the pub opposite, I'll follow her in.'

He nodded, said, 'No problem, mate.'

A few moments later and one of Charlie's very beautiful angels walked out wearing her very skimpy white outfit and a long overcoat on top. I was as professional as I could be, of course, but I do accept my jaw may have dropped open as those endless legs strode across the road in front of me, that iconic seventies hair dancing as she went. She stopped at the door of the pub, turned to the car, beaming, glowing, beckoning me to come her way. My heart skipped a beat. Maybe more. I asked Andy to sit for a few minutes. I got out, followed her in.

The goon followed us as she picked a small table in a corner. We both sat down as her minder took a stool at the bar.

'I'm Farrah,' she said, as if myself and everyone else in the bar didn't already know.

'I'm Ian,' I said, already enjoying my date with an angel.

'Where is your colleague?'

'That's my son,' I said. 'He's waiting in the car.'

'Well go get him!' she said, a million dollar smile, teeth as white as her outfit.

'Okay,' I said, and did so.

She ordered a fruit juice for herself and ordered Andy a Coke. I had tonic water.

'So why are you guys following me?' she asked, that silky, soft Texan accent.

'I can't tell you,' I said, 'but you have nothing to be concerned about.'

'Are you press?'

'Yes,' I said, explaining my client was press but I couldn't divulge their identity.

She looked relieved, said, 'As long as you are press.'

I nodded.

She said, 'I don't know if you guys know, but somebody tried to kidnap me in Mexico a little while ago. So, I'm kinda nervous.'

'Well,' I said, 'I can assure you neither our client nor we are planning anything like that. You could say we are here just keeping an eye on you. I'm sure you understand the situation.'

'I accept that,' she said. 'You seem like nice guys. But just so my security doesn't get all heated up, let me give you my itinerary.'

She reached into the inside pocket of her coat and handed me three sheets of paper. They detailed her movements over the following four days.

'Now you don't have to follow me everywhere,' she said, flashing those world-beating pearly whites.

I'd liked to have given her only good news at that point, but I didn't have any.

'Sorry,' I said, 'even with this, I still have to do what I'm being paid to do.'

She gave another easy, gorgeous smile, said, 'That's okay. I know you now so I'll feel more comfortable anyway.'

I offered to pay for the drinks but she wouldn't have it. Her bodyguard was already settling up at the bar. She shook my hand as we said goodbye. She put an arm around my son's shoulder, told him to enjoy the weekend. And, with her security guard at her side, she left, crossed the road, that feathered hair flowing, and went back indoors. We went back out to the car and sat for a while. Come 10 pm, with no more movement, I pulled away.

My motorcycling agent began surveillance on Saturday. The itinerary said she would be picked up at 6.30 am and taken to Granada offices in London. And it said that at 3 pm she would be delivered back to Belgravia. The details matched perfectly with the reality. After that, the itinerary said, the star had no engagements.

Soon after and another agent moved into position to join the biker for that Saturday evening. All of us felt it unlikely much would happen in the hours ahead, but we had to cover the property all the same.

Shortly after 6 pm, our men spotted a lady exiting alone. They weren't sure if it was Farrah at first as this had not happened before. She was wearing a long dark coat we had not seen before. But it didn't take long to work it out. Those lush blonde locks were unmistakable. It was Farah Fawcett Majors herself, high heels clicking as she made her way up the salubrious street and hailed a cab. Both agents tracked the vehicle as it made the very short journey to Knightsbridge. She got out, paid, and walked down some steps into a Chinese restaurant right next door to the Knightsbridge Sporting Club, a high-class Casino I knew from *Operation Unit Six*.

My agent called me. I sped to Knightsbridge. We met near the entrance. I couldn't go in, given she would recognise me, but the other two could. They smartened themselves up and walked down the steps. Inside, as they asked for a table, they scanned the restaurant. And there, in the corner, sat the beautiful actress with another screen star—Ryan O'Neal.

I called my client in America. He said to sit tight while he arranged for two photographers. They arrived within about twenty minutes and moved into position to get pictures of anyone who left the building. But soon after that, other snappers started arriving too. And then a journalist. And then more of each. The information was being leaked all over the place. Within an hour an army of hacks and paparazzi was camped at the door of the restaurant. And as the demand for the high-value photographs reached fever pitch, photographers broke ranks. A number made for the door, went right on it. Shutters clicked and flashes blazed as they grabbed every image they could of Hollywood's illicit couple having a chow mein. Management and staff intervened, tried to physically force the press from the restaurant. They got them out eventually, but it was a grim spectacle.

We sat on for a while as the melee died down. Eventually Mrs Fawcett Majors emerged from her dinner alone, walking up the steps, her head down, obviously upset as the cameras rattled all around her. She walked across the pavement, barely even checking for traffic, and across Brompton Road. She was almost struck by a car as she went, her mind miles from what was going on around her. She walked alone into a church via one door, made her way through and exited via another door at the side. As she emerged she hailed a cab and departed. I lost sight of her after that.

The National Enquirer had all it needed for the story. Together with the British press, it carried the details of her date with Ryan O'Neal, reported that her failing marriage to Lee Majors was finally over, that she had been coupled up with Ryan O'Neal for a while. *The London Evening Standard* approached and interviewed me, given I was identified as the man behind the agency which had initially cracked the story the US media had been waiting for. The assignment had been a success, *The National Enquirer* delighted that it could be first with the story across the USA.

Ryan O'Neal and Farrah Fawcett, who divorced from Lee Majors in 1982, had difficulties ahead but were a couple right up until her sad death from cancer in 2009. She was sixty-two. I have the fondest memory of meeting her, yet I can't get away from the guilt that comes with it. She was striking and gracious and, no doubt, was already resolved to closing down her relationship with her husband at the time. Yet the distress that came to her on that night in London was as a result of my work. Such contrasts between the personal feelings and the professional dealings are the lot of the ambitious PI.

As for *Saturn 3*, well it was released in 1980. A biographer for one of its stars, Harvey Keitel, said it had been 'the nadir of his career.'

Thinking back on that time, there have been moments where I have felt the same.

TWENTY-FOUR

The Fastnet Disaster (1979)

WE were some distance beyond Land's End when the storm showed itself. It had been smooth sailing, calm conditions as we enjoyed a curry and a couple of beers. But, over a short period, that all changed. The sky darkened and the sea began to roll in a way that suggested this was only the beginning. We felt the wind drive into us, getting stronger and stronger, soon too powerful to use to our advantage. We had no option but to reef down—cut back on the sail area to reclaim stability.

We braced ourselves for worse, experience advising this was more serious than any of us might have predicted. We strapped to the rails and waited. Soon enough the *Ocean Wave* was being shoved around in a force nine wind, the massive push and pull throwing the yacht in all directions like a toy in the bath. As we struggled to hold our footing, the mighty grey sea took to reaching right over us and our vessel, to crashing down on top. Huge waves, like apartment blocks all around, surged high and slammed over and over again.

But *Ocean Wave*, all forty foot of her, was not going to be disposed of easily. All six of us crewmen were breathless as the boat rode up the crests, hung on as hard as we could as it slapped back down into the troughs. The vessel was soaring and diving and shaking. We could barely even snatch glances of the terror on each other's faces. One mighty wave blacked out the sky as it reared up and smashed over us. We'd just been punched upwards by the sea and the forces combined to throw everything down hard. The thump burst apart the fastenings on the forward deck. They vanished into the turmoil all around. Water gushed through the open hatches, filling the bilges. The pumps were working overtime, spitting the sea back into itself as it kept on ramming its way back in over and over.

Posing for the Sun newspaper 1979

We stayed upright through the worst of it, nature's rage seeming to back away for a time. But it returned soon, another army of waves, bigger and broader than anything we could have prepared for, marching right at us again. We feared we were losing control of the *Ocean Wave*, turning our minds towards a mission to survive. We shrank the sail again when we had the chance, cut it to just a storm jib as best we could. But we were flooded, our limbs exhausted, the yacht's batteries soaked to death. We had no radio comms, no navigation lights.

When the sea's rage eased, our spirits defiant, we fired up the hob on the gimballed cooker. We boiled up hot coffee laced with shots of Navy Rum and clinked our cups, wished each other everything good in what lay ahead. We checked our position, rolling around in growling waters some miles from England, some miles from the Scilly Isles. We sank that potent, fortifying concoction and talked everything over. Should we press on? Or should we turn around?

Sailing had been a constant in my life, a hobby beloved since I was knee high to a grasshopper. Getting out onto wild salt waters had been like nourishment, mental and physical, through the good times and the bad. As soon as I had enough money to do so, I had bought a yacht of my own as a kind of guarantee that diversion was always waiting when I needed it. She was moored at Shoreham Yacht Club in Sussex and, through the seventies, my volunteer crew and I often raced across the Channel to Dieppe and Fécamp on the Normandy coast. We were no strangers to heavy weather between England and France and relished the challenge it presented. The often testing character of the waters could bring out the best within us. But 1979, at the twenty-eighth *Royal Ocean Racing Club's Fastnet Race*, was a different thing altogether. Fifteen yachtsmen and four spectators died in that awful storm. We were lucky to survive.

The race was 605-miles, a challenge known to sailors worldwide. It was first staged in 1925, the course beginning in Cowes, on the Isle of Wight, moving to Fastnet Rock, Ireland's most southerly point, then under the Isles of Scilly bound for Plymouth. I had not taken part before and getting invited onto the *Ocean Wave* as helmsman by skipper Jim Tozer was like a dream come true. She was a sleek glass fibre vessel owned by a London-based marine insurance company. Although a stable deep keel construction and capable of dealing with heavy weather, *Ocean Wave* was taken to her limits that day.

The forecast had given us some warning of storms, but no one could have foreseen the full power that came calling on that third day of sailing. We all liked the idea of tougher than normal conditions and we had joked about 'fair weather sailors' maybe not being fit for the course this time around. None of us wanted to be beaten by whatever threats the sea might pose. But we had no idea how serious it all would get.

After finding some relative calm, we had talked about what to do, how bad it had been, how bad it could be. We could not deny we were already struggling, that the comms were out, that we were damaged and the pumps were under pressure. An inspection revealed we had lost the hoists for two sails, the Genoa and Jib, at the bow, the fierce storm having ripped away the pulley wheels. We took a vote on what to do. We all knew it was best to throw in the towel and, though hearts were heavy, did the right thing. We set sail for Cornwall, the nearest port. It would have been madness to do otherwise.

It took some hours in cold and unsure conditions, strapped to the rail, for us to reach Falmouth. We found many others had also beat a retreat to the point that there was no room for us to moor. We anchored off and, in the welcome shelter of the coastal waters, roasted a chicken, drank the remains of the beer and a bottle of rum. All energy sapped, and still blissfully ignorant of the disaster, we slept.

Overnight our batteries dried out. We woke to the uncertain crackles of a BBC radio report which, when we could make it out, told of the most significant operation in the waters since World War Two. It said every available lifeboat and rescue aircraft was at work. It said yachts had been lost, that sailors, alive and dead, were being hauled from the sea. We were dumbfounded to learn this was the event in which we had been taking part.

We made our way ashore, numb and empty with the shock. We found a phone box and lined up to call our loved ones. All were waiting to grab the receiver, all aware of what had taken place, all with every reason to believe we had been lost. My father made clear his relief by bellowing down the phone that morning like a joyful Sergeant Major, 'I knew you'd make it, son! *Cesspits and roses! Cesspits and roses!*'

Of the 303 yachts setting out on that race, twenty-four were abandoned. Five were lost in what press reports called 'mountainous seas.' Seventy-five were flipped upside down and some 125 yachtsmen were pulled from the water. Tugs, trawlers and tankers had joined in that incredible effort.

It had been the most intense experience, thrilling, daunting, life-affirming, terrifying and tragic at the same time. It was a blunt and almighty reminder that all we are and all we have hangs by the thinnest of threads. I was one of the fortunate souls who moved forward with life from that dark day. I did so with a little more wisdom in my head, a little more gratitude in my heart.

TWENTY-FIVE

Mission to The West Bank: Recovering Sarah (1979)

An October phone call from Terry McGill, my partner in our US Agency, *Maryland Investigations Inc.* He had been contacted by a lawyer from Children's Rights, a charity for parents whose kids have disappeared, been abducted by parents or otherwise.

He told me the story of a lady called Lynn Durgan who had married a Turkish teacher. They'd set up home in America and were parents to baby Sarah. When Sarah was just sixteen months old, the marriage fell apart and they separated. Lynn was very fearful her partner, Dr Kanat Durgan, would scoop up the little girl and take her to Turkey. She went to court to prevent it. It ruled in her favour and mapped out monthly visitation rights for the father.

One day, about three months before the call to my office, he arrived at Lynn's house at the allotted time. He put Sarah into her stroller and took her for a walk. You can guess the rest.

Lynn called *911*. A search began, but nothing. US Immigration Services were called in, pictures were sent out, airports were put on alert, but there was no sign of the errant Dr Durgan and the small child. The child's mother knew it in her heart—Sarah was no longer in the USA. It was such a young age for a child to be taken from her mum.

Terry had gathered all the information he could and posted it over to me. My job was to advise on the options. The father had been a mathematics lecturer at a US university, had been living there after securing a Green Card allowing him to stay as long as he liked. The university advised there was no question about his legitimacy as a qualified lecturer.

It said he had been lecturing at a university in Istanbul before he moved to America. Fortunately, Lynn had an address for his parents in Istanbul.

I called a meeting with some of the more adventurous agents we'd worked with. It was a tactic I'd used before. It not only got the best available people onto the job, it also minimised risk. This was a job that would require considerable resources. Any single agency would go belly up if the majority of its staff were delayed, via jail, violence or any other matter, in Turkey. There was strength in numbers.

Children's Rights lawyer, Professor Henry Foster, joined with Lynn and her parents to review my plan for the operation in Turkey. It was a go. Lynn got herself to the airport, UK bound, saying that whatever was about to happen, she wanted to be in the thick of it.

Agent Roger Payne, a burly, decorated army veteran from our Belfast Office, left immediately to check the parents' address. He began surveillance early but, as the searing sun rose and set, there was no sign of anyone there at all. He established an address for Dr Durgan's brother and got into position for another day's waiting and watching. But nothing.

On the third day, downhearted, he went to the university where Dr Durgan had taught. Might they have a way to contact him? It was then that things began to turn. Roger found himself speaking to a young woman who handled reference and verification inquiries. She said that one week earlier she had been asked for a qualifications check on Dr Durgan. It wasn't the one made by my office, but by a university known as BZU. It was the University of Bir Zeit, a Palestinian centre of learning in Ramallah on the West Bank.

Roger called with the news and I went cold. Ramallah was, to say the least, an unstable place. Car bombs and street shootings were a regular fact of life there. Yet our task would be to get among it all and safely retrieve a child.

To be sure of my ground at the outset, I called BZU and asked if someone there might speak English. That was arranged.

'Is Dr Durgan available?' I asked.

'He is on campus,' I was told.

I called the US Embassy in Tel Aviv. They helped out with an English-speaking Israeli lawyer. He asked if there were outstanding alimony or maintenance court-ordered payments. I checked with Lynn, who was by now staying at my home. She said there was.

'Great,' said our Israeli lawyer. 'That's a breach of a US court order.'

He explained that a treaty was in force between the US and Israel allowing either state to enforce monetary court orders. We quickly reached out to the US courts and were forwarded the relevant documents detailing the rulings and sums involved. Dr Durgan had never paid a penny in support. We booked our tickets, packed our bags and steeled ourselves for some tough business in the West Bank.

Ben Gurion—Natbag, Israel's main international airport, is about thirty miles from Jerusalem, some twelve miles from Tel Aviv. We scoped it out, checked its location, layout and procedures, checked the logistics of getting back and forward. I always needed to be confident, anticipating the most pressing of moments, that I knew as much as I could about where I was going and what I would face there. Each arrival at the airport had their passport stamped. And to depart, one needed to show that same arrival stamp. This was not an issue for myself and Lynn, but for Sarah? Lynn had secured her daughter a new US passport. Obviously it would not have been stamped.

I rented a car and drove us both into the wonderful old city of Jerusalem. We took a small hotel in the Arab Quarter, basing ourselves on the route around twelve miles from Ramallah. The next morning we met up with the lawyer who had helped us so far. He confirmed the documents were satisfactory. One demanded payment of the outstanding maintenance, the other required Dr Kanat Durgan to return his child into the custody and care of her mother. But we would not be able to rely on the support of Israeli police to achieve our objective. They were not authorised to be in battlescarred Ramallah other than for protective security duties. And, we were advised, Palestinian police would not execute an Israeli court order on their own turf.

We paid a visit to the clerk's office at the High Court, a branch of the country's Supreme Court. We wondered if, with their endorsement and given the unusual circumstances, we could secure the services of any police at all to have Dr Durgan arrested as part of the enforcement of the order. While he was detained, we considered we might be able to locate little Sarah and get out of town.

We got to speaking with a judge, off the record, who suggested that if I was to be appointed as a Bailiff of the High Court, I could make the arrest of the good doctor myself. As a bailiff, there would be back-up from Palestinian police. I would be the one executing the order and making the arrest. They would be there to ensure my legitimate business was not hindered. Dr Durgan, after I arrested him, would be taken to Ramallah station as a matter of course.

So I was to be sworn in as a bailiff of the High Court. As I took the stand, a slight kerfuffle among the staff. A few sharp words of Hebrew were exchanged. I couldn't understand why the clerk was suddenly looking so anxious.

The judge turned to me, 'Mr Withers,' he said. 'It seems we do not have a Christian Bible. Would you mind making a statutory declaration instead?'

'I would not mind at all,' I said.

I made my vow and was provided with a certificate in Hebrew, Arabic and English pronouncing me a Bailiff of the High Court of Jerusalem.

Off we went into the West Bank town of Ramallah. On the way we could see the damage, the bombed out buildings and bullet marks of the seemingly eternal conflict of the region. I checked in at the barricaded police station. The man in charge was perfectly welcoming and immediately assigned two Palestinian officers to accompany me to execute the court orders in Ber Zeit. Lynn and our lawyer would wait behind while this official business was conducted.

I drove my rental behind the two officers. At the entrance to the university, they asked to see Dr Durgan. After some twenty minutes, he appeared. The police advised him I was a bailiff of the High Court. He was fluent in English. I served the documents and advised him I would be needing to hold his passport. He was not a happy man. He protested in the strongest terms to the police officers, but they told him there was nothing he could do. He would either surrender his passport or get arrested. Dr Durgan said there was no chance of him obeying their orders. And with that, a police officer took out the cuffs and I told him he was under arrest.

We went back to the police station and he was put in a room for inter-view. He was outraged and uncooperative and, frankly, not doing himself any favours with the local law. He fell like a stroppy teenager into a chair and complained non-stop while the cops looked on. His mood changed fast when a senior officer bellowed at him, roared into his face, ordered him to get up and stand to attention. Dr Durgan, who was just as shocked as I was, did it fast. Yet soon after he was protesting again, his body lan-guage again showing defiance in front of these no-nonsense coppers. Two officers seized him, dragged him from that room and into another. I could hear from outside that they weren't exactly taking him there as a treat. The roaring began once more, the shouts and screams of officers which must have been totally terrifying for the mathematics academic.

I waited, a little uncomfortable, unsure of what was going on. It didn't take long before the door opened and the senior officer appeared. He advised me that Dr Durgan had somehow changed his mind. I could accompany him now to collect his passport and two officers would go along too.

Dr Durgan appeared. He wasn't physically harmed but he had been through the mill all the same. During the roaring, he had been advised that Sarah's mother Lynn was in Jerusalem and that she was seeking to take the little girl back to the USA. I sat in the back of the police Land Rover with him as we drove. He wept as I outlined how it had come to this and told him it could still be resolved in a way that suited all parties. His life need not be affected too badly if he was to enter into talks with his wife. I said if he were to surrender his child voluntarily, I might even be able to get the incriminating warrants suspended.

He knew I was making sense and he knew too that he had been the one who overstepped the line in the first place. In the back of that Land Rover Dr Durgan agreed to surrender little Sarah to Lynn. We went to a house in a narrow street where he was living with a young woman and the child. Escorted by police, and still in cuffs, he collected Sarah's US pass-port, his own Turkish passport and handed them to me. He was taken back to the police station. I collected Lynn and our lawyer and brought them back to the house. Again, two officers escorted us.

Just before the reunion, our lawyer warned that Lynn could lose her case for the outstanding alimony if she went ahead and took the infant.

He said that, in his professional opinion, it might be unwise to go ahead with the meeting at this point. Our lawyer had been first class so far and we had great respect for his views, but this was unhelpful in the extreme. Poor Lynn had been dreaming of this day for months. She was stunned to hear any suggestion of opting to delay this any longer. She didn't know what to say. But I knew exactly what to say. And I didn't hold back. There was nothing more important and urgent in Lynn's life than being able to get her girl back in her arms. But the lawyer stood his ground, said we were messing up a legal process that could have repercussions, that it was his duty to say so. He said he wanted to speak to his principal in Jerusalem. And, given there were no phones in Bir Zeit at that time, he said we would need to drive back. Lynn was falling to pieces and I was furious. I just let him say whatever he wanted. In the meantime, we would do what we wanted.

We pulled up at the street where Kanat Durgan had been living. I got out and tearful Lynn followed. I took her arm as we walked to the house. A number of people had gathered around by this stage, word spreading fast of the arrest of the doctor and the arrival of Sarah's American mother. Dr Durgan's girlfriend answered when we knocked. She too was weeping as she handed over the child to her mother. Arab women who had gathered to witness this event began to cry as a wave of raw emotion seemed to envelope the little street. It was intensely poignant.

We walked back to my car and Lynn, her child held tight, climbed in. Amid the outpouring of feeling, the lawyer's face told a story of nothing but annoyance. I didn't care. He had chosen a ludicrous moment to interject so bluntly in such a delicate matter.

As we drove slowly out of the village, through the barricades and roadblocks, Lynn's smiling eyes were locked on Sarah's. It was an absolutely priceless image that stays with me to this day. After a few minutes, the lawyer leaned over my shoulder and patted me on the chest.

'I'm sorry,' he said. 'You were right. Perhaps we lawyers are just too cautious. You did your job.'

The next morning was spent in the court, signing papers amending the order and allowing us to take Sarah out of the country without any question.

SPERRY, WEINBERG, WELS, WALDMAN & RUBENSTEIN
6 EAST 43ᴿᴰ STREET
NEW YORK, N.Y. 10017

SAMUEL WEINBERG
RICHARD H. WELS
NATHAN J. WALDMAN
ROBERT M. RUBENSTEIN
MARVIN H. COHEN
ALLAN H. CARLIN
ROBERT A. SCHACHTER

HENRY H. FOSTER, JR.
COUNSEL

EUGENE E. SPERRY (1900-1945)
FRANK MOSS (1908-1920)
ISIDOR WELS (1908-1963)
—
(212) 490-1650

CABLE ADDRESS
"SPERRYANK"

March 26, 1980

Mr. Ian D. Withers
InterCity Investigations Ltd
181 North End
Croydon   Cro 1TP
ENGLAND

Dear Mr. Withers:

Thank you for your letter of March 5th and enclosed clipping on the Sheri Sorokos case. I send copies to Arnold Miller in Washington and Lynn Durgun in Seattle.

Lynn was in New York City a couple of weeks ago and brought Sarah to my office. She spoke most highly of you, as a person and as a professional, and gave me some of the details of the Israel adventure.

Congratulations on the favorable results you continue to achieve. Next time you are in New York City, it would be a privilege to meet you, so if possible give me a ring.

Sincerely,

Henry H Foster

Henry H. Foster

215

We were an hour into the flight to Rome en route for home when I was woken by a stewardess. She pointed at Lynn. I looked over. It was not good. It seemed as if she had fallen unconscious in the seat just across from me. I took Sarah and a call for medical help was made on the tannoy. Luckily, two doctors were on board. Both rushed over. One suspected appendicitis, the other believed she had kidney failure. She was laid out on seats at the back of the aircraft and screened off. After landing in Rome, she was rushed to hospital. Sarah and I were fast-processed and taken at speed by police to the same hospital.

We were there for three days, looked after by Alitalia with the greatest of consideration and care, while Lynn was treated. The severity of pain from kidney stones had caused her to black out, but we knew she would be fine. From there we went to London where Lynn stayed again with Phyl and I for a few days while she recovered some more.

Watching her playing and bonding once more with Sarah in that time was very special. As was the wonderfully kind letter I received soon after from Professor Foster of Children's Rights. He said that he knew on dialling the number for our office, he had made the right call.

TWENTY-SIX

Escape from Greece: Recovering Nikole (1980)

SHERRI Ann Jacque wanted to get out into this big world and do something important. The idea of joining the US Peace Corps seemed to be a way to live that dream. After training, she left her beautiful home state of Iowa and ended up based in the Aegean island group known as the Cyclades, southeast of the Greek mainland. It was here, on the splendid isle of Naxos, that she fell for fisherman Evangelos Sorokos, known to all as Angelos. Sherri became pregnant, made her way back to Cedar Rapids and, not long after, Angelos followed. He secured a student visa and the couple married and looked forward to bringing up their daughter Nikole.

Unfortunately, however, it wasn't quite all happily ever after. Angelos was a little too fond of other local ladies for Sherri's liking. The relationship faltered, things became quite bitter and he became aggressive. Nikole was two and Sherri was twenty-six when she and her family decided it would be better if Angelos wasn't around. They gave his name to US Immigration saying he had defaulted on his student conditions. He was given seven days to quit the US.

In that time Angelos took himself to the Greek embassy with his daughter's birth certificate. He had her added to his passport and, in October 1979, picked her up and vanished. When the police looked into it, they advised Sherri's family he had taken the toddler to Canada, then to Athens and then to his island home in Naxos.

Sherri was upset when she called me in November of that year. She said her child had been stolen and she would do whatever it took to get her back. As always, an important early question—was her case legitimate? And indeed it was. A US court ordered the immediate return of the American-born girl while custody was established.

Sherri agreed I would assign an agent to visit Naxos to confirm the location and to consider the feasibility of a recovery operation. I called up Roger Payne once more, the hugely trusted, towering ex-soldier from our Belfast office. He flew to Athens, took the inter-island ferry to Naxos and was able to confirm the location of the girl. She was in the care of Angelos' parents in a small rural house miles from anywhere. As for Angelos, he lived elsewhere with another girlfriend. We learned he came from a long line of fishermen. It seemed that almost all the many males in his wider family were hardy seafarers who disappeared into the blue yonder for three or four days at a time. They had connections across the island, knew the ground and the shore like the back of their collective hand. Taking a child from this family while way out in the sticks, transporting her safely through little Naxos and into mainland Greece was one hell of an ask. The risk was too high.

I broke the news to Sherri on the phone. One mistake, I said, and she might never see the child again. And my team could end up in jail or worse. The smarter move, I said, would be for her to temporarily rekindle that vanished love she once had for Angelos, go to Naxos, meet him, explain she wanted to restart their marriage and live forever on the island. And once that had been established, she would be in a much better position to safely retrieve her girl, get off the island and get home to Iowa.

That didn't appeal to Sherri at all. She really did want to be any way close to Angelos and did not want to be involved in such underhand doings. I agreed it was hardly a glorious way to go about making progress. But I said the retrieval of an abducted child was inevitably difficult. Sooner or later, I said, someone had to take the low road. And, one way or another, everyone gets hurt on the way to the resolution. That is just the way it is. She appreciated my advice yet I remember she put the phone down pretty hard. So be it.

A couple of months later, just into 1980, she called back. She had mulled everything over during a difficult Christmas and decided she would go for it. Her father spoke with me. He asked for my word that I would do whatever it took to safeguard Sherri and Nikole come what may.

'You have my word,' I said.

We were off and running. My first request was that Sherri get a second passport for herself, which she did. On January 14, 1980, she flew in and came to stay with Phyl and I at our house in Sussex. We went over the plan. It involved forging a Greek entry stamp on the older of her two passports, post-dated by one week, showing she had landed in Athens. Sherri flew out some days later using the new passport. It was stamped as she went through immigration. She posted that one back to me from Greece. She took the ferry to Naxos, checked into a B&B for a couple of nights and composed herself before going in search of much-unloved Angelos and much-loved Nikole.

Simply put, Angelos hit the roof when he saw her. He was aggressive, outraged, convinced she had come to steal the girl away. He demanded she give him her passport. She took it from her bag. The forged stamp said she had just arrived that day, suggested she had no other base on the island. And she told him she had no plans to leave. Angelos snatched it from her and, after a while, calmed down. He arranged for her to stay at his parents' home, allowing her to spend time with her daughter. She connected well with his mother and father yet for two weeks he came and went at all hours to ensure she was going nowhere.

It was an extremely tough time for Sherri. Angelos demanded she must submit to sex no matter what because she was his wife. He would arrive up drunk, belittle her, ensure she felt always unwelcome on his island. But in the end, after he had decided this was no trap, he went back out to sea. And it was via that same sea that I planned to remove Sherri and Nikole from Naxos.

Thousands of Europeans charter yachts each spring and summer and set off to explore the thousands of islands in the region. I would do the same, although earlier in the year than most. I would sail it into the Naxos harbour, stay a while, discreetly collect mum and daughter, sail east to a Turkish port and, via Istanbul, fly them home. I sourced the yacht in the Athens port of Piraeus and, to meet insurance requirements, secured various further navigational qualifications.

I lined up Roger Payne, who already knew the area, to come along. And I arranged too for Jim Tozer to get on board, a sailing buddy, an experienced investigator and a great navigator who had guided us to safety during the Fastnet Disaster. We set off on Tuesday, February 7, 1980, the three of us catching a flight from Gatwick to Athens and onto Piraeus to pick up our magnificent thirty-five-foot motor yacht. I was charterer and skipper and Jim was navigator. Roger's role was simply to be himself—an ex-soldier awarded the British Empire Medal for courage under fire in Northern Ireland. I had every confidence the yacht was fit for heavy weather, as was forecast, and that its crew was fit for whatever lay ahead.

We set off on the 130 nautical mile trip to Naxos, motoring at about ten to twelve knots. It would take the best part of twenty-four hours. The plan was to anchor in the harbour and stay for a couple of days so locals got used to the yacht. During this time, we would make contact with Sherri and get the timings together. It was, after all, still out of season and if we were to stay one night and leave at the same time Nikole disappeared, we'd be obvious suspects and potentially tracked.

We tied up firmly in the idyllic little port just ahead of a storm. And we'd been wise to avoid it. It came in fast, the rain belting down and the ocean rolling as we left for a walk into town. We grabbed some basic provisions and, streets flooding under our feet, headed back. I cooked a pretty decent Irish Stew on board and all was well.

At around 10 pm, just as I was about to serve up, a knock on our little door. What on earth? It was Sherri and Nikole.

'I've got to get away now,' she said, crying, rain still hammering down. 'I've got to get away,' she said again, holding the soaked child close to her.

We got them on board, cold, drenched, distressed. I said we were on the front edge of a massive storm, gradually increasing to force eight and rising to force nine, that there was no way in the world we could leave. Sherri didn't care. They both sat shivering as she explained she had spotted a foreign boat, assumed it was us and approached. But there had been no one on board. We had been in town. They had waited around in the downpour, returned to the harbour later and when they saw the cabin lights on they came knocking. She had taken the child that morning instead of leaving her to school. The police would already be sweeping the island.

This couldn't stand. I firmly urged her to go back, to make excuses, to return to her routine for now, that she had no choice. I said again that there was no way we could leave port in this storm. It would take three or four days for the weather to clear and she could not be on board this boat. But she wouldn't go. She said she couldn't, that there was nothing I could say that would make her leave. She said she had endured twenty-one days of sheer hell, that she had been physically and sexually assaulted, that she could take no more. So here we were, in the only foreign boat in the little harbour, the only yacht in the harbour at all, with the island's only missing child on board.

Incidentally, it all got slightly worse when, as we tucked into the much needed stew, I realised I'd flavoured it with baking soda instead of salt. Seems my reading of Greek in the shop wasn't up to much. But we ate it anyway.

Jim, Roger and I decided to get rooms in the hotel overlooking the harbour. Sherri and Nikole could stay in the boat, keep out of sight and, if anyone came looking, we could pop up and explain that it was our vessel, that we were seafaring Brits who knew nothing about a missing American and her daughter.

We all got some sleep and woke to a different scene. Police vehicles were everywhere, sniffer dogs were arriving from Athens, search parties were setting off in the still-stormy weather, the unmistakable throbbing of a helicopter overhead. In fact the chopper hovered above the portside hotel for some time before moving away and returning soon after. We tried to look confused about it all and watched, faces straight, hearts pounding, as the freshly-arrived canines were walked along the windy shore, the port and right up to our boat. Would they pick up on the scent? Would they alert their handlers that there were people on board? We discussed how best to proceed, how to minimise the possibility that the police might order us to open up. We decided to stay right where we were. After a few minutes the police came to the hotel in search of the crew of this unknown, untended yacht. We met them in the lobby, asked what was going on. They checked our passports, explained that a girl had gone missing and moved on.

'The downpour,' I said to Jim and Roger, relieved beyond belief that Sherri and Nikole had not been sniffed out. 'The waves were crashing right over the yacht for hours. It's killed off the scent.'

Time passed and, again, the dogs were walked around the port and right by our boat. The tension we felt was just the same. We could only hope they would once more miss the scent, that the two occupants would again stay still as stones. It took four days, among the longest of my life, before Jim said we had reached a point where our escape was a 'reasonable risk.'

We made the break at 2 am. Just as we had climbed on board, I heard Jim say, 'Police are coming.'

I looked up, saw a police van at the entrance to the port. Jim seized the small on-board axe. The knots holding us to the harbour would have been wrenched tight over the past few days. There was no time to untie. He chopped the first rope. The yacht swung wildly out towards a rocky outcrop. We could easily have struck it. But he was fast with the second chop. The bow was inches from contact with stone when the reassuring purr of the big diesel marine engine kicked in. Braking power was in place, steering controls in my hands. The bow turned to face the angry sea and we surged forward.

It was rough going, climbing the broad swells and falling slowly into the troughs, but we were in charge. As we evened our speed the keel was quickly cutting through the waves. Behind us, the police van rolled slowly through the port, uninterested in our secret escape.

We hoisted a gybe sail to steady the yacht knowing an uncertain journey lay ahead. We sailed a southerly course, tracking our way around the island, carefully navigating through numerous small islands and rocky outcrops. In time we switched course to head east towards Bodrum port on the south-west Turkish coast. In the cabin, Sherri and little Nikole clung to each other, hope in their hearts. Neither raised neither complaint nor concern about the rolling and yawing.

Our thinking so far had been that the Naxos fishing fleet would remain tied up given the conditions. But, after a couple of hours, we saw navigation lights to our stern. The radar picked up on the vessels heading out to sea, little green dots telling a story that we could not know. Could those fishing boats have an interest in us? But our yacht was as advertised—strong, stable and confidently ploughing onwards with a mighty head start. After some thirty hours of testing sailing, the three-strong crew were weak, famished, burned out. We had to rest. The weather had calmed yet we had drifted slightly south while heading east. To our port-side was the island of Kos. Jim navigated us closer inshore to a sheltered bay on its southern coast. We dropped anchor in the millpond calm and silence of the bay on a starry evening. We sipped on hot coffee, put a chicken in the oven, avoided the baking soda and charged our glasses. Everything was, despite developments, going okay. We would reach Bodrum in just a few hours come the morning. And, with that sentiment in the air, all on board slid into a pleasant slumber under the stars in the balmy breeze.

As dawn opened above us, we became aware of people shouting not far away. We looked to see, realised the yacht had dragged the anchor. We were just yards from the sandy beach, the keel already touching the bottom. People were shouting warnings, waving their arms. There wasn't a second to waste. We fired up that bullish engine once more and pulled away with a grateful wave back to the beachcombers. We needed to get beyond Greek waters.

In the open sea once more and our spirits were high. We mixed a couple of cocktails to sip on deck under the naked sun. Such were the politics of the time that, as we left Greece and approached Turkey, we had to navigate between gunships dispatched to eyeball one another where water borders met.

I requested permission via radio to enter Bodrum harbour but it didn't go down well. As we closed in, sirens rang out and port police cars pulled up at the shoreline. We watched as men with machine guns set their sights on us. It was tense but we were in Turkey now and had no reason to believe these officers were acting on any instructions from Greece.

I sipped on a G&T as we docked, gunbarrels tracking our movements. A port police chief, one of the most officious looking men I've ever seen, marched over. Polished jackboots, medals, oversized cap, large moustache and, most spectacular of all, yelling in Turkish and jumping up and down on the spot. It was like something out of a *Bugs Bunny* cartoon.

I put down my drink and asked if he spoke English. This seemed to surprise him.

'You English?' he said.

'Yes.'

He filled his lungs, ready to bellow some more.

'Why the fuck you fly Greek flag in our harbour!? It is an insult!'

Before another word could be yelled, Jim yanked the Greek flag from the mast, spat on it and threw it overboard.

The men with machine guns went, 'Hooray!'

From there we were escorted to the port's police station so our passports and papers could be examined. Within a few minutes we were very much being encouraged to make a donation to smooth our onward path. Such a payment, we were advised, would save us the trouble of having to pay formal fees to the Harbour Authority. We understood and coughed up.

We checked in at a hotel where we were the only guests. The manager allocated us a spacious two-level apartment with tiled floors and open tread stairs. It seemed only right that we all go for a bite to eat and a few drinks to celebrate, and that's what we did. And we made the most of it. I don't even remember walking back.

About 1 am I woke with Sherri shaking my arm and screaming.

'Quickly,' she said, 'Quickly!'

She led me to the stairs. One of the steps looked as if it had been chopped in half. A pool of blood was spreading across the tiled floor below. It was Roger. Unconscious, his head split open. Jim had dashed to find the owner and get medical help. I gasped as I realised just how much blood had been lost. Roger, six foot and more of him, had gone to get some water. He had made a wrong turn, had been coming up the stairs instead of going to his ground floor divan. Sherri, nerves on edge, had screamed at what she thought was an intruder. Roger had turned suddenly, his foot went straight through one of the weak treads, his leg plunged down. He had fallen backwards, a large man crashing to the ground from the stairs, cracking his head hard. The manager arrived, gasped at the sight. She said the nearest doctor was many miles away and made the call.

Between us, we lifted the sixteen stone dead-weight of Roger onto a divan. He was breathing normally but completely unconscious. I applied cold cloth compresses but while the blood slowed it was still spouting from his ear in small pulses. It took an hour for the doctor to arrive.

His face seemed to suggest it wasn't as bad as it might have been, but he couldn't be sure. Between us we communicated with the only common currency we had—very basic French. The doctor said he would come back in a few hours, that Roger was too drunk to assess. He added that the nearest hospital was in Izmir, some 150 miles away.

I sat with Roger and, worryingly, he remained unconscious and continued to bleed lightly as the long hours passed. The doctor returned at 7 am and gave him a shot to sober him up. At worst, he said, it was a fractured skull. At best, a burst eardrum. Either way he needed a hospital and, he said, an ambulance from Izmir would cost the equivalent of a £1,000. In those pre-credit card days, we didn't have that kind of money. If we had still been in Greece, and therefore in the EU, we could have accessed emergency treatment as fellow EU citizens.

The doctor excused himself as we held an urgent roundtable. Sherri and Nikole needed to get back to the USA. Roger needed a full assessment. We needed to arrange for the boat to get back to Athens. How would we progress from here?

Roger, reacting to whatever he had been given, was beginning to come around now. We talked him through it all. He understood what had happened, said he was embarrassed and sorry.

Jim suggested getting Roger back on the yacht, motoring him to Kos, in Greek waters, and taking advantage of the country's EU membership. But it was risky. If the Greeks had linked our yacht to the missing mother and daughter, both might well end up in custody there. Roger agreed it was the best option, that getting to Izmir would take just as long as getting to Kos. He said I should get Sherri and Nikole to Istanbul and onward as planned.

We checked with the doctor. He monitored Roger for a while longer and concluded it was not a skull fracture, although possibly a hairline fracture. He was satisfied that he could travel the two or three hours back to Greek territory. Back on board, we cleaned down the cabin, cleared out all traces of anyone other than the crew having been on board. And both men, plucky as you like, set sail.

It was two days before I heard. Greek police had been waiting with dogs. They searched the yacht. There was no indication of Sherri or

Nikole having been there. But they did find the charter contact naming me as skipper. Where was I? Jim said we had been in a car accident in Bodrum and that I, the skipper, had been flown home. Across five hours in police custody, he explained that no one had realised how bad Roger's injury was. He said he was returning the yacht to Piraeus but now needed hospital treatment for his friend.

Medics at the local hospital wanted Roger treated in Athens but he insisted on flying back to Northern Ireland and, eventually, got his way. But to get home Jim and Roger first had to get to the capital but no flights from Kos to Athens were imminent. They had to spend a night in a hotel which burned up the last of their money. My office arranged for flights to Athens the next day, for accommodation there and for the flights home after that. By that time news of the case was breaking in the British press, The Sun carrying an initial report. Jim and Roger were hugely relieved to board that British Airways plane and could not relax until it was beyond Greek airspace. Finally home, Roger went on to spend half a year in hospital in Belfast. He lost sight in one eye and hearing in one ear. It was a devastating blow.

Meanwhile, Sherri, Nikole and I took the 440 mile bus journey from Bodrum to Istanbul. For almost twenty hours we chugged our way through wide open plains and climbed treacherous, skinny mountain roads amid severe blizzards. We even had to get out at one point and lie behind the bus as we came under mortar attack from Kurdish rebels. Eventually a Turkish army unit ended the incident with little in the way of mercy.

A general strike was in full swing in snow-covered Istanbul, including a riot near the airport, and the taxis weren't for taking us anywhere. I went in search of the right man, shed a few dollars and soon enough we were on our way to catch the first available flight to London. After a few days' rest and catch up with Phyl, we were off again to the USA, stopping off first in Chicago.

Not for the first time in my life, a media frenzy. Wall to wall journalists and TV cameras awaiting our arrival. As we boarded for the short flight towards Cedar Rapids, six journalists and one TV crew were given the all-clear to interview us in the transit lounge. Landing in Iowa, an air hostess asked us to remain while the other passengers deplaned. A camera crew came on board to film us exiting and, outside, it was something close to unbelievable. Forty, maybe fifty or more reporters had gathered. It was extreme and emotional and unexpected. I remember clearly that Sherri's grandmother was there, Nikole's great-grandmother, and how the tears flowed.

I carried that bright little girl on my shoulder as her mother hugged relatives. And then we made our way to the homestead, towards the man to whom I had given my word that I would do whatever it took to get his daughter and granddaughter home safe.

Looking back on it, Naxos really encapsulates the highs and lows of the child recovery business in which I found myself. It was often fraught with danger, laced with the unexpected from both man and nature, and through it all I had the wellbeing of a young woman and child at the front of my mind.

From a publicity point of view, it was priceless advertisement for my services. Yet had something gone wrong, how quickly the media would have been to turn their righteous ire my way. From a purely financial point of view, the ever-present, ever-changing risk and reward did not balance out at all. But I know for sure that there are few things as rewarding in this life as successfully ensuring a good mother rightfully gets her little girl back in her arms. Just knowing I helped make that happen in this and other cases is where the biggest payoff is found.

TWENTY-SEVEN

Moving to Northern Ireland (1980)

I MOVED out of England. It was one of the single biggest decisions of my life, one that was the result of multiple events. And almost all of those events were related to the behaviour of my friends in the Metropolitan Police.

Forgive me, if you will, while I offer a quick refresher into what had been going on.

You'll recall that as I had left a London court in 1977, after receiving that wildly overcooked conviction for child stealing, I had been told in no uncertain terms I was not welcome in my own city. The gentleman delivering the message identified himself as a Metropolitan Police officer. I've no reason to think he was lying.

You'll have read that in 1965, less than a year after leaving my job at Surrey Police, it was the Met who took me to court. The ridiculous charge, under the old Larceny Act, grew from me having a bunch of keys. They lost the case.

In 1969, I had been charged after showing one officer a gift our office had received—a fountain pen gas gun—while he was there supposedly investigating a burglary at my office. They lost that one too.

Let's not forget the two Old Bailey Trials, both on charges for conspiracies which the police seemed to have dreamed up and threw everything at. The first, in 1971, for a *conspiracy to evade the purpose of the wireless telegraphy act*. And the second, in 1974, for a *conspiracy to effect a public mischief*. The House of Lords itself ruled it was not a known offence in British law.

In 1972 I had confirmed ahead of a court case that I witnessed the powerful Detective Chief Superintendent Kenneth Drury, head of the

Met's organised crime-busting *Flying Squad*, doing a little bit of business. I had the picture to prove it. Twelve detectives were jailed. And, after *Operation Unit Six* was blown open in 1977, I had been lined up to give evidence in a case involving corrupt cops.

Since moving to Brighton, neither I nor Stuart had a single brush with the local police. They understood we had a job to do and respected that. I felt the same about them. Yet in London, I knew men like Ginger Hemsley and his crew would have liked nothing more than to see me fail. And most of my business was still in London and routinely brought me to the capital.

In most circumstances, when you find an enemy turning his attention to you, there are ways in which you can fight back. Yet I had done all I could in terms of fighting the Met, and indeed had spent a hard-earned fortune in the battles to salvage my hard-won business which they seemed to be so intent on shredding.

An organisation like the Met has deep pockets, enormous manpower and can hold a grudge for longer than any rational human who seeks only to get on with his life. For an individual or lone agency to take it on is an almost existential decision. There came a point where, with my wife and young children to think of, I didn't know how wise it was to continue with my physical presence being so readily available to the Met, given they had a habit of cuffing me. There was nothing to suggest that I would not continue to be, as I feared they saw it, fair game.

It all really came to a head that day outside the court. When that brazen man stepped into my face and made it clear that they would be coming my way again, things began to crystallise. Phyl and I had talked it over, had a few days of deep thought. As the decade came to a close, Johnnie was five, Jamie was two. Neither of us could shake the idea that they, along with us, were living in the shadow of something unpredictable and beyond our control. Such was the nature of that long shadow, that it fell too on mine and Rita's daughter Debbie, seventeen, and our son Andrew, fourteen. Could my business be pulled from under me? Could the future of all my family be compromised in some way? The nature of my work meant some kind of interaction, pleasant or otherwise, with the Met was always inevitable.

Phyl became increasingly clear about what we should do. She was a Belfast woman, came from a big family, had a strong support network already built into the fabric of society in Northern Ireland. I'd been to Belfast many times and had opened an office there in 1972. I'd always enjoyed my visits, liked spending time with the extended family. Ironically, the Troubles were raging in that period and the most common interaction many local people were having with Englishmen was with heavily armed ones in British army uniforms. Yet I knew for sure at the same time that, despite the conflict, it was a welcoming, warm-hearted place.

To fill in the picture, I had secured two small offices in Ireland, one in Dublin also, in 1972. Both had a good client base, mostly law firms, and were turning a decent profit. Indeed, it was the looming menace of the Troubles which meant the island as a whole had less competition in terms of the PI trade. There was just one other firm in Belfast and a small handful in Dublin. That Belfast rival, *Gilbert and Company*, had been around for donkey's years and its sole interest was debt collection. In terms of investigations, we stood alone.

Most of the Belfast work was commissioned by various media outlets, banks, solicitors and courts. What we did not do was surveillance work, which I'll explain later, but we did everything else, often managing it all from Brighton. If myself or Stuart or anyone else was needed, one of us would jump on the so-called Belfast shuttle which jetted back and forward to London several times a day.

The frequency of my visits there, once every few weeks, was as a result of the needs of the courts. The courts' officers and related officials were required to attend addresses in what were seen as some of the most challenging of areas. These districts, largely republican areas, were simply not being serviced by either court officers or bailiffs, which presented a fine opportunity for me. Few wanted to be branded agents of the British state, a designation which could cause no end of trouble at a time of limited yet sincere insurrection. But I'd been called worse in my time.

On those visits, with the cooperation of the Royal Ulster Constabulary and British army, I would take a trip into the heart of west Belfast where support for the IRA was deep and widespread. I would travel up and down the Falls Road in my conservative suits and plain ties serving court process. On most occasions, I went up in the back of an armoured army Saracen vehicle. Yet there was not a single occasion when I had an issue with anyone and, likewise, no one had any particular issue with me. Most people I spoke with were polite and friendly and understood why I was knocking on their door.

For me, the main issue about considering any move over the water was that I could not escape the idea I would be taking yet another course of action as a result of the bloody Metropolitan Police.

I was in a quandary. We got ourselves to our lawyer's office in Brighton to see what might be feasible, to see what questions he might raise about such a move.

David Barling asked, 'If you were to move your business could you still operate as you do at present in London and Brighton?'

'Yes,' I said, seeing no reason why not. I would still be within the UK so in terms of the methods, legal system, tax system and everything else, not much would change.

About two years before all this, Stuart and I had decided to split the agency in half after differing on how we wanted to operate and expand. The agreed split included the franchised offices and client base. Those franchised offices were all operated independently, each paying a fixed royalty to use our brand and systems. After the split, Stuart retained the *Nationwide Investigations* name while I opted to rebrand initially as *Intercity*, later *Intercity Reliant Ltd* trading as *Priority Investigations*. All told, I held onto the offices in Belfast, Dublin, Maryland and one we had franchised in Jersey. Basically, Stuart and I were successful in different ways and it seemed to make sense to become friendly rivals. His way of doing things was more focused on sub-contracting assignments while mine was more hands-on, to be out on jobs while employing staff to run the office.

As part of moving things around, I had switched my administrative HQ to Sussex. If, as my lawyer had raised, I moved the admin HQ to Belfast, Brighton would then become a franchised branch. That would be all there was to it. But it had been a theoretical question, hadn't it? I wouldn't actually really move my HQ to Northern Ireland, would I?

David pressed on. 'So do you want to move your business to Northern Ireland?' he asked.

Phyl became slightly animated at the direction of the discussion, quickly answering, 'Yes. I mean, we could if Ian wanted to.'

Much as I knew she was excited, the stubbornness within me showed itself.

'No way,' I said. 'I'm not going to move my business just because the Met would like me to.'

And I had a point. But, to a point, I knew I was digging in my heels because of my feelings about that police force, not because of my feelings for my family.

I mulled it over across the next few days. Phyl and I talked late into the night about the pros and cons, the whys and why nots, really drilled down and mapped out what this might mean for each of us in the years to come. We went over everything, talked firmly with each other, fought about it, laughed about it, fell into long silences about it. And, when we had turned it around in every direction and looked at it from every angle, I un-dug my heels.

'Okay,' I said. 'Me, you, the kids, the business, everything. We'll move to Northern Ireland.'

My parents, brothers and others were baffled.

'Are you sure about this?' was a common question, and one that came from a good place in their hearts. They knew I was no stranger to Belfast, yet there were almost nightly TV reports about the violence and the situation was showing precious little sign of getting any better.

'We are sure,' I told them all, advising everyone it wasn't as bad as all that.

I wasn't so sure they believed me. You see, there had been an incident...

The Belfast office was the first floor of a converted house at Wellington Park in the pleasant Malone Road area of the city. One night there had been a ring on the main front doorbell. The duty operator, a young lady who had been advised never to open the door while alone, took the call on the intercom. She was talked into opening up by a man who said he was delivering mail for tenants in the office above. As she turned the lock, a masked man shoved his way in. He put a pistol to her head, ordered her to 'Get out of here now!'

Instead of mail, he had with him two five-gallon cans of petrol taped together. Between them, a crude detonator which would turn his improvised device into a fairly ferocious fire bomb. As he struggled with his terror cargo, our operator dashed back to the control room. In a very practical move, she had advised her visitor she was getting her bag and coat before she would run from the building. It must have seemed quite rational to him for he didn't object. The courageous woman used that time to trigger the silent alarm at her desk. The police were alerted. As she left she yelled for the two tenants above to get out. The bomber's main interest was to get himself out and, his device in place, he ran off. Within minutes the RUC had arrived. One young policeman spoke to our employee on Wellington Park. In a panic, she told him there were two tenants in the office above. The policeman raced inside, dashed up and called out to the pair still working away there. They came charging down, followed by the officer, and all leaped over the bomb in the hall. Just as the policeman was at the door, the thing detonated. Flames blasted out in all directions. The heat was so intense it melted his flack-jacket, sticking it to the back of his uniform. And such was the force of the blast, it sent him flying across the driveway, through a hedge and into the neighbouring garden. Fortunately this heroic RUC man had only minor injuries. Unfortunately, by the time the fire brigade had arrived, the building was well ablaze. Flames spread to the next-door property, where the French Consulate Legation was housed. Both buildings were completely destroyed.

The Provisional IRA later claimed responsibility. They said their target had been British Intelligence who, they believed, were based in the building. I can only assume they thought my firm, as a result of my travelling up and down the Falls Road with court orders, was a front for a British Intelligence unit. A stupid and dangerous mistake.

As I said, I carried out a good deal of work in the city but we did not do static surveillance. That would have been foolhardy to the point of stupidity. People parked up in cars watching other people or places in Belfast at that time were either one of two things—security forces doing a poor job or terrorists—either IRA or pro-UK loyalists—keeping an eye out for their next target. At least that was the prevailing train of thought in those dark days. Such was the atmosphere, if a thing like that was spotted along somewhere like the Falls, the IRA would learn of it soon enough. The consequences could be grave.

So, with all of that thoroughly considered, Phyl and I turned our mind to relocation and scouted out a few properties. It was clear that in terms of real estate in Northern Ireland, we could get a lot more bang for our buck than in England. And in 1980, with two boys and the entire contents of our home and office packed up, we made the move. We settled at a beautiful property with plenty of land in Dunadry, Co Antrim, about fifteen miles from Belfast.

Regardless of location, I vowed from the outset to aggressively grow my business presence far and wide from Northern Ireland. I set out to secure as much publicity as I could and the high profile and high-value assignments continued to come. One new client became the government of Seychelles, which was seeking research into a number of emerging individuals of interest. As our communications developed, I flew over a number of times to discuss these matters with very senior officials. This began eating up my time fast and, constantly seeking to expand to embrace the workload, I had to think of a way to ensure I always had quality, ambitious management in place.

Ahead of another trip to the Indian Ocean nation, I remember pondering the matter at the desk in my now head office on central Belfast's Great Victoria Street. I concluded that I could achieve all I needed by buying out, or buying into, another agency. That way, I could increase sales and, quite possibly, find a decent new manager at the same time.

Yet life has a way of disguising its opportunities. In my case I didn't buy into another agency, but instead bought out a small Belfast courier company. When I saw that it was for sale, it occurred to me that it could piggyback on the existing infrastructure and flexibility of the agency. Operating under the name *Priority Deliveries*, our smart white vans zoomed around the city picking up and delivering packages. We went on to land a contract to provide a scheduled delivery service for Northern Ireland's Education and Libraries Board, a daily service ferrying stock, stationery and internal mail.

A further opportunity came when an old pal and rival to our Dublin office got in touch. Liam Brady referred one of his contacts who wanted to dispose of a fifty percent shareholding in a security company. It took some haggling, but I secured the deal and the forty plus guards and store detectives who came with it.

With international travel now firmly on my professional itinerary, with business flourishing all around me, with not a single London copper in sight, things were truly sunny in my life once again. On the home-front, the kids were settled and the in-laws were regular welcome callers to our comfortable, happy home.

Content in my new base, I considered that I could merrily work hard and live well right where I was for the rest of my days.

Except that's not how things worked out at all.

TWENTY-EIGHT

IRA propaganda, John Downey and the Anglo-Irish Agreement (1980s)

DURING the eighties the Provisional IRA's uncompromising view of the world was being delivered in two key ways. The first was via its initially small number of political representatives in Sinn Fein and, the second, through its weekly newspaper *An Phoblacht*—or *Republican News*. As the IRA established new funding streams and its ruthless terror campaign sank to new lows, its cheerleaders were very much in the business of justifying the most horrendous of actions. Yet, although the political representatives and the newspaper delivered the thinking behind that illegal organisation and its deeds, they were doing nothing illegal themselves.

That situation became something close to untenable for the British government, led at the time by Margaret Thatcher. She was disturbed by what she called 'the oxygen of publicity' enjoyed by the IRA. It was only to be expected that the media would carry the words of Sinn Fein and, via *An Phoblacht*, IRA spokespeople after each attack. But the government saw it as being far too convenient for those who supported the murder of UK citizens in the UK. The pressure, from various sources, began to mount.

My view on this was quite simple. In a democratic country, the government has no business preventing people from voicing, watching or reading whatever opinion they choose. When a mature and liberal nation finds itself policing the marketplace of ideas, however unpalatable, it is time for it to take stock. I was an Englishman living in Northern Ireland throughout this period and I was very well aware of the obscenity of the violence carried out by the IRA, and by loyalist terrorists too. The only reason such groups existed was to take life and destroy property for political ends. And while that was as cruel as it was unnecessary, speaking or writing about it for whatever reason was a different matter.

The issue would reach a climax in 1988 when, in an extraordinary decision, the government banned the voices of terror group representatives from the British media. That tactic was ridiculed around the world and arguably backfired by drawing more attention to the words of Sinn Fein's leader Gerry Adams and others. The ban was lifted some six years later.

It was in the run up to the ban that British Airways took the decision to no longer carry *An Phoblacht* in its cargo. The paper was being printed in Ireland and a few hundred or so copies were being sent for collection and distribution in London. I could never have predicted that Sinn Fein would approach me in terms of helping them with their delivery problem. But then, at the time, I had taken over the courier firm and was rarely in the mood to turn down business.

The initial telephone inquiry did not spell out the details. A lady said only that she wanted goods moved from Belfast to London. They were newspapers, she said, which would need to be picked up and delivered to Heathrow airport once a week. I arranged for a quote.

We are not talking about large numbers here. The few bundles of *An Phoblacht*, destined for west London, fitted into a large suitcase. Sending as air freight would cost around the same as a return fare for a passenger. So, the deal done, that's how we did it. Our driver would pick up the bundles of newspapers, pack them into a suitcase and one of our team would fly over and deliver the goods to a waiting van driver.

It was an easy day's work for our staff of all political flavours, including those who were very much opposed to what Sinn Fein stood for. They would fly over, enjoy a drink in Heathrow, fly back. We didn't make much money from it at all, but in the spirit of good-natured cross community relations we carried on for as long as we were needed.

It lasted for about a year, after which time British Airways, the most regular carrier to London at the time, had a change of heart and accepted their newspapers once again.

What was bizarre was that during that year, while playing a part in delivering the IRA's printed message to readers in London and beyond, I was told of a threat to me from the IRA. I can only put it down to poor internal communications within the ranks. I learned of it via a request on the phone to meet an RUC Special Branch officer based at Mount-pottinger station. We sat in a cafe as he and a colleague advised they had arrested a man some hours earlier. In his possession were names of potential targets, including yours truly. He said I should advise my family and take extra security precautions. An RUC technical officer visited my house to install various alarms as a matter of course. There were seven in our wider family who served with the RUC, some of them very often at our home. An upgrade in security was a good idea in any case.

Among the murderous outrages of the times was the IRA's notorious double bombing of Hyde Park and Regents Park on the same day in 1982. Four British soldiers died, along with seven horses, when the Provisionals detonated a device beside the Household Guards on parade at Hyde Park. More than thirty people were injured. And seven soldiers on parade with the Royal Green Jackets died in the Regents Park bombing. A man called John Downey, from Co Donegal, was implicated as an 'active participant' in the Hyde Park attack. Unfortunately he had been able to slip out of the UK and into the relative safety of the Republic of Ireland.

Despite requests from the British government, it was always claimed that Downey could not be found. The same response came in other cases too where Irish citizens wanted for terror crimes had retreated behind the Republic's border. Times were tense. In 1983, IRA members (including my old Brixton Prison canteen customer Gerry Kelly) had escaped from the Maze Prison and some made their way across the border. Two years earlier, ten republican prisoners had died on hunger strike at the same prison. In 1984, Margaret Thatcher had survived an IRA bomb attack at the Conservative Party conference in Brighton. Five others were not so fortunate.

Political life in Northern Ireland was polarised and ferocious and murder on the streets was horrifically routine. Among all this came the strong sense the powers-that-be in Dublin were not minded to cooperate with Mrs Thatcher's government at all, plunging relations between Britain and Ireland into the gutter. At the time, Dublin had a constitutional claim to the six counties of Northern Ireland and it was, from their point of view, not at all simple to extradite Irish citizens wanted in the UK on crimes linked to the political conflict. It was perhaps simpler for the Irish to be unable to find the wanted individuals than to haul them into court.

It was after Mr Downey could not, allegedly, be located that I became involved in his case. In that week after the Brighton Bomb, I took a call from my long-standing client Barrie Penrose of *The Sunday Times*. He said he had a 'challenge' for me. Over fish and chips in Belfast he told me about a meeting he had attended with his friend Sir Michael Havers, the UK's then Attorney General. The issue of the mysteriously unlocatable IRA suspects had been discussed. Barrie told me Sir Michael Havers had said,

'You know your people in Ireland? I'd like to see if they can find this John Downey individual.'

Barrie said the Attorney General, and therefore the UK government, were seeking to embarrass the Irish government by finding on-the-run Downey without any Irish participation. There were many constraints on any official parties becoming involved in the search but, as Sir Michael had said, none at all on private citizens playing a part. I said I'd begin immediately.

Barrie provided Downey's full name, date of birth and told me that he came from Co Donegal. The first step was to determine if Downey was on record with the Pay Related Social Insurance, the equivalent of the UK's National Insurance Scheme. I would pretext as an official at the British unemployment benefits office, Department of Health and Social Security.

I recall being slightly nervous as I picked up the phone. This was an important case. I didn't want to bugger it up. I wanted to find John Downey. A man answered at the Dublin office and I introduced myself with a made up name.

'We are having trouble getting in touch with a claimant who has returned to Ireland,' I said in my best London accent. 'To Donegal, I believe. We have a final cheque for him and have no idea where to send it.'

A pause.

'Hi London, how are you doing? That's no problem. I just need the name and PRSI number.'

I said I didn't have the PRSI, just his UK National Insurance number.

'No,' said the guy, 'that won't do. Do you have a date of birth?'

Indeed I did.

A minute later and I was in luck. Lots of it.

'I have him,' the man said. He read out the address in Donegal and, even better, told me Downey was unemployed and signing on for benefits every two weeks. And, better still, he said he would be signing on at the Ballyshannon benefits office this Thursday, October 18, 1984. That was in two days' time.

This was an incredible information haul. With one phone call I had all I needed to know about the whereabouts of Britain's most wanted terrorist bomber. I'd only left Barrie an hour before.

It's worth saying that, during this time, talks had been ongoing behind the scenes in London and Dublin about securing a groundbreaking new arrangement between the UK and Ireland. The Anglo-Irish Agreement was an incredibly controversial idea, one that would technically give the Republic a voice in matters relating to Northern Ireland for the first time. Unionists in Northern Ireland wanted nothing to do with it, but both sovereign governments saw huge merit in striking a deal which would enhance cooperation over security and related issues. It would mean that crossing the Irish border might no longer mean one was no longer so completely beyond the reach of the UK authorities. The fact that I had located Mr Downey so fast spoke very clearly of the Irish government's unwillingness to track him down. It was clear that something needed to change.

Yet for my purposes, and those of *The Sunday Times*, the border was not standing in the way. I called Barrie who in turn called the Attorney General. Both were delighted. Barrie asked me to launch a surveillance operation in Ballyshannon and secure pictures of Mr Downey. I was already on it. A reliable agent from Dundalk, Co Louth, handled the job. He was in place from early on Thursday morning. Safe to say I spent those hours on tenterhooks.

A call in the early afternoon. My plain-speaking agent with an update. In a very matter-of-fact tone, he advised me he had spotted and photographed Downey. I met him in Newry, Co Down, at 5 pm that same day and collected the roll of 35mm film. Then I called Barrie to report our success. His words to me were said with passion.

'Secure that film.'

It was picked up the next morning, on Friday, October 19, 1984, and delivered to London. Barrie rang to say he was very pleased but wished the images had been slightly better. I wasn't about to apologise. He was sitting on a fantastic scoop and had nothing to complain about. Those bloody journos are never happy…

The photo was published on the front of *The Sunday Times* on October 21, 1984. The headline inside,

"Walking Free: Top IRA terrorist."

I had agreed to sign over copyright of the image from my agency to the newspaper for an additional fee. That turned out to be a mistake. That photo earned a fortune for *The Sunday Times* over the coming months and was reused many times by many outlets worldwide.

The days that followed saw uproar in the House of Commons. The Anglo-Irish Agreement talks went into overdrive. It was clear that the story was a catalyst for, in 1985, getting it over the line. It ultimately paved the way to an extradition agreement and led in the end to a number of arrests in the Republic.

That said, slippery Downey was not charged over the Hyde Park bombing until as late as 2013. He was tried at the Old Bailey but the case collapsed after it emerged that, in 2007, he had received written assurance from former Labour Prime Minister Tony Blair's government that he was not being actively sought by UK authorities. But that's a whole other story.

In December 2020, after a civil case taken by relatives, the High Court in London ruled Downey must compensate family members of 19-year-old Hyde Park bomb victim Lance Corporal Jeffrey Young. He was ordered to pay £715,000.

Back in the eighties, locating Downey led to my firm being commissioned by the same newspaper and other outlets to engage in similar tasks. We worked to track down a number of on-the-run prisoners, many to addresses in the Republic, in the years to come. Such was the nature of our work, at no point did we ever claim any of the glory.

In 1985, probably as a direct result of what I had been working on, the police in Northern Ireland were in touch once more. The IRA had again turned their attention to me, and this time it was more serious.

Special Branch advised that they believed I was being, or was about to be, actively targeted.

So we ramped up security once more. I changed my routines and kept all my senses sharp. I watched out for cars and people that seemed in any way out-of-place, ensured our home and office was secure and frequently checked if I was being followed. We ensured that both our boys were safe at boarding school in Dungannon, Co Tyrone, and overall met this development with the gravity it required.

The IRA had already blown up my first Belfast office. Before that they had blown up the transcript office of the Old Bailey, which led to me spending longer in jail. I was damn sure they'd already done enough damage to my life.

Yet they weren't the only armed and dangerous faction I would have to worry about the years to come.

TWENTY-NINE

Seychelles: An Invitation to Spy (1979/80)

IT was a few weeks before Christmas. I'd been out with the family, a treat they'd planned for me since the Fastnet Disaster of the summer. It was around 1 am. I'd just got in, merrily stuffed with Chinese food and a little worse for wear. The telex machine was clattering. A single sentence.

'Please call this number as soon as you receive.'

I ripped off the paper. The number started with 0039—the dialling code for Italy. Who wants to talk to me in Italy? And why so urgent? It was past 2 am there. I was too curious not to do what I had been asked.

A woman answered.

'*Pronto*,' she said. 'Mr Ian Withers?'

'Yes,' I said. 'I've just got your message.'

'My name is Angela,' she said, a lively accent within a silky voice. I had, she explained, been highly recommended by someone. Would I undertake round-the-clock surveillance on four people in central London? Starting immediately? For the next seven days?

'Are you able to deal with this?' she asked.

I was busy, my agents already committed to a great deal of work. It would be a logistical nightmare to commit to such a job on the spot. So, of course, I said 'Yes.' I rarely knew the word 'No' when it came to work. I'd worry about how to fit it all in later. I added, 'What can you tell me?'

She gave me four names: Sir James Mancham, Robert Frichot, James Michel, Gérard Hoarau. The first three had been in London for a few days, the fourth had arrived a few hours ago from his home in South Africa. The names meant nothing to me.

Angela said on completion of the task, my invoice should be sent to Mr G Mario Ricci at his GMR Group in Italy. I had to tell her it wasn't going to be that simple. I knew already that an operation as intensive as this would take at least ten agents. And while she sounded perfectly genuine and pleasant, I would need more than just instruction. It would cost, I said, something like £30 an hour. On top of that, there would be fees for vehicles, mileage, other emerging expenses. She listened carefully. I wondered if she could tell I'd been drinking.

'Could you,' I asked, 'arrange for a £1,000 advance?'

I had to ask. I wasn't about to get tricked. The prospect of another long and bruising legal drama to claw back what I was owed did not appeal at all. Once bitten...

'Yes Mr Withers,' she said. 'A £1,000 advance is no problem. I can give you travellers' checks. Do you have someone in Rome that could meet with me to collect?'

'Yes,' I said. 'We have an agent in Rome.'

I had no such agent in Rome, but I wasn't going to let a little thing like that get in the way of a great business opportunity. Besides, there were no credit cards and no other immediate way to sort out issues like this. I was used to adapting fast, to ensuring people got from place to place for such dealings. I said I'd have someone meet her in the morning. She should present them with photographs of the individuals and the retainer.

And so it was an early start for my good friend and colleague Barry Trigwell. He took the 8 am from Gatwick to Rome, met Angela at 3 pm, collected as discussed and flew home. Meanwhile, me and my hangover got to work on lining up a team. I advised my secretary Lynne Ford that she would be needed almost constantly to write up the reports and prepare the daily logs.

The week that followed went like clockwork. We found and ID'd all the men, stuck to them like invisible glue. We took excellent photographs of each with other people and while alone. And from their hotels, we pretexted copies of bills. In respect of James Michel and Gérard Hoarau, that included all the phone numbers they had called. Angela rang my office two or three times each day. She wanted live updates about where they were, what they were doing, who they were with. We delivered it all, right down to the fine detail.

At the end of a demanding but successful job, I prepared the final reports for her and our unseen client. We could all meet for lunch, Angela said, at the five-star Carlton Towers Hotel, off upmarket Sloane Street.

I put on one of my sharper (yet still conservative) suits, bundled up the reports and photographs and took the train from Brighton to London. Angela introduced herself as Angela Ricci. She was olive-skinned, slim, attractive, stylish, in her mid-thirties. She shook my hand then leaned in, presenting her cheeks to be kissed. I did so. She took my arm, guided me to a corner booth in the plush restaurant. Three men were chatting, waiting, each with a glass of white wine. As their faces turned my way, adrenaline exploded.

What was this?!

One of the men I had been trailing for a week was looking right at me. Angela squeezed my arm to calm me. She had sensed my shock.

'James Michel,' she said, gesturing towards that familiar face, a man of about thirty-five years. 'Minister of Finance for the Republic of Seychelles.'

One other man was her husband, Mario Ricci, the full-bearded, middle-aged chairman of GMR. The third was Giancarlo Lauro, an assistant to Mario.

'Call me Lauro,' he said, smiling.

She told the men I was Ian Withers, the security specialist who had been assisting in London. Mario, grey-haired and easygoing, did not speak English. As he talked, Angela translated. He said Mr Michel had been included among the four subjects to see how well my team performed when it came to surveillance. Mr Michel had remained unaware he was being watched at all. He said he was impressed we had secured the room and phone bills, and more that we had called the numbers and blagged our way into finding out which individual or what organisation was on the other end.

We all ate, drank wine and Cognac and, towards the end, I presented my bill. It was something in the region of £3,000. And it was, shall we say, a little creative but then I was as much a businessman as I was a PI. At first they had no interest in it. They spoke with each other in Italian. Occasionally a question came via Lauro, James or Angela, and then they would discuss my answer. Yet no one looked at the invoice.

As the coffee arrived, Lauro finally asked me to pass the bill his way. He took a quick look, passed it to Mario. Neither showed any reaction. Mario waved a hand by way of instruction and Lauro lifted a briefcase from the floor. He counted out the balance, all in crisp twenty pound notes. Before handing it over, he added another £500.

He said, 'Mario says thank you for the good job and excellent result. The little extra is for having been so very helpful.'

I thanked the men and Angela, shook hands all around and took my leave. The job was done. The bonus was fantastic, just in time for Christmas. And, to the best of my knowledge, that was the end of that.

As the new decade opened, and the inevitable bleakness of January took hold, I couldn't help thinking about that assignment. Usually I would present the report, collect payment and just move along. But, in the case of that Italian job, the circumstances had fired up my curiosity. What was I doing meeting the Finance Minister of the Republic of Seychelles? I couldn't help but ponder who had been pulling the strings and why. I couldn't help but wonder where the buck stopped.

I'd discovered that G Mario Ricci was a well-known Italian business tycoon. He had interests in numerous enterprises across Europe, the US and Africa, and at the very least had a sizable tea plantation in Seychelles. If he was the well-heeled main man in terms of sanctioning a little surveillance here and there, it made sense that I should let him know I was reachable. Cheekily enough, I'd sent a telex to his office wishing him and his wife a very Happy New Year. But I'd heard nothing back.

Then, in March, I did. Would I, a telex asked, be able to attend a meeting at Mario Ricci's office in Milan? Might I consider a discussion with my previous client? There was nothing to consider.

Off I went to Milan. Lauro met me at the airport outside the city and we walked briskly to a bright red, open-top Alfa Romeo. In the following hour he piloted that car along the beautiful roads of Lombardy and into the city like we were fugitives, as if traffic laws were for other people. My heart was pounding and hair restyled as we pulled up hard at a luxurious residential complex. Lauro led me to a ground floor apartment. Just as I got my breath back, I found myself stepping into the most extraordinary home. It was beautifully decorated and packed with a huge collection of the oddest curios. I saw sharks' jaws, tigers' heads, huge stuffed snakes. The place was like a natural history museum. The walls featured paintings and photographs of various animals, of huge reptiles, of the most striking of creatures which I wasn't even sure I could name. Mario and Angela appeared, hands were warmly shaken and cheeks casually kissed. I was introduced to their two daughters, five-year-old Mariangela, already speaking good English, and baby Rebecca.

A typically fine Italian lunch was served before we adjourned to a more formal boardroom in that enormous apartment. Before we went any further, it was made clear that Mario was a close personal friend of a chap called France-Albert René, the President of the Republic of Seychelles. Mario, via Angela, said he had been asked by René to find a suitable candidate for the role of National Security Advisor. I was told that Seychelles, while remaining a British Commonwealth country, had become a single party socialist state. René had seized power in an almost bloodless coup in 1977, one year after independence from the UK. The first elected president, and now deposed, had been a bloke by the name of Sir James Mancham. Mancham had founded the Seychelles Democratic Party, taken power in 1976 and appointed René as prime minister. While Mancham, viewed as a playboy with extravagant tastes, attended a Heads of Commonwealth meeting in London ambitious René had seized control. Mancham, of course, was one of the four I had been asked to surveill in London. One of the others I had been watching was Gérard Hoarau. He headed up an anti-Seychelles government organisation called MPR— Mouvement Pour La Résistance, and later a political wing known as the Seychellois National Movement (SNM). Its aim, Angela explained, was to overthrow René and reinstate Mancham. Hoarau had been jailed in Seychelles over his political stance and had since left to live with his parents in South Africa. The last of the four I had observed was Robert Frichot, a lawyer exiled from Seychelles by René's government. A co-founder of the MPR, Frichot had set up home in London.

Angela, listening carefully to Mario, turning it all into perfect English, said René's government had become convinced that securing a National Security Advisor was now imperative. She said Hoarau and Mancham had ramped up their plans to raise funds, destabilise the government and seize power in the former British colony. The country, made up of 115 small Indian Ocean islands, had historically been fought over by Britain and France until the Brits won and it formally became a full crown colony under the Treaty of Paris in 1814. Now it was being fought over again.

I was fascinated as it was explained that the MPR had been able to some extent to get France on board in terms of supporting their cause. Indeed, just a couple of years back in 1978, the French navy had sent a small gunboat with about fifty marines to Seychelles in what Paris had termed a 'courtesy visit.' They had sought to arrive at the capital, Victoria, on Mahé island, and dock at the port before doing what it was they planned to do. However, as they made their way, their radio transmissions were intercepted by a Russian fishing vessel in the Indian Ocean. And when I say fishing vessel, you should picture a Soviet navy ship in disguise. The Russians, who were well disposed to the path on which René was taking the Seychelles, established that the French courtesy visit was to be nothing of the sort. The marines were to take over the Police HQ in Victoria, arrest President René and hand back governance to Mancham.

As the Russians informed René, troops were airlifted from Soviet-backed Tanzania on the east African coast. It took them around five hours to arrive—and they were there in good time. As the French marines dropped anchor in Port Victoria, they realised a well-armed welcoming party was waiting. The crew were arrested and various French officials based in Seychelles were rounded up and booted out. The gunboat was seized and became the founding vessel for the Seychelles Navy (part of the SPDF—Seychelles People's Defence Force).

René's government, having made that bold and defiant step, went on to make another. It said this had been an illegal French incursion into British Commonwealth waters and requested that the UK assist. It wanted London, as was the case with a number of Commonwealth nations, to provide shared intelligence services to ensure this kind of thing did not happen again. However, London was not so keen. Seychelles, it said, was a one party, left wing state with no elections in sight and in the midst of flirting with Marxism. It would not be appropriate for Her Majesty's Government to lay on such resources. What it did do, however, was quietly slip René a list of private agencies and individuals that might be of use in terms of intelligence gathering. My name was on that list.

I sat for a moment, all eyes on me, as I absorbed the last of what had been said. I was calmness personified on the outside yet my brain was fizzling like a stick of dynamite. It seemed as if I really was being asked to act on behalf of a nation. It was the most extraordinary request I had ever received. I had many questions.

'So,' I said, clearing my throat, 'when you say National Security Advisor, what exactly do you mean?'

Mario, in serious tones, via Angela's serious tones, said, 'The MPR dissidents live in different parts of the world but London is effectively their base. What would be required is to gather intelligence as to their sources of finance and to learn with whom they enter into agreements. To monitor and photograph them. To find out who they talk with. To learn what we need to know in order to protect the Seychelles government and the country itself from invasions, attacks or dangerous internal dissent.' He said the job would be to find out 'anything helpful' to support the current regime.

I nodded, followed up with, 'Is the current regime legally recognised around the world?'

'Yes,' he said, explaining it's a legitimate British Commonwealth country with a legitimate, recognised government. He said President René has many detractors given he seized power, but his right to hold it was not disputed at government level. His coup d'etat had been a sudden but largely non-violent event, marred by the death of one policeman and one insurgent when shots were exchanged at a Victoria police station. He said all the major powers have Embassies, Consulates or High Commissions in Seychelles, that there is diplomatic and trade interaction between all.

I asked a few more questions but I was already satisfied, and more than a little thrilled, with what I had heard. There was nothing unethical here, nothing illegal. In fact I was being asked to take on what was a role familiar to almost all countries around the world. The USA has the CIA, the UK has MI6, and now Seychelles would have me. As I say, it was the most extraordinary request.

But I wasn't quite in the door just yet. I was invited to prepare a proposal. It would serve as the foundation for a mission statement and, potentially, a formal contract between myself and the government. It should note that I was to be responsible for the provision of external intelligence, reporting exclusively to the Ministry of Defence in Victoria. It would outline feasibilities, methodologies and budgets. I said I'd get right to it.

A variety of documents were passed to me, reading material for the way home, background to help me draft my blueprint. I left soon after, a little dizzy yet totally determined that I would seize this amazing opportunity with both hands. I knew I must absorb everything I could about this nation whose name, to that very day, had summoned up only images of a tropical paradise.

The files were practical, told me Seychelles was part of the continent of Africa, had a population of some 63,000, that the people were of mixed racial and cultural origins, spread over the islands. I read that until the sixteenth century the islands were uninhabited, but traders from Europe changed that as the nation became an invaluable stop-off point on long journeys across the Indian Ocean. French and English, I read, are both official minority languages in the country yet the most widely spoken tongue by far is French-based Seychellois Kreol. The papers talked of a mostly Catholic population, of farming, fishing, sweet potatoes, coconuts, cinnamon and various other spices. They talked of giant tortoises, endemic plants, of the jellyfish tree. I read about the rainforest, the weather, the music, the cuisine, tourism and government spending. I learned how atop one mountain near the capital sits a US Air Force space tracking station which had been watching the skies above since the early sixties. And the documents dived into the politics, into René's coup and the dozens and dozens of suspects believed to be plotting against his government. It took a week to get through it all.

I met with my solicitor David Barling in Brighton, asked if he would check if any legal or policy issues might impact on me signing a contract. He got back to say the Africa Desk at the Foreign and Commonwealth Office had considered the matter and had no concerns. He said they had told him it was they who recommended me and that they'd appreciate it if I kept them updated on any matters of interest. I was given the name of a contact in the department—WH Wenban-Smith.

I completed the proposal, signed an agreement and posted the lot to G Mario Ricci's Office in Milan. There was no reply. I feared for a time I might have overquoted, that perhaps I had blown it. My idea had been to keep things simple, to charge a daily management fee of £500 with expenses on top—international travel, sub-agent hire etc. It was a hefty enough sum at the time but had become comparable to what I could earn with a hard day's graft manning the agency. And my life would be all over the place, working to their different timezone, potentially flying off to any corner of the world to monitor any dissident at any point. I thought I had made a reasonable offer. I hoped so anyway. Fingers and toes were crossed.

THIRTY

Seychelles: Meeting the President (1980)

Two months passed and nothing. Then, early one Monday morning, a telex. I was making coffee, getting my head together. I tore off the paper, had a quick read. It wasn't entirely clear, but I was being asked to attend a meeting in south London to finalise arrangements. I sat down to read it again. It did seem as if I had landed the contract. But who, I wondered, was I to meet in Victoria? Why, I wondered, were they asking me to confirm early plans to travel somewhere within such easy reach?

One slug of coffee and it hit me.

'Bloody hell,' I gasped. It wasn't Victoria in the English capital but Victoria, the Seychelles capital.

Within a couple of weeks I was touching down just south of the equator, some 5,000 miles from home, about 1,000 miles off the east coast of Africa. I was met at the airport by the smiling Mario and his beaming daughter Mariangela. The smart little girl translated while her cheerful dad drove for about thirty minutes to Bel Ombre on the north coast.

The clock that chimes twice, Victoria, Seychelles

We went through the busy little capital, the administrative centre of the islands that make up Seychelles. We passed by the tiny Big Ben-style clock in the centre, the shining silver painted wrought iron tourist attraction erected in memory of the British queen whose name the city had carried since 1841. Mario, via his daughter, said the locals call it *Lorloz*, that it's a much loved timepiece, one that chimes twice. If you don't get to count the chimes the first time around, they told me, wait two minutes and trusty *Lorloz* will repeat it.

The unrushed people of the archipelago all around were smiling and chatting as we went, the aromas of Kreol cuisine being prepared for the day. We sailed up and over the hills beyond, cruised along the coast, the sands white like snow, the bright blues of the water, the lush greens of the tropics, all new colours for my jetlagged eyes. And on we went north into Bel Ombre, pulling up outside a hotel. Mario, via Mariangela, told me Residence Danzilles was owned by his group of companies, Gruppo GMR, and I would be made most welcome.

Staff showed me to a room with a balcony overlooking the ocean and I was hypnotised. I found myself watching palm trees swaying in the warm breath of the trade winds, heard myself thinking how I could fall in love with a place like this, asking myself if I was sure this was all real, if I was sure this wasn't some hugely elaborate long con to isolate me in paradise. Yet I was so lifted by the scenery and so exhausted from the flight that the details didn't matter. All I did was chuckle, enjoy a few moments of nature's boundless magic beneath the forever sunshine, lie down and slip into a nourishing sleep as the waves swished below.

I woke around four hours later, approaching midday. A receptionist rang, invited me to lunch in the hotel's restaurant. I showered and dressed for the weather before tucking into tropical fruits and spicy grilled fish. Not my usual fare but fresh, delicious and delightful.

A car picked me up and we returned to Victoria, driving through the big, elegant gates of State House. A winding road took us up towards a number of white, colonial-style buildings. We stopped outside the Ministry of Youth and Defence. Inside I was introduced to a youngish looking man sitting at a large desk smoking a cigar. He seemed very pleased to see me, stood up, shook my hand thoroughly.

'Ogilvy Berlouis,' he said, 'Minister of Defence and Youth.'

He was charming, warm, friendly, talked casually about Seychelles, about the quality of life there. Then the next leg, the short walk to State House, the president's large, two-storey portico-fronted offices. The entrance was around the back and guarded by two armed men wearing plain clothes. They searched my briefcase and patted me down. Inside, we took the stairs to the second floor and into a large reception area where a young lady sat at a desk with a bank of phones. Berlouis introduced me to Bernadette, the president's secretary. Mario and Angela arrived soon after and, a few minutes later, we were called in to meet France-Albert René, the president himself.

It seemed like everyone in Seychelles smiled so much of the time, and the man at the top was no different. He was forty-five, seemed cheery, easy-going and said he was very pleased to be finally meeting me.

'I have heard a lot about you,' he said, his hand shaking mine, inviting us all to sit.

The first thing he did was hand out some high-end cigars, an act that I'd learn was something of a trademark among Seychelles politicians. René, Berlouis, Mario and myself lit up and, in a few seconds, the president was saying he would take me fishing on my next visit, show me around, ensure I got to see the best of his beautiful home. I said that would be great.

His behaviour was perfectly decent, totally informal. And at the same time it was clear he was in charge. He had a strong voice, strong features and subtly dominated the proceedings through authoritative body language. He was, I observed, the most relaxed man in the room, in a room of largely relaxed people. It was something close to impressive. Yet his tone would change when staff came in to speak with him or do some duty. He would snap, fire out a couple of quick orders in Kreol and they would absolutely obey. I noticed too that Berlouis was extremely respectful towards René, that the pecking order was crystal clear.

We got onto the proposed contract. The conversation centred for a while around the reach that my work would require, that dissidents were to be found across the globe. The president talked confidently about it all, as if none of it really bothered him. He very much set the tone and pace of the discussion before turning to me, looking me in the eye.

'I am pleased with all of this,' he said, which I was happy to hear. 'So I welcome you to the *Overseas Intelligence Unit of the Ministry of Defence*.'

It was to be an agency of government which the president had very recently created. The new unit was to be headed by me as *National Security Advisor* and would be part of the *Seychelles Security Service*, the islands' internal intelligence unit under the command of Defence Minister Berlouis. The president initialled the contract draft, as did I, Berlouis and Mario. This meant it had been accepted in principle but the formal contract was not signed on that day. It was a minor matter. And, among all the cigar smoke, the conversation moved back to fishing, to life on the island, to advice about the best beaches, the best views, the best places to dine, to drink.

From there, the question of payments came up and how they would be made. I knew there were issues with foreign currency. Sterling was essential to enable other agencies to be paid around the world, yet hard currencies were often in short supply, the availability very much dependent on how many foreign tourists had been around. Mario, with Angela translating, said he would guarantee payment of bills and expenses in Europe, that his companies in Italy and Switzerland could more easily secure sterling.

After that, we were back to fishing, the climate, the locals, the music, the wonderful lifestyle of which the president was clearly very proud. We sat for around two hours chatting, drinking never-ending espresso, mixing business with pleasure in the most convivial high level meeting I'd ever had. Yet René had, in his own casual way, impressed upon me the importance of the work I was being asked to undertake, had made it clear that he loved his homeland and that he wanted to move ahead with his plans. He was a lawyer, an accomplished speaker, a charismatic leader who it seemed had earned the admiration of a majority of citizens. Yet, in terms of those who sought to campaign against or directly interrupt his journey, exile was to be expected. I had already known that René had a bold, brazen blueprint to create a kind of far flung socialist paradise, that from his small outpost he had caught the attention of Moscow, Washington, London and others. Indeed he was in a position to play one off the other, to secure funds via various agencies in exchange for promises of adjustments to his behaviour, and I suspected he was wily enough to be doing just that.

I left with Berlouis. He took me back to his office and opened the conversation about specifics. He handed me a list of immediate tasks. I was to locate and verify the current address and phones for various MPR members based in London. The names of interest, so far as I can recall, were James Mancham, Eddi Camille, David Joubert and some others who were encouraged to part ways with the islands following René's coup three years before. Berlouis said I should find them, surveill them, develop whatever information I could. Ideally, over time, I was to establish the identities of all those in the network, find out what they were planning to do, when they wanted to do it and uncover who was paying for it. I was also asked to work out ways to intercept anti-government propaganda which was being smuggled into Seychelles. And I was to carry out background checks on potential investors seeking to set up in business. And to background check journalists on working visits, to establish their agenda in terms of requests for interviews with politicians, officials or business people.

Berlouis said I should be aware too of ongoing low level, dissident incidents within Seychelles itself. Buses and bus depots had been sabotaged, sparking widespread complaints about the government's handling of an important facet of local life. One annoying little constant was to use a coin to rig a light bulb so when the bus station's old-style light switches were flicked, the fuses blew. It could take hours to find which light was doing the damage. In other cases, sugar and salt had been put into the fuel tanks of some buses. The saboteurs knew that once a bus was fully loaded and climbing one of the many hills of the islands, the mixture would filter rapidly through the mechanisms and the bus would come to a non-scheduled stop. People would have to walk, be late for work and the inevitable grumbles about the government would follow. In one worrying incident, a petrol bomb had been lobbed at a hotel popular with tourists. A blaze followed and damage was caused before staff took control. What flowed directly from that, as intended, was the suggestion

The Ricci family – circa 1985

that more attacks directed at tourist venues or even tourists themselves could follow. René wanted to nip it all in the bud.

After I left Berlouis, I changed and went for a barbecue with the Riccis at their home in Glacis, about twenty minutes along the coast from my hotel. Staff there kept the wine and beer flowing and served up fish and meat curries of a standard beyond anything I had ever had. I hadn't known that the Kreol cuisine of the Seychelles was so rich with unique island curry blends. For a fan of the more spicy menu like myself, it really was as if I had arrived in some kind of nirvana. I'd go so far to say India could learn a trick or two from the curry chefs of the Seychelles. Sorry, India.

Back at my hotel, I closed the day with a couple more Seybrew beers at the bar while tuned to the infectious rhythms of the Seychelles dance music—one lively style known as *Sega*, and its calmer cousin *Moutia*. I hit the hay around 2 am after an amazing day one in an amazing location, the comforting night sounds of the islands carrying me off to sleep.

In the morning, as the sun came to enrich once more, I was collected and driven across the Sans Souci mountain range. We passed by a tea and coffee plantation owned by one of the Ricci's local companies. Beyond the hills, I met with Mario and his family once more, ate well at a beach barbeque and dived into the warm, turquoise ocean. I lunched on grilled fish, tropical fruits and chicken curry before heading back to the hotel for a well-deserved afternoon siesta. That evening I was collected, driven to the airport and took to the skies with a smile on my face that was going nowhere fast.

Picture the scene, if you will, the following day as I recounted all of the above to Phyl. I told her, with perhaps a few tears of joy in my eyes, that I had been to the most truly beautiful place. She was astonished at how easily it had all unfolded, at the fulsome generosity of those I had met, at the idea that I had confirmed my status as the National Security Advisor for Seychelles. I could barely believe it either.

But now, with the sweet memory of those bewitching two days fresh in my mind, I had to get to work. I hadn't been brought over because they wanted to do me a good turn. No. They had shown me the very best of themselves in the spirit of the deal we had made. And now I had to return the favour.

THIRTY-ONE

Seychelles: Uncovering a Coup (1980)

AT first it was relatively straightforward. I did as Berlouis asked and began looking for the addresses of the men who had been singled out. I launched into the research of journalists with an interest in Seychelles and began looking at the issue of the propaganda making its way onto the islands in an MPR newspaper.

A further request followed as I was getting stuck in, and it was perhaps more unexpected. I was to provide intelligence training facilities to Seychelles military, police and intelligence officers. The aim, Berlouis explained, was to develop strategies to better ensure the country knew of any upcoming attack.

As I began producing the results required, I got to learn some more about the finer detail of what was going on. My targets located, myself and a number of agents were beginning to tune into their conversations to get an idea of their plans. There was no particular mystery as to how we were doing most of that. Merely being in close proximity to the plotters was often enough to get a good sense of what was going on. They seemed remarkably comfortable to speak, perhaps naively assuming that because they were beyond the borders of the islands their conversations were beyond reach.

We were able to firm up, simply by being in the right place at the right time, one important fact. MPR leaders Gérard Hoarau and James Mancham had gone some distance in terms of arranging for the services of a mercenary force. They had already opened communications with an apparently aggressive unit which had previous experience at mounting a coup d'état. Their plan was at a relatively advanced stage, way beyond what Berlouis and René might have expected. We were playing a very high stakes game of catch up.

We moved ourselves closer to our targets, agents tuned into their conversations by human ear and electronic bug. Their funding source, an investment of around £1M, was via Saudi Arabian Oil and arms billionaire Adnan Khashoggi. He was a close pal of former President Mancham and had invested in Mahé after independence. Along with Mancham, he had drawn up by now shelved plans to turn its beautiful north coast Beau Vallon Bay into a Vegas-style strip laden with casinos. Personally speaking, it was an endlessly vile idea which would have destroyed the natural beauty and surroundings of one of the most breathtaking beaches in the tropics. It seemed the guy wanted to fund a coup so, at least in part, he could get some casinos in return.

Lots of agents were employed from my own agency and others to keep tabs on all that was going on among the London exiles. It wasn't a round-the-clock operation by any means as the more we learned, the more agile and precise we became in terms of picking our moments to tune in. At first, I kept myself to some extent physically distant from the intel gathering, not wanting to become a known face among the men I was tasked with watching. But as the weeks passed, I began to play a more regular role in all of this. There were social events and other doings in London which I knew would be useful to attend and it was important for me to personally get a sense of everything. Very often Gérard Hoarau would be there. I got to know his face and voice and style and character quite well. Inevitably, he got to know something of mine.

Hoarau had trained as a priest in Rome before, fluent in Italian, returning to his homeland. He decided against a life in the church and began a career as a civil servant where he became a significant figure in advancing tourism. He was charged with arranging Seychelles' 1976 independence celebrations and, with the backing of President James Mancham, went on to be promoted to a key post in Foreign Affairs aged just twenty-five. Beyond all that, he was a top flight footballer, captain of the Seychelles national team and coached in the local league. Perhaps ironically, he was also a relation-in-law to President René, a nephew of his wife Geva. In 1977, Hoarau had been at the Commonwealth Heads of Government meeting with then President Mancham when René launched his coup and seized control. After getting to know Hoarau, even as an observer, it seemed to me that the intellect, passion and energy that made him the man he was had turned exclusively towards ousting René in any way he could. And that is precisely what was going on when I first analysed his conversations.

Day by day, we filled in the picture. It was clear this was no pie-in-the-sky insurrection plot. The coup was to be led by former British army Major 'Mad' Mike Hoare, a redoubtable South Africa-based gun-for-hire who had spearheaded campaigns in the Congo in the sixties. He was a fervent anti-communist with global contacts, including in the USA, and had been the inspiration behind the 1978 mercenary adventure flick *The Wild Geese*. We came to know that Irish-born Hoare despised René's regime and, despite many believing he was planning to retire, was keen to get involved. Among his band of around fifty ex-South African and Rhodesian special forces and former Congo mercenaries was South African conflict veteran Colonel Jerry Puren, another formidable operator who had the experience and reputation which chimed with that of Hoare's.

We kept working. We were onto something of paramount importance and there was no room to bugger it up. Piecing together scraps of intel furnished by various agents, we came to know that the dissidents were not only close to finalising their plans, but also fiercely confident they would succeed. Not only had they secured significant funding and recruited that experienced mission leader, they also had backing right from the heart of the South African government. Suffice to say it wasn't a fan of left wing societies sprouting up in its part of the world. Those of us looking to a future for President René were facing one hell of a challenge. Our details were not perfect, but they were enough to put the Seychelles on the highest state of alert.

But there was a hold up in the plans—a funding problem. Sir James Mancham had not received the finances he needed to pay the mercenaries. It seemed they had asked for everything to be prepaid. Given everything had been moving fast, I welcomed the idea of decent delay.

I liaised with Berlouis constantly from the UK. We talked over hiring an ex-British army expert who knew a thing or two about dealing with armed factions. The man had years of service in Northern Ireland under his belt and knew exactly the sort of weak points the enemy was looking for. He jetted over to Seychelles and examined the ports and airports before drawing up recommendations to boost defence capabilities. We did not know if we were facing an initial assault by air or sea. Based upon his advice, the port area in Victoria was fitted with a more powerful radar system. Changes were suggested for the locations of military posts and weapon arsenals. And he recommended we install discreet x-ray equipment at the inbound baggage hall in Seychelles International Airport. He advised all arriving checked luggage be x-rayed and any suspicious luggage to be marked with chalk. When a passenger reclaimed a chalked bag, the Customs team would request a search. And another x-ray machine was cited at the post office to identify any incoming arms, detonators or any other suspicious materials.

Further advice on the airport centred on the runway. Discarded military vehicles should be parked at the far end and an anti-aircraft gun should be installed nearby. In the event of an emergency, the old vehicles were to be moved out to block the runway. Airborne enemy reinforcements would be unable to land.

And, as part of the overall counter strategy, I needed to work with the Seychelles Security Service to identify residents in Seychelles who were involved in anti-government activities. They could be useful links for the mercenary force and may also be assisting in those ongoing and escalating attacks which were threatening to hit the country's economy.

The MPR was also behind the importation of anti-government newsletters which not just backed actions against tourist hotels, but gave a guide on how to make petrol bombs. They came into the country from London, packed into the cases of people acting as tourists. We were also able to establish that, later on, members of Air Seychelles cabin crew were a link in the chain, bringing in the newsletters on the weekly flight from Gatwick. Once in the islands, it was quickly disseminated.

As we created something close to a 3D intelligence picture across the summer and into the autumn of 1980, I did what the British Foreign and Commonwealth Office had asked of me and kept in touch. But before reporting to Wenban-Smith at the Africa Desk, I cleared it with President René. He had no issue. I would advise my FCO contact of what I was doing, who we were interested in and why. It was good in a way to get his blessing, and indirectly the blessing of the UK, as I outlined my methods and plans and the dangers we faced. Our connection was good, with enormous potential for being extremely beneficial to both parties. Friends in high places, and all that. Indeed, as things developed, the FCO advised me from time to time. Wenban-Smith even asked me on occasion to influence the Seychelles government in one or other particular direction and, at my discretion, I did so.

My agents in London managed to establish excellent and consistent intelligence. They infiltrated the exiles, made their way into the conversations they were having and filled in the vital blanks. They established in time that the money which had put everything on hold had been signed off and that the mercenaries were to get paid in advance. Their mission, we learned, was all ready to go. It was scheduled for November, 1980.

Conversations were taking place almost daily between the London dissidents and their military contacts in South Africa.

Sixty-three-year-old Hoare's team of mercenaries were planning to send an advance group, acting as tourists, to Seychelles. The group would link up with MPR supporters. They would act as back-up for the key military strike force when it moved in. And between all the arrivals, the weapons would be smuggled in via passenger luggage. The main attack unit would arrive on a private flight after everything else was in place. They were to land in Victoria, acquire vehicles and fan out in small teams to seize the critical points—the radio station, the airport and the presidential State House itself. The entire government would be isolated, ordered out of power, told to wait. Once they had effective control, Mancham and his new team would jet in from Nairobi, a squad of Kenyan soldiers on board. The Mancham team had been working with controversial Kenyan government minister Charles Njonjo who had given his full backing to the coup. And, when Mancham was back on Seychelles soil, it would be broadcast to the country that he was president once again.

November came. We were fully braced for attack. But we knew whatever they were going to throw at us, it was not going to land as they had hoped. Our intel had hamstrung the plotters before they even knew it. It had removed from them that great military advantage—surprise. We were in possession of their plan, of their identities and we knew they were coming. The police were ready, the defence forces on full alert, the airport poised to identify and see off any arriving usurper. And when the London-based dissidents began changing their habits and melting away into the ether, it made clear to us they were moving to the next step.

The Republic of Seychelles got into position.

THIRTY-TWO

Seychelles: Foiling a Coup (1981)

NOTHING happened.

I was braced every day in November for a call, rushing to the telex each time I heard it come alive. Yet paradise remained uninvaded. Had we got something wrong?

The month closed and, slowly but surely, the dissidents began returning to their old haunts in London and elsewhere. We got back to work, hugely curious as to what we would hear next. As ever, they had plenty to talk about among themselves and, as ever, they had plenty to (indirectly) tell us. We had been right, but there had been an eleventh hour problem with the funding. On the cusp of the coup, Mad Mike still had not secured the full amount and pulled the plug. The MPR attack had been shelved until he got his money. But this was, the dissidents said, nothing more than a setback, albeit a little embarrassing. Word came through that the invasion would instead take place at the end of 1981, one year away.

On the islands themselves, few were any the wiser. Life continued on much as normal. Berlouis stood down the SPDF from intensive duties until the next time. We were confident we remained on top of things with new systems in place and a continuing firm grip of the intelligence picture on and off the islands. And we remained ready to respond.

Sure enough, almost a year to the day later, the postponed invasion finally got the green light. It was Wednesday, November 25, 1981. A scheduled Swazi Air flight from South Africa touched down in Victoria. On board were forty-five mercenaries, some in the guise of a visiting rugby team and the rest pretending to be members of a charitable drinking club called *Ye Ancient Order of Froth-Blowers*. In reality they were all on a mission to take over an isolated nation—they called it *Operation Angela*.

Unfortunately for them, they never got much further than the airport. Thanks to the advice of our ex-British army military advisor, their bags—laden with bulky toys ostensibly for orphaned children—were put through the x-ray machines and trained staff knew what to look for. If they had got through, the idea was for the men to scatter around Mahé, pretend they were generously delivering the toys and launch into action as René held a cabinet meeting a few days later. It didn't go to plan at all. That said, most weapons did get through. Expertly-designed false bottoms had effectively concealed rifles in quite a number of cases. But not in all. As one suspicious item with a chalk mark was collected by one of the final group, Customs officers approached and an AK-47 was discovered. In a blinding panic, the man pulled the loaded weapon from the case and legged it. He fired a shot as he dashed towards the bus which had already been boarded by some colleagues. Weapons were drawn and Seychelles police and military moved in. A six hour gun battle began, the local forces pinning down the invasion force and ensuring the bus could not leave the airport.

The mercenaries held the runway for a time, opening fire on an armoured vehicle which approached. Its commander, Lieutenant David Antat, was killed. They took the control tower, directed an arriving Air India plane to land despite the armoured trucks on the runway, and hijacked it. They refueled and demanded the Boeing 707 be flown to South Africa. On arrival at Durban it was impounded. Mad Mike and his hijackers were arrested, tried and jailed for air piracy. One mercenary had been killed in the shoot out and two were wounded.

At the height of the action, I had been taking dozens of calls—most of them from Minister Berlouis at the Ministry of Defence. They needed to know how many mercenaries had arrived and how many had departed. They wanted confirmation of the locations of the MPR leaders—Mancham, Hoarau, Camille, Chow and others in the London group. My contacts in South Africa, those I knew from my work with the country a decade before, came up with the goods. They passed me the passenger manifest, all the names of the men who had flown to Seychelles from South African soil. And, balancing that with the hijacked Air India plane arriving in Pretoria, we knew exactly who and how many were still at large on the islands. I'm just not the sort of guy to ever lose a useful phone number.

Six mercenaries were held in Seychelles and later tried for treason. All were sentenced to death under an old British law which, though struck from the books in the UK, remained in force in the former Crown territory. I was asked by the FCO to do what I could to influence President René in the direction of commuting such dire penalties to life sentences. The UK did not want a British Commonwealth country executing anybody, and certainly not in the glare of publicity.

I asked for a private meeting with René. I said how I knew feelings were running high, that the mission had caused the death of Lieutenant David Antat and people were angry. But, I asked, was he sure he wanted to execute all the captives? René listened closely, drew on his cigar then assured me there was no way he would execute anyone. He also said he was a man of 'the church,' which was news to me. Anyway, the mercenaries would not be executed, he confirmed, but they would spend some time thinking they would be. That was good enough.

In the aftermath of the whole affair, a pre-recorded tape surfaced in which James Mancham could be heard announcing he was taking power in Seychelles once more having rescued it from René.

Numerous books and reports have since told the story of *Operation Angela*, the damp-squib coup that went so embarrassingly wrong for the MPR, for Hoarau and Hoare. Much of the material bolsters that which we had already known.

What remains unclear is what the US might have known about it all, given we had reason to believe the CIA was interested in anonymously nudging René out of the way. There is an island called Diego Garcia, around 1,200 miles from Seychelles, which serves as a very strategic American air base. In the midst of the Cold War, its proximity to René's socialist state can't have been comfortable for Uncle Sam's new man in the White House, Ronald Reagan. What had played out in Seychelles on that day could have been much worse, yet it was still, I am sure, part of a wider international power game. It's just that no one really wanted to become officially involved, to get their hands dirty and become shackled to a coup in the Commonwealth of potentially huge global significance.

Yet the involvement of South Africa cannot be disputed. The assault on Seychelles took place with the knowledge and tacit approval of its government, to put it lightly. A UN investigation into the whole thing would say as much. And indeed, a year after the event Hoarau and Mancham told MPR supporters that Pretoria had endorsed the whole thing both to oust René and protect landing rights for South African Airlines at Victoria.

And, as if that wasn't enough, in October 1985, René asked me to fly to South Africa to meet the Minister of the Interior there. The objective, he said, was to agree a compensation payment from that government to Seychelles as a result of the damage to Seychelles International Airport sustained during the failed coup. The negotiations had been going on for a while and on-the-quiet as direct talks breached the Organisation of African Unity's anti-apartheid sanctions. I was happy to do so but since signing up to work with Seychelles, I had been served a 'Banning Notice' meaning I was not a welcome man in South Africa. I called up my old contact Major Craig Williamson at BOSS who cleared my path. At a later meeting in Pretoria, I accepted the offer of US$1,000,000 as full and final settlement of any further claims for reparations.

Yet what had happened in 1981 was not the end of the attempted coups. An urgent call from Berlouis in August 1983 advised me that the island's own defence forces had launched a coup of their own. It was taking place right at that moment. He said to immediately enhance surveillance of MPR dissidents, suspecting they might be involved and be coordinating things from London. Was there any sign of them heading for Seychelles with the aim, as ever, of reinstating their man?

My agents were on the case. They got themselves to the right places, asked the right questions. But nothing had changed. It was pretty clear that the MPR's key players knew nothing of the mutiny. We soon learned that this was a sudden, stand-alone attempt by some disenchanted SPDF troops. They were being led by Sergeant George Nicholes who issued a statement saying a coup was underway and that he was the President-in-waiting. There was violent action as a number of hostages were taken by his men. He threatened much worse if President René didn't stand down. Nicholes seized the radio station and issued a statement picked up by global media calling on the MPR to support his action.

The MPR heard his calls for back up. But they were unprepared and, as we had suspected, had known nothing of the event. And their power-base was too far away to be of any help. Besides, they had their own idea of who should be the next president. What happened instead was that sitting President René sanctioned a call-out for support to Tanzanian troops stationed at the time on Mahé. They didn't mess around. They tore into the renegade Seychelles soldiers, put down the rebellion and took back the radio station inside three days.

Regardless of the facts, the MPR, still licking its wounds from the failed coup of 1981, launched a cynical bid to gain credence by saying it had played a part. It had become desperate.

Eight people were killed and twenty-two injured in that mutiny. A terrible and most unnecessary waste of life.

THIRTY-THREE

Seychelles: Placing a Mole, Foiling Another Coup (1983)

THROUGHOUT the coming months and years, I'm proud to say my agents shadowed the Seychelles dissidents with the highest quality tradecraft. We never let up because the plotters had no plans to quit either. They were constantly discussing fresh ideas for a coup d'etat and seemed compelled to have another go. And wherever they were, there was always a good chance of picking up intel. The key figures of Hoarau, Eddie Camille and Paul Chow had evidently never heard the useful old wartime saying *Loose Lips Sink Ships*. We weren't about to tell them.

The relationships between my guys and their guys only grew. Agents became friends, posed as supporters, donated small sums to the cause. They worked their way into meetings, penetrated right to the heart of the MPR conversation.

One agent became particularly friendly with Hoarau, telling him he had been a mercenary in his past life. Naturally the MPR chief was interested. The agent

Barry Trigwell (Jim O'Boyle)
– murdered in Birmingham

went by the name of Jim O'Boyle, said he was an Irish citizen and had a valid Irish passport to prove it. In reality his name was Barry Trigwell, my old cellmate from the hellhole prison in Argentina. Barry was a most talented operator who had been based at my Brighton office for years. In the greatest traditions of a brilliant double agent, he won Hoarau's confidence to a remarkable extent. When the time was right, we agreed he would ask the MPR leader to send him to Seychelles on something of a recce, as well as to help rally and organise the ill-disciplined and uninspired support base there. Hoarau allowed himself to be persuaded that it was a great idea. Trigwell, aka O'Boyle, set off with bundles of MPR leaflets and newsletters in his luggage. A secret meeting followed with Berlouis and President René. From there Trigwell went onto build a network of MPR-supporting contacts who would meet, often at barbecues on Mahé and also on the island of Praslin, to discuss the latest regime change plans. Every word was fed back.

As National Security Advisor, I knew Trigwell's placement was a fantastic strike. His work enabled the military and police to pinpoint caches of explosives and weapons across the islands. I felt it was important that those who had plans to use such materials should not be arrested but instead discreetly watched and used to expand the overall intelligence picture. Berlouis agreed and in the period that followed the value of the information just kept on climbing. But we were never complacent.

Meanwhile, in terms of the MPR in London, the intel kept on coming. We were learning, towards the end of 1983, that Hoarau and his colleagues were growing ever more restless. They wanted a breakthrough, were anxious that René had settled into his role and that they were on the backfoot. Another attempt at taking power was in the early planning stages. Once again Mancham was organising the funds and once again mercenaries from South Africa were being recruited. Security was tightened in Seychelles, luggage scans were intensified and document checks enhanced.

Defence Minister Berlouis called one morning. A lone South African tourist had arrived. He was relatively young, fit and with a military bearing. The intelligence team on the ground went to work. They filmed as he travelled around photographing various military and government installations in Victoria. Berlouis was minded to have him arrested or certainly pulled in before he left the archipelago, but I felt otherwise. We had the suspect's departure details and could trail him from the moment he arrived back in Johannesburg. With some effort, I managed to ensure he left unhindered.

I sent Ken Williamson, a fine London-based agent, off to South Africa. I asked him to ensure I got daily updates not just in terms of keeping me up to speed with any developments, but also to prove he was okay. We had no idea what might be ahead. Ken hooked up with Paul Armussen, a South African sub-agent who had been sent images of the mystery man. Both agents watched as our suspect was picked up at Jan Smuts International Airport by two fit looking men. They followed the trio to an isolated military-style compound about an hour beyond the city. The place was surrounded by security wire, had fearsome guard dogs chained inside and the only road around ended at its gates.

The agents backed off, parked in a clearing around half a mile away and worked out the logistics. They crept back through the bushy terrain and, with binoculars and zoom lenses, managed to get a view inside from higher ground. There were a dozen or more men staying there, all military-looking types. Over a number of days, they filmed the mercenaries using a cardboard cut-out of a helicopter, clearly war-gaming an attack. They feigned jumping from this mock chopper, automatic weapons in hands. They would then charge towards a large wooden structure before opening fire at human-shaped cardboard silhouettes. The information we were picking up in London only confirmed what we were seeing in the photographs and film. The mercenaries had arranged to get themselves a small cruise ship and modify it with a helipad. It was to head, ostensibly as a tourist vessel, towards Mahé. An assault was to be launched from a helicopter.

President René and his ministerial team at the Assembly and State House had little doubt what they were seeing. They were sure the helicopter would be landing right at the country's parliament and the cardboard figures, they believed, were themselves. There was every suggestion he and his cabinet could be cut down by gunfire outside the building. When we matched up all the raw intel, the picture cleared yet further. The attack was to take place at the State Opening Ceremony of the Assembly. It was no secret that the entire top rank of government, the president included, would be posing outside on the steps for photographs.

The good news was that we were on top of the issue from early on. The bad news was that one day Ken didn't check in. After a couple of hours, I called his hotel. They were snappy about it, citing guest privacy. I wasn't having that. I demanded to speak to the manager, told him I had been the one who booked and paid for the stay. He rolled over and told me what I really had not wanted to hear. Ken had been spotted near the compound, watched by police for a while and then arrested. He had been brought back to the hotel, had his room searched and the last he saw of him was him being led away in handcuffs. I knew it could only be that they had picked up Paul Armussen too. At first hearing, the whole thing stank. South Africa, at a high level, had shown its interest in toppling René in the previous coup. It felt like this might be happening again. Were its police working in tandem with the mercenaries?

I called Wenban-Smith at the FCO. He assured me he would see to it that Ken Williamson was properly represented. A couple of days passed and I heard nothing. Two men were missing. I was really starting to worry. What else could I do? Should I reach out to my contacts there, spill the beans about running an operation on their turf? Was this latest planned coup d'état something they were involved with? It was a bloody mess, but the wellbeing of my agents had to take priority. I bit the bullet, put in a call to Major Craig Williamson. I came clean, told of my agent (and his namesake) and sub-agent working in his backyard and pressed the need for some information. It wasn't good. He told me South African Security Police had arrested the entire bunch—those inside the training camp as well as the two men observing outside. I put my case very diplomatically and, I'm glad to say, the pressure on both my men was very much reduced. My suspicions that the South African government had been linked with the planned assault on Seychelles were unfounded.

Ken Williamson was ultimately deported from South Africa. He was met by a wall of journalists in London working on a story about a 'Seychelles Spy' foiling another coup. It had ended messily, but we had been successful. The coup was foiled. What was being planned had shown every sign of being a bloody affair.

But, although rumbled and beaten again, the MPR remained determined.

THIRTY-FOUR

Seychelles: Lies Told in Room 412 (1982)

I COULD only guess how many hours I spent flying back and forth over the equator in the first years of the eighties. Calls would come early in the morning, in the middle of dinner, in the middle of the night asking me to get to Seychelles fast. In the scenarios where the intel team on the islands had picked up on something awry in their line of sight, there would be no time to waste. Such matters were potentially existential developments for the government there, of critical importance to the people I had come to know. The issues faced by the regime of President France-Albert René could barely be overstated. I've said before that I found most Seychellois to be easy-going, laid back souls. Yet, make no mistake, among those I knew, the commitment to their vision for their country was rock solid.

As with any client, I didn't want to let them down. When the calls came, I acted accordingly. It was what I had signed up for. I could be off at something close to a moment's notice three or four times a month, slamming the brakes on everything else in my life. My travel bag was always packed, the flexibility to travel 5,000 miles at the ring of a phone inbuilt into everything I was doing.

The flights were not always easy to arrange. In some cases I would have to get myself to one European city or another to connect with one airline or another to get myself Seychelles bound. One journey, late in the September of 1982, saw me fly from Gatwick to Frankfurt to snatch the only seat left on the last available flight to Victoria. I boarded that Somali Airlines 707 in Germany for the long haul south, a stopover of several hours lined up at Mogadishu, Somalia. It was an older, weary-looking plane, packed to the gills and I did my best to sleep. I thought of the meeting that lay ahead, of how significant or otherwise it might be, of getting whatever it was resolved. And, as I always did on those journeys, I looked forward to the moment of arrival, to stepping out of the stale, steel tube and into the sunshine, to feeling the fresh, clean Seychelles breeze on my skin, of pulling it into my lungs.

After twelve hours we touched down in Mogadishu. The captain urged us to disembark saying those onward bound for Mahé could stretch our legs. We were led to the departure lounge but there wasn't much to be said for the place. It was hot, humid, packed, stuffy, noisy. I found a seat, closed my eyes once more and pictured my destination, thought of the Kreol dishes I might soon be enjoying, wondered if I would get a chance to get some fine sand between my toes. As the song says…

'I'm going back to the Seychelles,
'Where the Clock Chimes Twice,
'I'm going back to the Seychelles,
'Isles of Paradise.'

An airport official with a loud hailer arrived in the middle of our restless group. He announced, with a lot of apologies, that we were going nowhere. The Somali president, he explained, had an urgent trip to make. His office was commandeering the aircraft. We would, he said, be put up in a hotel overnight. The plane would be back in the morning. Sorry, sorry etc.

It was frustrating. I was a mere 800 miles or so from Seychelles. That plan for a curry on the coast was fading fast. Yet I had some relief in knowing I would at least, to some extent, have my own space and perhaps be able to get out and about a city I didn't know at all. I'm not going to say that Mogadishu in the eighties was an ideal tourist destination, but it was certainly more interesting than its airport. However I couldn't get my mind off the fact that I needed to be in the Seychelles as soon as possible. I suppose I felt that the pace of my journey was letting down my client. But nothing could be done.

I rose at 5 am, was bussed back to the airport, boarded with no problem and, with all kinds of relief, set off for my most beloved of workplaces. Security staff were at the steps as I disembarked at SEZ, Seychelles

International. I was ushered through the VIP building, offered fruit juice and coffee while my passport was stamped. The government car whisked me through the tiny capital and past the clock. We drove the mountainous road, heading north towards Bel Ombre and this time to its luxurious Fisherman's Cove Hotel. I was left to freshen up, change into the bush shirt and shorts I liked to wear on the islands, before the car swooped back to speed me to Victoria and through the imposing gates of the State House complex. I was delivered directly to Ogilvy Berlouis' office at the Ministry of Defence.

The welcome was typically warm, the espressos typically strong and the conversation had that familiar balance of convivial and constructive. There had been odd developments, he said, involving a strange, emerging connection between Mario Ricci and Gérard Hoarau. It had reached the point that President Rene, Mario and himself had hatched a plan to hoodwink Hoarau into believing Mario might switch allegiances to the MPR.

This was a startling development and, I was told, something that had been brewing for a while. I knew of rumour already knocking around on what the islanders called *Radyo Bambou*, or *Radio Bamboo*—the local grapevine. Gossipers had been saying the government was planning to acquire some of Mario's properties and tea plantation company on Mahé. Mario knew this was all nonsense, the president had made it clear it was all nonsense—but such was the resilience of this fake news that Mario had decided to have a bit of fun with it. He had invested a great deal in Seychelles, was a close friend to the president and he began to dwell on the idea that dissidents were thinking he was being shafted. Indeed, such was his playfulness, he had already made a number of friendly phone calls to Italian-speaking Hoarau at his home in South Africa to discuss matters of business and politics. Hoarau, I was told, had been nibbling at the bait. He had wondered if Mario might meet him and some others in London, if he might want to spend a while mulling things over. Hoarau said he was planning to spend a week or so in the English capital as he had some business to attend to. Mario said he too enjoyed the occasional visit to London and he could arrange a hotel. The men had agreed that Angela and Lauro would accompany Mario, and that Edi Camille, Paul Chow and Sir James Mancham would come along with Hoarau.

My clients were, it's true, surprised at how well Mario's sub rosa plot had worked so far. It came, co-incidentally, at a time when Hoarau had been informed by the South Africans that his residence status was not going to be renewed, that his presence was now considered *contrary to the public interest*. That decision came after his well-publicised role in the attempted coup two years before. The whole thing had been an embarrassment to South Africa. Hoarau, re-energised, recommitted and thinking ahead, had mentioned to Mario that he would be applying to live in the UK. That was enough to suggest high level meetings with the MPR were inevitable in the times ahead.

Fired on espresso and intrigue and with night drawing in, Berlouis and I left his office. Over spicy grilled parrotfish in town, he said he wanted to involve me at this point. We agreed that, in the guise of a booking agent, I would find a suitable top-class hotel in central London, one with a secure meeting room, and that I would gain access to where Hoarau would stay before his arrival. I was to bug the room to ensure all conversations and telephone calls were captured. The Cognac flowed as we talked it over, played out the risks and rewards as best we could. Berlouis was particularly excited.

After dinner, exhausted and a little drunk, I crashed hard. The next day I was gone again, more double digit hours in the sky, this time on Air France, bound for Paris, onwards to London.

The venue would be the five-star Carlton Towers Hotel, near Sloane Square, where I had first met my new employers. It prided itself on its confidentiality and security and, from the MPR perspective, should hit the spot. Mario gave the location the thumbs up and off we went with *Operation Carlton Towers*.

The meeting was set for three weeks ahead. I used *Reliant Business Services*, the Jersey commercial investigations agency I'd bought out that year, to do the deal with the Carlton Towers. A secretary reserved a conference room and two luxury suites—one for Mario and Angela, one for Lauro—for seven days. On the same group booking, we included two separate single rooms, next to each other, also for seven days. Then a separate booking specifying a single room one floor directly above the two single bedrooms. Again, for seven days.

Arrival day was Sunday, October 17. I pitched up early with an agent and a secretary from our London office and checked in for all the rooms. Now in possession of the keys, I sent the sub-contracted electronics team to the single rooms to be occupied by Hoarau and Paul Chow. They installed a bug on the telephones and two separate transmitters in each— one of each pair to serve as back-up just in case. Receivers and recorders were installed in the single room above. The closest proximity helps secure the cleanest reception.

I arranged then for a transmitter to be installed in the conference room, its frequency matched to a receiver in Lauro's suite. The Ricci team, if required, would be able to leave the conference from time to time and listen in to what Hoarau's team were saying in their absence. It was an old trick I'd picked up in Hong Kong. We tested everything. All was well. We were ready to go.

My company secretary dressed in a smart dark two-piece suit, just like that worn by hotel staff. We borrowed a gold coloured *Welcome Team* badge saying it would be handy in terms of greeting those attending our conference. Lauro, already on the way with Mario and Angela, called with news that Hoarau was en route from Heathrow and would arrive within the hour. A final check of the rooms to ensure no debris had been left, that the towels were perfect, the bedsheets smooth. We placed a bunch of flowers and a fruit bowl in each room as part of our welcome.

Mario, Angela and Lauro arrived and got themselves out of sight. Our fake hotel employee got into position and waited. Minutes later, Hoarau and Paul Chow entered, cases in hand. She moved in, welcomed them to the hotel and presented them with the room keys. There was no need now for them to go to reception. Hoarau seemed delighted with the treatment which he believed was courtesy of his new friend Mario Ricci. He and Chow were happy to be escorted to rooms 412 and 414. As for me, I was on the fifth floor, directly above, ears pinned back.

Importantly, it wasn't just me and my agents who were tuned in to what followed, but also my old friend Barrie Penrose of *Sunday Times* fame. As we had closed in on *Operation Carlton Towers*, President René had expressed a mix of concern and excitement. His key concern was that, however it played out, it was possible that very negative press could follow if his people were seen to be entrapping Hoarau. Given the attempted coups and the mutiny, there had been quite enough headlines and he was fearful of the damage to both Seychelles' reputation and tourism. As such, we had given Barrie access to what we were doing and allowed him to set up a recording station of his own, via his own newspaper. Whatever followed, he could serve as an authoritative and independent voice. He would have a window on what took place when MPR activists gathered in secret and would be much more easily believed than people like Defence Minister Ogilvy Berlouis. In effect, Barrie Penrose was an insurance policy.

Across the following week, as expected, Sir James Mancham, Edi Camille and others visited with Chow and Hoarau. We recorded many phone calls both in Kreol and English and sometimes both. Among the more alarming interceptions was a conversation between Hoarau and Chow on the transportation of explosive detonators. We learned they were to be sent as cargo on a British Airways flight from Heathrow to Mahé. Mario wanted to bring in the police but instead I asked Penrose firstly to confirm the information and then, as a *Sunday Times* journalist, alert the cops. My fear was that if an alert came from me, it could compromise our ongoing operation at the hotel. The next BA flight out was grounded and searched yet nothing was found. We later learned we were too late. The explosives had been on board a plane the day before.

Across the week, the MPR were very pleased with themselves. They were hugely buoyed by the idea of meeting the Ricci camp and each evening talked excitedly of a plan coming together to finally overthrow René's government. In fact, they were in such a tizzy it felt at times as if they were losing the plot. They revealed they were developing plans for the CIA to bankroll their next run at a coup d'etat, that they had as many as 300 mercenaries to do the deed. And, as part of their general strategy, they were badgering Mancham about bringing his acquaintance actress Brigitte Bardot on board as a contributor to the cause. And they talked easily of chilling plans to set up 'hit squads' to eliminate fellow Seychelles exiles who refused to cooperate with the MPR's idea of the way forward.

On Wednesday, October 20, 1982, we sat listening to live conversation from Hoarau's room between himself, Sir James Mancham, Paul

Chow and one Bernard Verlaque. The subject was a meeting earlier in the conference room with Mario Ricci. The phone rang in the room and Hoarau answered. He spoke for a moment in Kreol, then fell silent. What he had heard had shocked him.

'What's wrong? What is it?'

Mancham and Chow were both asking it. The tone in Hoarau's voice had changed. He had become upset, was briefly unable to voice the news. He put the phone down.

'My God,' he said. 'Two of our people have been killed.'

Complete silence in the room.

And then, Mancham, 'What? How? Who has been killed?'

'Mike was demonstrating priming a bomb. It exploded and they've both been killed.'

Confusion, anguish.

'What? No. Who? Who?'

By now we were also in shock, looking at each other as the dramatic conversation played out just a few feet below.

Hoarau, extremely upset, said, 'Simon Denousse and Mike Asher are both dead.'

He put a call into Mario, told him what had taken place in Seychelles. They spoke for a while and Mario seemed to calm him down. After that, he spoke again with his colleagues in the room. He said Asher was a South African mercenary bombmaker, a man he had brought in to train the MPR in constructing the deadly devices.

The men, distressed but working their way through it, talked everything over. Chow said the MPR should issue a press release to take maximum advantage of this tragedy. His idea went down well. He and Hoarau began drafting their lines. When the form of words had been agreed, Chow began making calls to the press saying—

"South African Mike Asher and Seychellois Simon Denousse had been murdered by Alert Rene's Security Police after having been arrested, tortured and then taken to a deserted beach where they were killed, and their bodies put into their car which had then been destroyed by a bomb."

I said at the time and I say again now that it was a shameful state-ment. It was absolute rubbish and, perhaps worse, massively disrespectful in terms of the two men who had only just died. Their bid to twist the truth to gain instant political capital from tragedy was straight from the cold, cruel playbook of terrorist organisations the world over.

As Chow was spinning his tale to newspapers, a loud knock on the room door. Hoarau opened. It was Barrie Penrose. He too had been tuned in. We were a little shocked. He launched into a series of blunt ques-tions about the deaths in Seychelles. Hoarau was dumbfounded. Former President Mancham excused himself, pushed past, said he had another appointment.

Penrose's team had called in the Metropolitan Police who arrived soon after to raid the MPR's rooms. I advised Mario that this could get messy, that the police would be looking for the bugs, and would likely find mate-rial with his name on it. He and Angela wisely took themselves shopping. In the end, the police never did seek to interview them.

In the meantime, my team packed up what we could and quietly made our way out. Heading through the lobby, I spotted Sir James Man-cham being interviewed by police. Nearby sat Barrie Penrose and others from *The Sunday Times*. I nodded at Barrie and Barrie nodded at me.

On October 24, 1982, *The Sunday Times* ran a front-page report demolishing the MPR's lie. It said South African Mike Asher and Sey-chellois Simon Denousse died when a suspected type of plastic explosives they were handling went off accidentally. The paper said, in a feature inside, that it had uncovered a plot to stage a coup.

Quoting from the recordings, it said bombs would 'destablise' the Seychelles administration before a 300-strong mercenary force would 'confront the regime directly.'

It went on to say that scores of MPR propaganda leaflets along with two grenades, an assault rifle of a type not used by the Seychelles military and an empty magazine were found near the wreckage of the vehicle in which the two men had been preparing the explosives.

Mario took the tapes home where they were later played on *Radio Seychelles* in a series of one hour programmes. It was via their own words that the true character of the MPR was fully exposed to its own people. Listeners heard Hoarau and Chow plead with Mancham, known for his flamboyant lifestyle while president, to ask his friends for money to finance the coup.

Hoarau asks, 'How about your friend Brigitte Bardot? Assure your friends that their money will be well spent!' And they heard all the plotters talk of seeking CIA funding by trying to prove that René was pro-Soviet and pro-Libyan.

The MPR's support base, financial and otherwise, took a critical hit.

Not long after I was urgently called to the islands once more. I grabbed my bag and set off on the first leg of that familiar journey, Belfast to London. Arrival at any British airport from anywhere in Ireland was closely monitored at the time given the ongoing IRA threat. Yet I'd never had a problem before and was typically just nodded through. But on this occasion something changed. I was approached that morning by two men as I made my way to the check-in desk for Seychelles. They identified themselves as Special Branch officers from the Metropolitan Police.

'Ian Withers?' I was asked.

'Yes,' I said.

They arrested me on the spot under the Prevention of Terrorism Act. They did not allow me to use a phone and advised me that I would be held incommunicado. I was cuffed, led to an unmarked people carrier and guided into the back. I was joined by the stony-faced cops among windows so heavily blacked-out I couldn't see where we were going. When we arrived, I recognised enough to know I was in Paddington Green, west London, at the HQ of what was then called the Anti-Terrorist Branch, or SO13. Inside, while all my property, including reports and bills for the Seychelles Minister of Defence, was examined, I was locked up. They left me alone overnight and into the next day before I was taken for interview. It was all about the Carlton Towers Hotel and specifically about what had taken place in room 412. I declined to answer any questions and insisted I be allowed to speak with my solicitor. After about an hour I was taken back to the cell and locked up again. And, after a while, they came to get me once more and the same thing happened.

After being served with what you might call a light lunch, I was advised I could call my solicitor, David Barling. I'd been in there for over twenty-four hours by that point. Barling said to sit tight and that he would have someone there fast. He would be sending a brief called Nick Perkins, a partner in his firm. And, he added, he would contact Wenban-Smith at the FCO. I was relieved. From there, while waiting for someone to show up, I gave a little ground. I confirmed my address and that I was contracted to the Seychelles government as a security advisor. They pressed me on the events at the Carlton Towers but I said I'd be saying nothing until I had legal representation. And, returned to the cell, I waited. As night fell, no solicitor had arrived. I bedded down once more.

The next morning I was advised that solicitor Nick Perkins was in the building. Indeed, as I would learn, he had been in the building the day before too but had been refused access to me. He was not happy. We sat together in the interview room as he said, under the circumstances, I should be allowed to leave immediately without answering anything else. The most senior police officer there said that was about to happen. He had received a request from the FCO that I be released immediately with no further action. My journey to Seychelles continued.

In the early 2000s I was at a PI conference when I met one of my Paddington Green interrogators, a man who had since retired from the force. We spoke about my arrest on that occasion and he was candid about it all. The questions I was due to face had been crafted by people above his head, he said. The objective had been to get me to admit that I had bugged the hotel. As before, I told him nothing.

THIRTY-FIVE

Seychelles: God's Banker, Bodyguarding and Eavesdropping in Edgware (1983-85)

THE damage caused to the MPR through the exposure of its own lies and brutal fantasies was never going to be fatal. But it did slash its fanbase down to a hardcore of Hoarau's most loyal.

As well as forever flying up and down to Seychelles in the early eighties, I flew elsewhere too. Seychellois exiles, as well as expats minded to endorse the MPR, could be found in small groups across the world. I had, as often as not, a good understanding of what they were up to. I made frequent trips to Australia, South Africa, Mauritius and right across Europe to update that insight. Indeed my office at *Maryland Investigations Inc* became an ideal base from which to monitor Hoarau when, as serendipity would have it, he began making frequent trips to Maryland and Virginia to visit a knot of die-hard dissidents there who wanted to hear his message. Yet London remained by far the busiest location, effectively the ground zero of resistance to René's government, the place where the decision takers dwelled.

Supporters would at times visit the islands themselves too, flying in from all over the world to touch base with friends or family. Very often they were tasked by the MPR with photographing military bases, police stations and other facilities to keep their intelligence picture as live as possible. My job was to be one step ahead of them or, often quite literally, one step behind. It was always important where possible to work out who was funding their trips. And there were also times when we were just plain suspicious of people for one reason or another.

Surveillance in Seychelles – 1985, Sunday Times

Towards the end of 1983, Berlouis asked me to urgently investigate and monitor a businessman who had just touched down in Seychelles. The new arrival was seeking a meeting with the president and other ministers about a joint, two-pronged venture. His key aim, he said, was to invest in a tuna processing project. But he also wanted to secure licenses for oil exploration in Seychelles waters as part of the deal.

I needed to fly over. Ahead of that, I gathered what details I could. He had a Panamanian passport naming him as Francesco Donato. On his arrival card, filled in ahead of landing, he said he was Italian. His address was given as a suite at 30 Rockefeller Plaza, New York. He was booked to stay at the Vista Del Mar Hotel in Glacis, a district of Mahé.

Two days later, with the help of a member of security staff, I was in his room. I installed a simple thirteen-amp adapter plug with a built-in transmitter and ensured it was working. I took a quick look through his luggage and photographed various documents on the table in the room. A couple of days later, I was back in London.

The documents I'd snapped revealed Donato used the alias of Pazienza. He had connections to a Sicily-based aerial photography company operated by an Alvaro Giardili. We established that Giardili was connected to Roberto Calvi, a senior Vatican banker who had been found hanged from Blackfriars Bridge in London in 1982. His pockets stuffed with rocks and cash, he had been the chairman of the Banco Ambrosiano which collapsed in one of Italy's most significant political scandals. Around $3M had vanished from the bank. How the man known as *God's Banker* met his death was by no means clear. But he didn't do it himself.

I engaged my US partner Terry McGill, asked him to research this mysterious Italian from his end. He found out he was a wanted man in his own country. The Americans had been asked by the Italians to keep an eye on him in New York pending extradition proceedings. On December 19, 1984, I advised Berlouis that our man was a fraud suspect in relation to the Banco Ambrosia case.

Back in Seychelles, the mystery man was making interesting calls to the USA. One was to a business associate in New York. We arranged for the associate to receive a carefully pretexted call in which he confirmed a chap by the name of Pazienza was living in a rented apartment at 420 East 80th Street, New York. That address had two unlisted phone numbers, both in the name of Frank D'Anato, very similar to the Panama passport name Francesco Donato.

On the strength of what we had gathered, Seychelles wisely turned down his proposal. He checked out of his hotel and, according to his itinerary, set off for Panama. I advised Terry McGill who set up loose surveillance on the address we had traced in New York. In early January 1985, Pazienza re-appeared at that apartment. The NYPD Extradition Unit was informed and he was arrested.

A few weeks later at one of our regular round-table meetings in Seychelles we discussed the latest intelligence picture. We got to talking over Pazienza's investment plan. It was possible he had a real interest in tuna processing or searching for oil. It was also possible he just wanted somewhere to secure himself with government consent in the hope he would not be extradited. Yet sources in the US did point to something we had not considered. Pazienza, in his time, had been a senior official in Italian military intelligence and a senior participant in the P2, or *Propaganda Due*. It was a highly secretive right wing Masonic Lodge of which former Italian Prime Minister Silvio Burlesconi had been a member. It shut down, it's said, in 1981. While with P2, Pazienza had been able to exert the right pressure and secure the rescue of a top US diplomat kidnapped by the Italian terrorist group known as the Red Brigade. The CIA were forever grateful for his work, apparently handing him the right of residence in America and that Panamanian passport as a reward. The passport was in the anglicised version of his mother's maiden name, D'Anato. Yet it seemed Pazienza had become tangled up in providing support for a Turkish right-wing extremist Mehmet Ali Ağca—the same chap who tried to murder Pope John Paul ll in Rome in 1981. The shooter would later claim Pazienza, who had his fingers in all sorts of dirty pies, was his contact. It was a murky business and fortunately our involvement was limited.

However we couldn't help but piece it together as best we could. We ultimately established that Pazienza was in London at the very same time Roberto Calvi was hanged from the bridge. Berlouis instructed me to pass all that information to the City of London Police who were probing the Calvi murder. Pazienza was extradited from the US in 1986 and, in 1993, was convicted for his part in the Banco Ambrosiano scandal. The point is, my job wasn't all about people seeking to overthrow the government. It also allowed me to assist in terms of quality control when it came to who was and who was not allowed to do business in Seychelles.

In December 1984, with our focus on the MPR, we spent some time filtering raw intel from around the world into a single picture, as we often did. There had been an upsurge in low-level but hugely damaging activity including two calls to the *Manchester Evening News.* The caller had claimed bombs had been placed on state-owned Air Seychelles planes. The aircraft had to make emergency landings and the government had to pay for everyone to stay at hotels. The whole business led to long, costly delays. I did manage to get a tape of one of the calls and identify a likely suspect in the UK, but nothing came of it.

But it was during this time that we began picking up on something worse, something in which the desired aim was somehow sharper, clearer, crueller. Hoarau and the MPR were discussing a plan to have a hitman assassinate the president. Also to die, they had decided, would be Minister of Finance James Mitchel and their influential hate figure Mario Ricci—a man the press had dubbed *eminence grise* and who locals liked to jokingly call the *vice president*. Once again I was clocking up the air miles.

On arrival I was taken straight to the President's private office. Berlouis and Mitchel were already there. Hands were shook and out came the cigar box and espressos. I presented the latest reports from London together with our analysis. We discussed the information and compared it with the very latest findings from the Seychelles Security Service, much of that intel from our undercover agent Jim O'Boyle (Barry Trigwell) who had surrendered to living full time on the islands. One picture complimented the other. The information was matching up. We went on to consider that most pressing point—an assassin, posing as a tourist, might already be in Seychelles.

The president at that time had a private group of heavily armed bodyguards led by a Belgian ex-mercenary. He said he was confident no one could get to him. Ogilvy Berlouis joined in to say he too was happy with his security detail from within the SPDF, even though there were questions about the loyalty of some others in its ranks. But what about the Ricci family? Mario was not a state employee. And to provide SPDF in any case would involve some intense vetting given the full range of circumstances. The president asked me to get involved. I was to arrange for someone to handle the family's protection right away. And what of Finance Minister Michel? Might it not be easier, swifter, less complicated to have me look into his security too? Personal responsibility had been put into my hands. I assured René I would take care of everything.

I got in touch with one of my many nephews, Billy Clarke, an ex-police officer from Northern Ireland. He had left the RUC after a close shave with an IRA bomb which killed his colleague. He had worked for my agency in Belfast, at one point managing it, and went on to lead intel-gathering in London. He was solid, reliable, sharp and could handle a problem or two. I asked if he wouldn't mind spending a while in Seychelles. He didn't mind at all.

The issue with the MPR, it was clear, was that it was not going to magically fade away. Its coup attempts could be hamstrung and its propaganda countered, yet our intelligence revealed over and over that the nucleus of its support base remained firm. Our thinking had to be not just that the president, Mario, Michel and others were in danger, but also that the danger they faced was there to stay. At this point, after all their failures, it felt as if the MPR were desperate for a scalp. I would need to get used to the idea that I'd be spending a lot more time in Seychelles.

My licence and training to carry a concealed weapon, secured in the USA, would prove useful. Berlouis arranged for me to be issued with a .357 Smith & Wesson revolver which I wore in a waist holster, hidden by the bush shirts I'd typically wear at the time. Across much of 1984 Billy, also kitted out with a handgun, and I were on security detail. We very often escorted the children of both Minister Michel and Mario Ricci to and from their schools and ferried the families to and from various events. On hundreds of occasions we slept at their homes. There was a very real possibility that an experienced hitman could move in at any time, anywhere, and I spent those days in a state of readiness, ready to do whatever it took, handgun at my side. For a time, my sleeping became shallow, more a case of power down than power off. I would wake in the night at the tiniest sound, be fully engaged with my environment all through the day. The duty of guarding parents with young children is a heavy one. The duty of guarding young children, heavier still.

As our senses heightened, so too did those of our colleagues. I remember, early in February 1985, taking a call from Berlouis. Internal security had identified two suspicious tourists. Both men had arrived alone, one booked for a two week stay, the other for three weeks. Single tourists were an unusual thing in a destination marketed as a hotspot for lavish honeymoons and young families. We had no specific information, but we were in no position to take chances. The men were identified, tracked and checked out in terms of what risk they might present right until the day they departed. Neither turned out to be a hitman or dodgy in any way. And neither ever knew they had been under suspicion.

But the intel was still saying that Hoarau in London and his friends wanted to do something. Had they shelved their plan to send a hired gun to Seychelles? We didn't know for sure. We would get a sense even from the tone and tempo of their meetings, their conversations, their travel plans, that something new was in the offing. Our bases were covered but, as I told Berlouis at the Ministry of Defence, it was inevitable that there would be gaps.

In March, 1985, Berlouis took the bold decision to plug those gaps. He asked if I would be able to set-up a permanent telephone monitoring facility in London? Would it be possible, he said, to record every single telephone conversation taken and made by Gérard Hoarau? And all those by Eddie Camille too? And two other individuals he named as well? He said, given all the signs were these guys were not letting up on their plans, that the scale of such an operation had become commensurate with the risk. At the time I was living in the Ricci home in Barbarons. I wouldn't be able to personally carry out the assignment from there, but I knew a man who could.

Bill Underwood had assisted me with a string of jobs in London. His background was rich in intelligence work for both the US and UK security services. He ran a company which specialised in tapping telephones, bugging vehicles, properties—you name it. His surprising client list included those who perhaps might not have wanted to get their hands dirty. His work had taken him deep into business and political worlds. I knew his discretion and professionalism were beyond question. I linked Bill up with Berlouis and they made their own deal.

Bill and his team did what they were asked to do, wiring up junction boxes to intercept calls. In a short time Bill was complaining that he was bogged down with the sheer number of recording hours he was dealing with. The four targets were all talkers, all chatting away daily on the phone to each other as well to dozens more friends and contacts. They spoke for the most part in Kreol and it was clear only a native speaker would be able to extract the raw intel detail. Such material can easily remain undetected by those who don't have an instinctive understanding of the words, the pace, the tone. The tapes would need to be flown to Victoria. I was tasked to arrange, via my courier company in Brighton, a weekly collection and dispatch via Air Seychelles freight handling agents at Gatwick.

But the issue of the sheer quantity of the work rose up again and again. Bill and his team were covering four addresses in a relatively small area of Edgware, north London. They were parking up in cars and vans, tuning into the frequency coming from each property and recording from the vehicles. There were times when they simply couldn't get parking close enough to secure a clear signal. And given they didn't want to miss a single word, it was a problem. Bill called me in Seychelles one morning to say he had a solution—as long as the government agreed to it. There was a house for sale, he said. It was close to all the properties in question. Given this was a long term operation, might it be worth me trying to persuade Berlouis to make an investment in a monitoring station? It seemed outlandish, but I gave it a go.

To my surprise Berlouis, on behalf of the government of Seychelles, agreed. He said I should go ahead and arrange it.

As usual, I wanted to tread carefully. My name had been published many times in connection with the security of Seychelles and other high-profile cases. It seemed smart to keep it off the books in terms of buying a house along the road from the MPR. Identifying myself as John Douglas, I agreed a price with the estate agent and used my company in Jersey, *Reliant Business Services Ltd*, to buy the house. I'd owned RBS since 1982, a commercial investigations agency I purchased from a competitor as part of my own business expansion. The Seychelles government transmitted about £55,000 to *Reliant Business Services'* account in Jersey and I transferred that to the vendors for the cash purchase of the property. During all of that, I put a call in to my contact Wenban-Smith at the FCO, just to let him know broadly that the Seychelles government had invested in a house as part of its ongoing intelligence work in London.

But it would turn out not to be a long term investment. Within a year, I had sold the house on the orders of René's government. What lay ahead, in the winter of 1985, changed everything.

THIRTY-SIX

Seychelles: The Assassination of Gérard Hoarau (1985)

A DAMP, overcast morning, the chill of an English December in the air. Gérard Hoarau left his lodgings in Edgware, northwest London, to visit his doctor for a flu shot. He was just thirty-four, yet it was something he did annually. The appointment had been arranged almost a year in advance.

He attended, received his jab and returned to the home of the La Porte family, his accommodation since his right to remain in South Africa had been revoked. As he approached the front door, loud cracks rang out from across Greencourt Avenue. His killer had opened fire from a garden opposite. It is said that an automatic weapon was used, that dozens of bullets were aimed right at him. Eight struck his chest and arm. Hoarau fell to the ground. Emergency services raced to the scene. The victim was alive yet unconscious. Medics fought hard to bring him back from the brink. They could not be certain at first that the injuries were fatal, but in the end they could not save him.

Police began seeking witnesses to this broad daylight murder on a residential street. Had anybody seen the gunman? Was anyone able to offer a description? They asked for information all day, knocked every door. One elderly lady said she had heard what she thought was a car backfiring. She told how she saw a man wearing a longish overcoat walking from where the backfiring appeared to be. In a statement she said he was 'swarthy skinned with a Mediterranean appearance, about five feet eight inches tall'. It was the only description they had and was circulated immediately.

The victim's status as a political activist led to the swift involvement of the Anti-Terrorist Branch of the Metropolitan Police. They searched inside and outside Hoarau's address. The detailed examination included checking the telephone wires leading into the property from a nearby telegraph poll. It was there that they discovered an unusual electronic device. They were quickly able to ascertain it was being used to intercept all calls into and from the La Porte household. And, quickly again, they established it transmitted the calls to a receiver which they knew must be nearby. After some investigation, they established two things. One was the address of the property which I had purchased on behalf of the Seychelles government—the operating base for the recording of the four dissidents. The second was, after tracing the transmitter's signature details, they worked out where the device had been sold from and to whom.

One week after the shooting, police arrested David Coughlan, an ex-BT Engineer. He disclosed he was working with two other men on an assignment for the Seychelles government. In due course, the police arrested Bill Underwood and a third team member. All three, the police said, were 'under arrest on suspicion of the murder of Gérard Hoarau.'

Around the same time, after becoming aware that I was the contracted national security consultant to the Seychelles, the police raided my home in Co Antrim and my offices in Brighton and Belfast. They arrested my secretaries and removed them to the operational HQ of the Anti-Terrorist Branch in Paddington Green. In what the search warrant said was a quest to find one or more weapons, they went through everything I owned. They broke cupboards apart, pulled up the floors and dug holes in my garden. They were ambitious in suspecting that, during one of the most intensely policed eras of Northern Ireland's Troubles, I had been willing and able to bring an automatic weapon from London to Belfast. And the idea that I would do so before burying it in my back garden has always seemed fanciful to me. But they did what they were duty bound to do. As for my secretaries, well they were held incommunicado for six days under the Prevention of Terrorism Act before being released without any charges. I'm sure that wasn't at all necessary, but nothing could be done.

I was not at home at the time of the raids. I had arrived in Seychelles on the day before the murder having spent most of the year there without my wife. I had been home since September, catching up with Phyl, with a mountain of mail and taking part in a Security Industry Convention in

Belfast. I had a stand at the event to showcase some of my products and services, something I had booked months before.

Police inquiries confirmed Gérard Hoarau's telephone had been compromised for some time. They knew tapes were being collected each Wednesday by courier for dispatch to Seychelles. I was the owner of the Brighton-based courier service involved. Each Friday those tapes were being placed as cargo onto an Air Seychelles flight from Gatwick and collected at the other end by a government official.

Before I outline events in my life on that day, and the days and years that followed, I want to say something about Gérard Hoarau. You won't expect me to say he was any kind of a friend, yet he had become something of a fixture in my life. While I actively opposed what he was doing, I never found myself disliking him on any personal level. In his own way, he was a character, the furtive mouse to my observant cat, and on those occasions when we eyeballed it was as if each of us had some understanding of the other. On one occasion, we co-incidentally checked into the same Paris hotel while I was tracking him at a weekend event. He had spotted me over breakfast. I watched as, sitting with another man, he looked up and saw me eating toast. He looked away, then followed up with a classic double take. He nodded and I nodded back.

Some time later, in an MPR magazine, he would say, *'Wherever I was, Withers was there. I was driving down the motorway in London and looked out the window. And Withers was in the car next to me. I was in Paris at a meeting, and I looked across, and there was Withers having breakfast in the hotel.'*

He came to know my role as I had come to know his. Despite those quite sickening dreams he harboured of having my clients and friends executed, I had a measure of respect for his commitment, some respect too for the charisma which brought people to his side to engage with the wildest of ideas. In many ways he was not a natural revolutionary and not at all any kind of a gifted plotter. But he was a friend to many and, in a fashion all of his own, a decent man.

The manner of his murder was as ruthless and as public as it could be. It was so far beyond the character of anything I was ever involved with that I have always known from instinct, from experience, from the inside of the security apparatus for which I worked, that it was not connected to the people I knew. Our vigilance had proved remarkably proficient and was knocking down every post Hoarau put up as a result of good old fashioned intelligence gathering. Indeed, that ongoing operation to record his every word said on the phone advanced our position to the point that the idea of wanting to blow everything out of the water by gunning him down was ludicrous. No such thing was ever sanctioned against anybody on my watch. And the idea that such a thing would be given the all-clear from the top, by some of the few people who already knew our electronics were in place at his home, just does not stand up to any kind of scrutiny at all.

It has been said before that Horeau owed money to a number of very serious men in South Africa and was, by order of its own government, not going back there. He had more dealings with cash-hungry mercenaries of all kinds of mindsets than anyone I ever came across. It might make more sense that someone with a grudge to enact, as opposed to the security and reputation of a nation to protect, would involve themselves in such an obscene, damaging and visible act.

And likewise, as I would learn, a US link to the murder should not be ruled it. It was no secret that America had an interest in not just toppling René but in maintaining full control of its strategically invaluable mountain top space tracking station on Mahé. The killing took place, after all, during the closing days of the Cold War, a time when American might and pride was on show like never before via NASA's space shuttle missions. Indeed Soviet Russia had shown an interest in damaging the Seychelles station, four degrees south of the equator, and it's said it used laser beams to try to interrupt communications between it and a key satellite.

Such dramatic global level thinking may seem far-fetched at first glance but it was certainly entertained by the Met's counter-terror police. In 2018 they would confirm to me that a single fingerprint in the Edgware property was evidence of there having been a CIA presence there. But we'll get to that later.

In the week before the murder of Gérard Hoarau, Defence Minister Ogilvy Berlouis had been on a trade mission to the USA and I was preparing to fly back to Mahé. Phyl was coming with me. I had promised her a break on those *Isles of Paradise*. She had heard me sing Seychelles' praises often enough that it really was time for her to see it all for herself.

We had left from Belfast on Monday, November 25, for two nights in London. Berlouis, fresh in from the USA, was arriving in town around the same time and we had arranged in advance to meet the following afternoon at a hotel in west London. On the evening we arrived, Phyl and I enjoyed a rare dinner together in London. And on the following day, Tuesday, November 26, we met Berlouis for a late lunch at the hotel. He'd had a busy week of talks and negotiations in America and had much to discuss. He told me he had negotiated the initial soft lease of a Boeing 757, which would ultimately become Air Seychelles' first large aeroplane. And he'd also arranged some matters around securing more university places for Seychellois, some military training and some financial assistance too.

Most significantly, he had renegotiated and renewed the contract for the rental of the aforementioned space tracking station in Seychelles which the US government considered of vital importance to its overall space programme. He was full of beans and thrilled at bagging what he called 'prizes' for his country. He said he would be spending a few days at his base in London and was then looking forward to getting home.

He asked about a request assigned to me the previous week. I had arranged for our London agents to observe an event at the Seychelles High Commission over the weekend of November 23 and 24. The MPR had been planning to hold some demonstrations. His office wanted photographs of all those at the protest. I told him the job had been done. That kind of thing was something close to routine in my world at the time. The images, including pictures of Gérard Hoarau and Paul Chow, had been delivered to me at the hotel just before the meeting. I passed the package to Berlouis. After that, we went our separate ways.

On the morning of Wednesday, November 27, Phyl and I checked out and made our way to Heathrow. We flew Business Class on Kenya Airways to Nairobi before connecting with the Thursday flight from Nairobi to Seychelles. Our nephew Billy, still on bodyguard duties, met us at the airport on arrival. He drove us to the Barbarons Beach Hotel and I took Phyl to watch the sun set, to enjoy the cool evening breeze as night closed in, certain it would cast a spell on her as it did on me. We were going to have a couple of weeks to ourselves and I knew there was nowhere better to be.

After a lazy, slow start on Friday, November 29, Phyl couldn't resist getting onto the paper white sands on the beach right next to us. She got to work worshipping the sun and wandering around while I, more used to those idyllic island days, caught up with work. I had planned for a quick debrief with Billy, a rundown of what had been going on since we last spoke. And I'd asked deep cover agent Barry Trigwell, aka Jim O'Boyle, to join us at my hotel if he could safely do so. It was constantly vital that he was never seen in my company.

The three of us had coffee and juice in my room as they filled me in with the latest chatter, rumour and developments that informed the direction of our work. I wanted to get up to speed fairly quickly given I'd be meeting Berlouis again when he arrived back at the weekend. The plan was for the minister and I to go through a few matters ahead of an upcoming meeting with South African VIPs. My BOSS contact Major Craig Williamson, his wife and a government minister were due in for informal talks following the settlement of the compensation agreement for the mercenary damage to the airport.

After lunch, at about 3 pm, as the three of us continued chatting in my room, a phone call. It was Brian Lewis, ex-CID with Sussex Police and the franchisee of my Brighton office. He sounded upset, even shocked. There were news flashes, he said. TV and radio. All the reports were that Gérard Hoarau had been shot dead that morning in London.

I went faint. I had to sit on the bed. My mind was racing. I told Billy and Barry, barely believing what I had heard. I remember being confused. Phyl came back to the room soon after and I recall the distress on her face as I told her. I did what I could to collect myself, knowing I had to make an urgent call to President René. I was put straight through and told him the news. His voice was typically calm, but I could pick up on a difference from the outset. He said he already knew, that the British High Commission had just informed him. He asked me to come to his office immediately. Before I left, Phyl spelled out something important. She said I could find myself being dragged into a murder investigation.

I was at State House by 4 pm. Bernadette took me into an ongoing meeting in the president's office. The commissioner of police was there, some State House staff, some agents of the Seychelles People's Defence Force too. Everyone was shocked. René looked pale, appeared weaker than I had ever seen him before. It was obvious he was upset. Hoarau might have been his enemy, but he was also a former associate, a relation-in-law and a fellow high-profile Seychellois.

The objective of the meeting, I was told, was to anticipate what lay ahead when the people of Seychelles learned the news and to hammer out ways to respond. Would there be outrage? If so, where would it be directed? Could this brazen daylight killing hit tourism in the year ahead? Could it lead to ill-informed international condemnation? We all talked for a time, listened to each other. There was no doubt we all knew where the finger of blame would point. Yet, despite the workmanlike character of what took place in that hour, at no time did the shockwave dissipate from the room. Something no one could have imagined happening had happened and it would take a while to adjust to the news. Questions about who did the deed and why were secondary to what was on the stated agenda, yet they were of course at the front of everyone's mind. No relief of any kind was taken from a gruesome public execution that no one in that room would have wanted.

I called the British High Commission. I said I needed to put on record that I was in Seychelles at the time of the killing. And I called David Barling at Weekes, Legg & Dean. He contacted the Metropolitan Police to advise that if I could assist in the investigation, I was willing to do so. Having agreed it with René, I let them know they were welcome to come to Seychelles, at Seychelles' expense, to interview anyone and everyone they liked. They were told that no one would hinder their investigation in any way. But the Met didn't seem interested. They were more keen to dig my garden and question my secretaries.

The arrest of Bill Underwood and the other two on his team was big stuff in the British media. It was of course leaked in advance, which in my experience was something close to standard when it came to the Met. Then, in a truly explosive development, they were charged with murder. That stunned me. And when the trial opened at the Old Bailey, I was stunned some more. The prosecution withdrew the murder charges. A plea arrangement had been struck. The men, it emerged, had removed a bug targeting Hoarau after the shooting and therefore interfered with the police investigation. They would admit obstructing the police but with the caveat they were acting in the full knowledge and tacit approval of the UK Foreign and Commonwealth Office, which I had personally made aware of the property purchase.

The FCO's interest in events in Seychelles, the court was told, was that the UK wanted to minimise Soviet influence there to ensure the USSR didn't get a foothold on the Indian Ocean. In a statement an FCO witness told the court hearing, *'It is not the policy of HM Government to confirm or deny any involvement.'*

The three agents received short jail sentences. Via my solicitors, René's government paid their legal bills given they were employees at the time.

The Met's next move? As far as I could tell, not much. There had been major media interest in developments so far, yet a good deal of it was about the arrests and what followed. It was as if the murder and murderer of Hoarau slipped from their radar. In fact, it very much seems to be the case that it remained off the radar for thirty-three years.

My next move? I was on the horns of a dilemma. I could go back to the UK, get back to work in Belfast where I employed some thirty people and owned various companies and properties. After all, my two younger sons were at boarding school in Northern Ireland. But what would living in Belfast be like for me now? Would I be arrested, come under intense scrutiny, would it all be damaging to my business? Would I be held for a week under the Prevention of Terrorism Act the minute I set foot in the UK?

Yet if I stayed in Seychelles, I could ride out the aftermath and controversy around the murder. Beyond the deal I had for payment via Mario's firm, René's government at that point owed me a lot of money, something like £200,000 from debts I had settled worldwide with various agencies over many months. Yet the government had been struggling to give me foreign currency. So it was possible too that I could stay put, gather that money up, reshape things back home as best I could in the meantime.

Over the next few days I met with Ogilvy Berlouis and President René. They advised I should stay on, at least for Christmas. There was a chance that the Met might be making quiet progress with the case. If they were to identify and arrest the real murderer, it would take the heat not just from me, but off the entire Seychelles government. René had, very plainly, been accused of sanctioning the murder in myriad claims in myriad news reports.

I took their advice about the festive period. My children flew over from Northern Ireland and we all spent a rather unusual tropical family Christmas at the Coral Strand Hotel, courtesy of the Seychelles Ministry of Defence. Very sadly, just after Christmas, Phyl's dad passed away. She and the children returned to Belfast for the funeral.

Back in Brighton, my solicitor David Barling continued seeking to establish if the Met had any interest in me. Did they want me for interview? If so, where? When? But no answer came back. That silence spoke volumes. I became convinced that if I went home they'd nab me. The press would report my incarceration, I'd be directly linked with a murder, my reputation would take a dive and my business would be hit hard. I can't say I felt thrilled about setting all that in motion.

Everything had changed. The murder of Gérard Hoarau did not just devastate his loved ones and outrage those who supported his beliefs. From my perspective, it had a hugely negative impact on everyone I knew in Seychelles, on everything I had achieved in my life, on everything I hoped to do in the years ahead. I was left having to decide exactly when I should fly home to feed the machine that I was sure would chew me up.

THIRTY-SEVEN

Seychelles: Life and Death Threats on the Isles of Paradise (1986-91)

THE cigar box came out once more at the office of President France-Albert René. He was very concerned that the reputation of his beloved country would not recover. It was January, 1986, a time when people were planning their annual breaks, when Seychelles was seeking to be front and centre as a world class tourist destination. But it was as if every mention of those *Isles of Paradise* was tied tightly to the suggestion that its government was behind a bloody and brutal daylight killing in a world capital city. René's demeanour had lost some of its strength, his character lost some of its force.

I needed to make sure I did the right thing by myself and my family. I was certain my name and my business were already damaged. It was one thing to bounce back from previous overblown negative press coverage around various work-related issues, but quite another to reemerge amid whispers I was linked to a murder. Even that old *no such thing as bad publicity* adage had a limit. I told Renè that, as with him, I didn't know what the future held either. What I did know was that I needed my money.

I asked, 'When can you pay me?'

It annoyed him. He was curt, sharp.

'There is very little foreign currency,' he said, more dismissive of me than ever before.

'Well what are the options?' I asked.

'You can get part paid in rupees.'

That was not acceptable. It was just too complicated, time consuming and expensive to convert up to £200,000 worth of rupees. In terms of maintaining my business in the UK, I needed hard currency. Sterling was best but any European currency would be an option. Yet help from Mario in that department was dwindling. He'd spent Christmas in South Africa. It was no secret he was planning to stay, to quit Seychelles altogether. Another handful of lives changed forever by the killing of Hoarau.

I explained to René that rupees were not an option for me. He blew out some smoke, cleared his throat, said, 'But if you get paid half in rupees you can live in Seychelles.'

It took me by surprise. He was saying I could live in the country and, over whatever period, get paid fifty percent of the sum I was owed in the local currency. He went further, said I could earn more continuing to work there and wind down things at home towards retirement. Me and my family could completely relocate, he said. To his mind, and by now mine too, you could do a lot worse than call Seychelles home.

I knew of course that it suited him for me to stay in terms of getting me paid. But he was also anxious to avoid further damaging publicity and my return to the UK could keep the situation fired up.

As I factored everything in over the coming days, the fog of dilemma began to clear. Avoid the trauma of potential arrest in the UK while the Indian Ocean lapped at my feet, the Kreol music, song and food in my life every day?

I suggested to Phyl that we do it. She was immediately taken with the idea. She'd fallen for the place too. There was enough in the bank to continue funding our boys' education at Dungannon Royal in Co Tyrone. And I could free up money by selling some of the interests I had acquired over the years. But we didn't have to commit to anything right away. And given I was going nowhere fast, Berlouis arranged for me to get a formal ID card and had me empowered to interview suspects and witnesses. The MPR, after all, now had itself a powerful martyr figure. Its supporters were anxious to act in his name.

With the invaluable help of our undercover man, Barry Trigwell aka Jim O'Boyle, we began picking up on fresh plans to smuggle in explosives and weapons. Based now on Mahé, I began working closer with the police and Seychelles Security Service staff. But I had been the London-based lead, head of the Overseas Intelligence Unit who had all of a sudden become a Seychelles-based contributor. My role had changed and, frankly, after a while I felt a little surplus to requirements. Barry's role changed too. He was asked to move to South Africa and later Australia to watch MPR members before he was paid off. By the middle of the year René, Berlouis and I agreed there was no point in staying on as National Security Advisor. The government had by then paid me half of the debt. It was as if everything was pointing in the direction of me, at the age of forty-five, taking that early retirement. Or, I should say, retirement of a kind. I applied for two Gainful Occupation Permits to allow myself and Phyl to remain and work on the islands. I knew neither of us weren't quite ready to sit around doing nothing.

As for the boys, summer was coming, they would be out of school and they couldn't wait to get back to Seychelles. I wanted to have everything in place. I bought a house in Turtle Bay from Berlouis and began looking for a business to buy and run, something to keep the cash coming and keep me active. I found it startling that, as I was making all my plans, the visa applications were declined. I had to wonder what wheels within wheels had come to the conclusion that I wasn't the sort of bloke they wanted there. Anyway, I had friends in high places. The president issued a directive to override the decision and five year permits were granted.

I bought two cars and a beautiful, fast fishing launch of about seven meters, with twin outboards, and re-named her '*Felisya*,' the Kreolisation of Phyllis. We had a fine summer as a family, everyone adjusting with the

Fishing boat – *Felisya*

greatest of ease to their idyllic new lifestyles. In fact the boys showed zero interest in returning to boarding school in Northern Ireland. That wasn't too difficult to understand. We looked at all the options before deciding what to do. For the term ahead, we enrolled Jamie, nine, at the primary school in the village of Ans au Pins where he quickly learned Kreol. He assimilated well and in no time it was as if he had turned native, was running around barefooted, picking and chewing raw chilli-peppers from the roadside bushes. He was the only white kid in a school of hundreds and got himself the good-natured nickname 'Milky Bar.'

He'd disappear at weekends, stay up in the mountains with local families, devour the wonderful local grub and he made many friends. When we saw him with his pals, he'd speak in Kreol before turning to us to speak in English with a wonderfully rich accent.

We enrolled Johnnie, twelve, at the International School in Victoria, which was on par with the boarding school back home.

He too adapted well and could be found most weekends on the beaches among his new pals. He became interested in scuba diving and literally immersed himself in the wonders of the shores of Seychelles.

As they were settling in, a business caught my eye. La Perle Noir was a very fine French-Kreol restaurant on the truly astonishing Beau Valley Bay. It made perfect sense. I loved the food of the islands, adored

La Perle Noir
Restaurant

the beauty of the beaches—buying La Perle Noir was combining two of my greatest loves. And, when Phyl and the family agreed with the idea, everything fell into place. In September of that year I began a whole new life as a restaurateur. We redecorated, purchased new kitchen equipment and retrained and uniformed the existing staff of twenty-five young women and four men. Phyl designed the outfits, fitting the girls with French-style black dresses with frilly white aprons and hats. We took on a new chef too to run the kitchen alongside the long-serving cook.

With the right investment, attention to detail and customer focus, we really made a go of it. In the coming months the table bookings grew and stayed constant, busy right across our new seven-day rota. I learned a great deal about the cuisine, picked up a good smattering of Kreol and managed to get myself the nickname *Tonton*, or uncle, among locals. We were particularly packed out at the weekends and if you had no reservation you were out of luck. The bar became an oasis for the British expat community. Around 4 pm every weekday, a bunch would congregate for beer, snacks and darts and very often for a bit of singsong in the evenings.

Meanwhile, Jamie was to be honoured at his school with a visit from the Pope. He was the only Protestant in the place and wasn't exactly up to speed on John Paul II. Around 5,000 gathered at the National Stadium after His Holiness touched down on Air France Concorde in the most torrential tropical storm recorded for years. With the world's TV cameras watching, he greeted the long line of children, each kneeling in front of him before taking and placing the communion bread on their tongues. But Milky-Bar Jamie hadn't a clue. He put the bread in his pocket. The Pope shrugged and that was that.

Johnnie's International School did not challenge him and, with Jamie moving into secondary education, both boys went off to board at St Andrews in Turi, Kenya. Johnnie outgrew that option too, returning to Seychelles where he began giving scuba lessons to tourists at Marine Divers school by the Beau Vallon Bay Hotel. He really got into his stride fast in terms of his capabilities and popularity. The school was operated by Rick Howatson, one of the many expats I had researched ahead of him investing and residing in Seychelles. Rick saw real talent in Johnnie and recommended he take more advanced training.

Across the next three years we relished our work at La Perle Noire, a stone's throw from the most gorgeous beach. It was a fun mission at one point trying to broaden the client base by luring in locals. We renamed Wednesdays 'Curry-day' and served a variety of excellent local dishes and tropical salads at the right price and it worked a treat.

Beyond that, I opened a company called Corporate Services Limited based in Victoria House, a firm aimed at helping other local businesses improve. One client was a small air-conditioning company which I rebranded as Ekonomikool, and I ultimately bought it myself. I arranged for it to import Taylor USA ice cream and slush machines for the many hotels and shops around Mahé and on the nearby islands of Praslin and La Digue.

I also took on a twelve-month contract to rescue and run a tourist ship abandoned by its previous British management. *Seypirate* was a beauty, a magnificent old ninety-foot pirate schooner. I brought it up to a good standard, put bands and pirate-style dancers on board and marketed it

Seypirate crew and dancers

to tourists. It was great fun and, I'm glad to say, did great business across that year.

In 1989 a man called Paul Lewis, who owned the Casino des Seychelles on Mahé, asked if I might sell La Perle Noire. I mulled it over for a few weeks and let it go for a handsome cash profit. Around the same time Phyl, a licenced casino inspector and dealer in the UK, received an offer. A second Seychelles casino was opening within the new Plantation Club Hotel complex on Mahé and its management hoped she might train up staff and run the business. She took it on and did a fantastic job.

Every now and then I'd take a call from René's secretary Bernadette. The occasional issue would emerge and I was glad to help out where I could. What was particularly interesting was when I was asked to look into a suspected 'betrayal' of the president by Ogilvy Berlouis. It seemed another coup was being planned and that this time the Defence Minister himself wanted to seize power. It was an astonishing claim. I dug down and discovered Berlouis and a handful of senior officers in the Seychelles People's Defence Force were indeed planning to arrest René when he returned from a trip to Zimbabwe. Wily René used the information to outfox his treacherous friend. He arrived home early and deplaned at the other end of the runway. The next day, as wannabe President Berlouis and his men waited to nab their leader, they were surprised by René's own troops. Berlouis and his co-conspirators were lucky not to have been jailed. Instead, they agreed to resign.

I was tasked too with looking into the circumstances around a series of anti-government documents and leaflets being imported into Seychelles. Through London contacts, I identified the publisher and, from there, the Malaysia-based printer. I took a flight to Kuala Lumpur where the management were led to believe I was the customer who had ordered the sizable printing job. I paid for the lot and they released it all, including a copy of the contract. This identified the MPR member who had made the order in the first place.

And when the team from US television's influential *60 Minutes* programme visited, René asked if I might act as a spokesman for his government. I already knew of considerable media hostility towards the president and of his view that there was nothing he could say that would not be somehow used against him. I agreed to the interview and spent a day with the late world-class reporter Morley Safer. It was definitely more of an interrogation than an interview but I did what I could.

The resulting programme was called *Spies Island,* a play on *Spice Island*. It was notable for challenging a lot of the MPR's wilder claims about René and his government, including long-running allegations he had sanctioned rights abuses and even the murders of dissidents. I knew of zero evidence for such claims and, as I had come to learn, the MPR was no stranger to distortions for its own ends. The programme was a much-needed counterweight and went on to win an award. The president was chuffed, evidenced by the arrival at my home one morning of a bottle of single malt.

And then, in 1991, Bernadette called to say René wanted to meet in his office. I immediately had the feeling that something was up. The president stood as I entered and it wasn't like him to do that. He turned, motioned towards the cigar box on his desk and sat back down. The espressos arrived. He told me, as politely but firmly as ever, I should leave Seychelles. He said I should attend to my business, pack up my things, gather my loved ones and go within 'a few days' if possible. It was shocking, confusing, hard to take in. But, unfortunately, it made sense. As he explained to me, my life, and the lives of loved ones, were about to be put in serious danger.

It all boiled down to the fallout from the murder of Gérard Horeau six years before. The USA, UK and France had all got to talking about Seychelles and had been presenting an increasingly united front behind the scenes. The Berlin Wall had fallen, the world was changing and the west now wanted change on the islands, wanted movement from a stubborn president who had no interest in elections. René had beaten back coup after coup and had, they knew, enjoyed a good run. Now it was time to bring in democratic reforms and reach out to his sworn enemies. If necessary, the pressure such nations could have brought to bear on a small land like Seychelles would have been immense.

René said his cabinet had agreed to overhaul the system of government. Seychelles had been effectively a one-party state since 1977. He said that from December 1991, seven months away, changes would come into play. There would be multi-party elections the following year, he said. And, he added, he had agreed that the opposition groups, including exiled members of the MPR, would be permitted to return before that.

There was nothing for me to argue over, nothing I could protest about. I sat there, cold, my mind racing. I had so much to do, to undo. My whole life had just been flung into the air. The businesses I had been building, the investments I had been making, all the plans to live forever in Seychelles suddenly in freefall. He said he wanted to thank me for my years of service.

I don't know how many emotions I was dealing with as I left his office, can't say how many thoughts and concerns and complications were colliding in my mind. The idea of having to get the hell out of there fast was enough to consider, but I had burned so many bridges back in the UK that, with all my unserviced businesses being wound down by the banks there, I didn't even know where I would go. I tried to work out a way to deliver the momentous news to my family as I drove back.

Phyl was there. So was Jamie, then fifteen and on summer holiday from the Kenyan boarding school. My eldest son Andrew, then twenty-six, was there too. I gathered them all and put a call into Johnnie over in South Africa where he was training to be a diving instructor.

'I have some bad news,' I said, and I hated having to speak every word that followed. Our future in Seychelles, I told them, was our future no more. It was heartening that they all took it well. There was no rage or blame, just acceptance that there was no way around this. And very quickly we were all talking of looking forward to the next phase after our wonderful adventures in the middle of the Indian Ocean.

One key issue was that Jamie had begun a relationship with a Seychellois called Natalie, whose father ran the National Lottery on the islands. Although I suspect Mr Ah-Mane would have been delighted to see the back of young Jamie, I really didn't want him to suffer anything like a broken heart. In the end we agreed he would stay on until the last moment and that Phyl would return immediately. She would not be going to the UK, but a different jurisdiction to look for a house. We would move to the Republic of Ireland. The contents of our previous home were in storage in Northern Ireland and we talked about getting everything out and dusting it down. Even the car that would be knocking on a bit by then. We had a meal out at La Scala in Bel Ombre on that last family weekend and on Sunday June 2, 1991, my wife left Seychelles for the last time.

Despite the emerging risk, I had a good deal of work to do to dispose of my businesses there, many loose ends to tie up. It was going to take weeks, maybe months. I had taken René's advice on board but I was under no obligation to quit right away, regardless of any emerging threat. I was going, but I wasn't going to run. And Johnnie, then seventeen, had his own way of looking at things too. He had work lined up as a scuba instructor with Rick Howatson and after returning from South Africa said he'd like to stay a while.

So I got to tidying things up. I sold Ekokomikool lock, stock and barrel to an English couple who had previously been on holiday in Seychelles. The ending with *Seypirate* was a different kettle of fish. My lease had been for twelve months and I knew now that, very sadly, I could not extend it. Unfortunately the crew didn't take the news well and damaged the schooner before demanding wages in lieu of notice. It was a maddening act of vandalism and I wasn't about to pay money to people who had wantonly destroyed part of the boat. The whole thing ended up at a tribunal and, my focus elsewhere, I lost. *Seypirate* was not repaired.

Three months flew past and I was still seeking to sell my home too. But by now exiles were returning from around the world. They were meeting up with MPR supporters to build support for opposition parties which would go on to unify as the SNP—the *Seychelles National Party*. As part of their battle cry for future votes they were, rather chillingly, pasting my image in windows, on walls, around the market in Victoria and other places. I'll never forget the wording:

'Wanted Dead or Alive for the murder of Gérard Hoarau.'

A red line had been drawn through the word *Alive*. I knew I had to get my skates on. René's office got in touch to say I would get round-the-clock police protection until I left. It became clear at the same time that locals knew Johnnie was my son, that even though he was teaching scuba he was in danger. I arranged to get him out in early September. Jamie and I were still there, him still in love and me still trying to wrap things up. We packed our cases, ready to bolt at a moment's notice if we had to. But I needed just a little longer.

They ambushed me outside my office on Statehouse Avenue. It was late afternoon. I didn't see it coming. Around forty people surrounded me like a blizzard out of nowhere. They blocked the way to my car while brandishing placards, shouting my name, calling me a murderer, demanding I go home. And that was just the polite stuff. I stopped, stood my ground, looked at all the faces in search of whoever might be leading the crowd.

I called out, 'Why do you wait for me? Who wants to speak with me?'

There was some muttering but no real response. I left it at that and pressed forwards, the same direction I had been going, to my car. They moved. I got in, started the engine and nosed carefully through the mob and away. It had been frightening yet there was no serious aggression. But that was it for me. I had left it long enough.

With heavy hearts and a tear in the eye, Jamie and I left Seychelles on December 1, 1991, making our way to our newly-purchased home in rainy Dublin. A warm fire and warmer hugs were waiting as we met Phyl and Johnnie. They'd worked hard to make it all beautiful, and it worked. It was lovely, comforting, homely, and just what we needed.

That December had all the signs of being an awful month but it turned out well. It was the first time in close to seven years that all of us, including my parents, were able to break bread together as a family. The new year came, we enrolled Jamie in a top Irish school called St Gerard's and, shunning any temptation to stay idle, I got to work. I wouldn't have lasted long in any case if I didn't start generating some good income. So, with Johnnie's help, I set out to restart my Dublin-based agency. We took an office in Dame Street in the city centre, ramped up the advertising and, after a few months, relaunched my old businesses in Belfast, London and I bought out my old Brighton franchisee.

And the MPR turned their attention my way once more. Word spread that I was advertising and, often in the dead of night, threatening phone calls came. It was distressing for us as a family but there was not much could be done. The calls continued for some time. The frequency faded here and there, but they kept coming. If you asked me when they finally stopped for good, I'd have to tell you I don't yet know.

There was no way I could avoid traveling. I would have to cross the border into Northern Ireland, have to go fly to England on business from time to time. So I just got on with it, just came to the conclusion that if the Met ever did express any sincere interest in speaking with me they could do so. Yet at no stage whatsoever did they approach me or my solicitors.

I went back to Seychelles twice to try and recover my abandoned assets. In February 1992, I was met at the airport by police officers who escorted me throughout the time I was there. I went back to the apartment and packed up my personal bits and pieces, abandoned the house and moved into the Auberge on La Misere using a false name. While there I was advised that my life was at risk and the phone calls came again. I did manage to recover a few of my assets, some cash and lots of promises. And, after a chat with René, I accepted about £50,000 as full and final settlement of any further claims against his government. It was the best he could do.

A few years passed and, after the Good Friday Agreement of 1998 and the diminishing terrorist threat, we moved back to Northern Ireland. I switched our head office from Dublin back to Belfast and Dublin became a franchised branch.

I became the co-founder and chairman of WAPI, *World Association of Professional Investigators,* holding the chair for seven years. I became heavily engaged in the proposed licensing of private investigators in the UK, representing the trade many times in various arenas. I went to London on numerous occasions, had meetings with the Home Office and gave evidence at the Leveson inquiry and to the Home Affairs Committee of the House of Commons in the 2000s. In fact I bought a house there for Jamie and even dealt with the Met on a number of occasions in terms of my work at the franchises which, I'm glad to say, really did begin to thrive. I did some work for *The Sunday Times* and other newspapers, traced fugitive terrorists for exposure. As a result of all that I had a number of meetings with British intelligence and Special Branch figures. And, just to be crystal clear, at no stage whatsoever did the Met make any approach to me about the murder of Gérard Hoarau.

As for Barry Trigwell, who had operated so successfully undercover, he returned to the UK after he was paid off and began working with my brother Stuart's agency *Nationwide Investigations*. In a horrific development, he was murdered in his home in 1995 by a hitman hired by his wife. She was jailed for life and died from an illness soon after her release on compassionate grounds.

As for France-Albert René, he continued to maintain his country's status as Africa's most developed nation. He also continued to enjoy the widespread support of his people after transition to a multi-party state. Despite opposition at the polls from the man he ousted, Sir James Mancham, he remained President of the Republic of Seychelles until he stood down in 2004, making way for James Michel. René, aged eighty-three, died in 2019.

In 2018 I gave evidence to the *Seychelles Truth, Reconciliation and National Unity Commission* which is examining claims of human rights violations as a result of René taking power. As above, I said I was aware of allegations, theories and straightforward lies surrounding his tenure, but I was aware of no evidence whatsoever.

THIRTY-EIGHT

Murder in Sri Lanka: Searching for Sandra Valentine (1989)

THE memory of that day I discovered a murder remains vivid. Sandra Valentine was far from home, had been missing for some time, yet there had been every hope she might still be alive. Unfortunately, all that was found was her body, alone, isolated and partly-decayed in a Sri Lankan mountain stream.

Having searched for her for some time, that outcome and the image itself weighed heavily on me. And for her family, it plunged their despair yet deeper. There was no immediate sign that her life had been taken, just the suggestion that no one had been there when she died. Her parents, unable to bear laying eyes on the remains of their much-loved daughter, asked if I would identify her corpse in the morgue. It was then that I noticed a detail which confirmed the very worst of all our fears. Sandra had not been alone when she lost her life. Someone had killed her.

I had taken a call from Terry McGill in Maryland in the spring of 1989 while living in Seychelles. A lawyer from New York had called to say he and his wife did not know where to turn. Their daughter seemed to have vanished after taking a year out to travel.

Terry advised that the man had been distraught on the phone. He had told him Sandra was his only daughter, that she was thirty-years-old and it was very unlike her to drop out of sight. He said she was a successful young woman, had launched into selling photocopying machines in New York after graduating from Georgetown University and had a natural gift for closing deals. She had bought an apartment and car, learned

Japanese and, with the world at her feet, could not resist leaving the US to see some of it.

She and a girlfriend decided to visit as many countries as they could. They got themselves a few *Lonely Planet* guidebooks each, made detailed plans and set off on their adventure in July 1988. They went west, making their way through New Zealand, Australia, Japan, China, Singapore, Thailand, Nepal and onwards.

Each week postcards and letters arrived, excited descriptions of the cultural riches of lands neither young woman had ever seen before. Eight months into the trip, one postcard from India was a little more downbeat. It advised that Sandra's travel partner had taken ill. The young woman's family had insisted she return to the US right away and she did so. But Sandra had no plans to cut short a dream trip that was firing up her every sense. Africa awaited and she didn't want to miss it. Her parents understood. Then the postcards stopped.

I was at the time in the right neighbourhood, globally speaking. I called Sandra's father, law firm partner Richard H Valentine, to get more detail. He said it had been two weeks since that last card, postmarked from Bombay, now called Mumbai. An itinerary she had left at home, along with notes on one of the guidebooks, suggested she would have flown to Colombo, Sri Lanka, on a flight from Bombay on March 20. It appeared she would explore the country for ten days before returning to Bombay and then on to Delhi. From there she would fly to Addis Ababa in Ethiopia and travel south to Nairobi in Kenya. She was due to fly back to New York via Pan Am from there.

I remember very clearly how distressed Richard was. I took his urgency on board, of course, yet I felt hopeful that this was not necessarily as bad as he feared. There could have been a holdup in the post, or perhaps Sandra had taken ill herself and was being looked after somewhere. He agreed that nothing was yet known. However he needed this matter to be resolved fast. I said I would check with all the airlines involved, confirm if she was or was not due on board and do what I could to establish if she showed up for any flights. If there was still no news, I would have already made my way to Nairobi to wait for her to check in for that final voyage home. It could be she had changed her plans, that she was making her way to Nairobi by some other method. But, of all the flights she was due to take, we were sure that the flight home was the one most likely to see her checking in.

Off I went to Nairobi, a three hour flight from Seychelles, arriving on May 25, 1989. Still nothing had been heard. I based myself at the 680 Hotel and copies of Sandra's postcards, a copy of her passport, receipts for her flights and a formal letter of authority to act for the family were couriered to me there. I went to the Air India offices in the city, bringing with me a letter of introduction from their agent in Seychelles. I sat with the regional manager as the Bombay to Delhi flight was boarded, and then the connecting flight to Addis. The check-in supervisors, as requested, called us after each flight had closed the door. They reported that the manifests for both had Sandra down as 'No show.' She was still somewhere in Asia.

Back at the hotel, I drew up a plan. I created posters from her photograph offering a reward for information. Air India kindly went on to circulate them to their offices and agencies. And I sketched out a timeline of her journey, based upon the letters and postcards. Factoring in all she

Sri Lanka – Sandra Valentine search

had written, it seemed to me that there was nothing to say she had ever left Bombay nor arrived in Sri Lanka.

Richard, becoming increasingly desperate, asked me to go to Bombay. An immediate problem with that was that I would need a visa, but I pleaded extraordinary circumstances with the Indian High Commission in Kenya and they were very helpful. The visa came through in a few days instead of a few weeks.

I flew over and found a cheap B&B near where Sandra had been staying, right beside the five-star Taj Mahal Palace. I checked all the lodgings that she had marked or highlighted in the *Lonely Planet* guide. Sandra was not, and had not been, in any of them. Her last postcard had been sent from a hotel business centre. A member of staff there told me a Sandra Valentine had prepaid to receive and hold mail for occasional collection, and handed me a whole bundle of them. I sat with a coffee and read through them all in search of a clue. One friend in New York had written noting Sandra's plans to go alone to Sri Lanka. But if those plans had been enacted, how did she travel? And, if that had happened, was it possible she had returned as planned to India in preparation for that flight from Delhi to Addis?

I could tell from my communications with Richard and his wife Nancy, Sandra's stepmother, that they were getting ever more desperate. They were waiting for news not just every day, but every hour. Their anguish was palpable. I remembered an Indian PI agency which I had used over the years and put a call in. They connected me with a journalist at the Indian State Broadcasting Service SBS, the equivalent of the BBC. I was invited to broadcast an appeal on behalf of the family, talking of the reward I had already arranged.

A couple of hours after that broadcast, arriving back at my hotel, a member of the reception staff handed me a note. It was from the police. I called immediately. He said there had been a train accident in Kerala State in southern India on July 8. There were still some as yet unidentified foreign female bodies in the local mortuary. I was told that I would be able to check the bodies to see if Sandra was amongst them.

A day later, I flew down, met the police and was told of the horrific incident at Peruman bridge over the Ashtamudi Lake. Ten carriages from a train from Bangalore to Thiruvananthapuram Central had derailed and tipped into the lake. In all, 105 people had been killed.

The cold, full smell of death was thick in the air at the police mortuary, the atmosphere heavy among the fifty-seven unclaimed bodies laid out for inspection. The refrigeration system whirred as I walked among them in search of the missing American girl. There were five light-skinned females, all a similar age to Sandra, each looking like a wax doll, skin hardened and ice-cold. But she was not there. I took some relief in knowing I could not confirm she was dead.

I had news for Richard, that his daughter had not died in the train disaster. And he had news for me. Mail had arrived from Sandra months after it had been sent. A letter was dated March of 1989, postmarked Negombo, northern Sri Lanka. It told how much she was enjoying herself, how different it was to India. And a postcard had arrived too, dated April 9, 1989, sent from the capital Colombo. It proved she had been there and that she had jumbled up her itinerary along the way.

Back on the road. The vicious war raging in pockets of northern badlands between Tamil Tigers and the Sri Lankan authorities prevented both air and sea travel from southern India, despite the relative closeness. I had to get back to Bombay. I arrived in Sri Lanka on Tuesday, June 6, 1989, and checked into a central Colombo hotel. First, I generated an updated poster, circulating it to all newspapers, the radio station and police HQ. And second, I needed to get myself a vehicle, a translator and someone with excellent local knowledge. Years of experience told me that there are few better people for ticking all those boxes than a local taxi driver. I quickly found the perfect man, agreed the rate we got started the next morning.

We went to the American Express offices in Colombo where I was told it would take time for them to trace paid travellers' checks on their system. Next, I stopped off at the country's Immigration Department who sanctioned me to inspect the many thousands of Immigration Arrival and Departure Cards filled out by everyone touching down or taking off. I took a seat, got to work and eventually found an entry card for a young American called Sandra Valentine. But there was no card to say she had left.

We drove to Negombo and checked at all of the B&B's listed in *Lonely Planet*. It was a case of third door lucky. The landlady recognised Sandra by name, said she had stayed for two nights. She said she had talked of visiting the tourist hotspot of Kandy, that she had wanted to explore the Buddhist sites and Tea Plantations in the peaceful, hilly terrain of that breathtaking part of central Sri Lanka.

The next day myself and my trusty companion were in Kandy, again knocking the doors. We found a small house on a side street close to the lakeshore and were able to confirm that was where Sandra had stayed on Monday, March 27, 1989. That was nine weeks ago. The woman seemed relieved someone was asking questions. She said Sandra had promised to come back for her stuff, but never did. The landlady retrieved the American's rucksack. She said she hadn't known what to do with it.

Sandra had left Kandy on the morning of March 28. She was to take a bus to the tea plantations around the hill town of Nuwara Eliya. We followed the route, passing astonishing waterfalls, an orphaned elephant nursery at Pinnawala and then, unexpectedly, came across a large, angry crowd that was blocking the highway.

'A political demonstration,' my driver said. 'Sit still.'

So we sat still as it played out. There was shouting, then some pushing and shoving. I spotted through the crowd a youngish, fearful looking man who was getting a few knocks. His arms were grabbed, twisted behind him and he was being forced through people to the edge of the road.

I couldn't help myself. I pushed the door open, pushed through the crush—then a horrific sight. The mob had seized him, had each arm twisted backwards forcing his chest to protrude forward. A large middle aged man stood in front, a knife in his hand. He raised the blade and thrust it through the victim's chest. It was surreal, almost as if in slow motion. I saw the victim's eyes open wide, saw the sheer terror on his face as the knife was rammed into him. With both hands on the handle of the knife, the executioner twisted it. The young man collapsed to the ground, murdered in plain sight. His killer pulled the knife from his chest and, with his foot, shoved the body into the ditch. And the crowd began to disperse.

I felt a hand gently take my arm.

'Come,' my driver said, appearing from nowhere, 'we must go before the police and military get here.'

'Okay,' I said, deep in shock.

'The man was a spy,' he said. As we left the scene he explained the victim had been working for the government against the interests of the Tamil minority. I had never before seen a murder take place in front of me and never felt so fully helpless.

Nuwara Eliya, in the Central Province, means City of Light. It sits around two thousand metres above sea level, a magnificent landscape and a perfectly cool climate. We began checking the visitors' books at the tea plantations, advising we were searching for an American who may have stopped by around two months earlier. No luck at the first, no luck at the second and then, at the third, The Labookkellie Plantation, I saw her name.

Tuesday, March 28, 1989.
Sandra Valentine, USA—11.00 am.

I copied the two names above and three names below her signature. All were German and all had signed within fifteen minutes of her arrival. There were addresses but no phone numbers. From the town centre I called my office manager in Brighton. Brian Lewis, an ex-Sussex CID Officer, wrote to each of the Germans. It would take a while to hear back, but I needed to get that moving all the same.

After that, we toured the area leaving posters in a number of hotels and the train station at Nanuoya. At the Grand Hotel the manager showed some recognition when he saw the image. She had been there, he said, on March 28, 1989, the same day she visited the plantation. She had not been a guest, he said, but had walked in with a request. He took me to a receptionist, showed her the poster.

'Yes, she was here,' the lady said. She remembered Sandra had bought a cold drink and asked to buy time to make a phone call.

I asked, with no real hope of a useful answer, if she had any idea who Sandra might have called. And one of the most efficient receptionists on the planet flicked through the pages of the petty-cash book for that month. All the details were there. Sandra had made three phone calls. One to a

Canadian friend in Colombo and one to the boarding house in Kandy. The third was a nine minute call to Air India. I called the same number. They were able to confirm that passenger Sandra Valentine had altered and rebooked on that day, cancelling her original flights from Colombo to Bombay to Delhi to Addis. She rebooked Colombo to Bombay connecting to Nairobi to catch her Pan Am flight to Frankfurt and on to New York. It seemed clear she wanted to spend more time in Sri Lanka.

I updated Richard in New York. He and his wife made plans to fly over. In the meantime, we got on the tourist trail lined up in the guide book—temples, monasteries, the National Park, to see if we could learn anything more but no.

I arrived back at the hotel in Colombo on Thursday, June 15. There was a message from Brian in Brighton to say one of the Germans had replied with a phone number. He and his wife had taken Sandra for lunch in Nuwara Eliya. They said she had bought a souvenir doll at the plantation gift shop, a gift for her niece. After that, they had dropped her off at the Grand Hotel. Both assumed she was staying there.

I called the manager at the Grand. He rechecked the hotel records to see if Sandra might have stayed under another name, but nothing. He said he would let me know if anything came up.

Richard and Nancy Valentine arrived in Colombo on June 16, 1989. I brought them up to speed on everything. Their minds full and exhausted, they both went to bed. I felt the same way.

I woke some time after 10 pm, the phone ringing in my room. It was the manager of the Grand Hotel.

'I am very sorry,' he said. 'We have found your missing girl in the grounds. She was in a river and appears to have drowned.'

I sat bolt upright, wide awake.

'Where is she?' I asked.

She had been taken to the mortuary at Newara Eliya Hospital, he explained. I said I'd be there in the morning with her parents. I expected it to be the worst day of their lives. I called the Newara Eliya Police. They couldn't help with any details saying it was too late in the day. All I could do would be to visit between 10 am to 8 pm the next day to ID the corpse.

The next call was a tough one. It was about 1 am on Saturday, June 17, 1989. I called the room of Mr and Mrs Valentine with news of their daughter. Richard listened silently. I was invited to repeat what I'd said, to say once again the words which I knew were crushing him. He waited a moment, collected himself, asked if I would come to his room, if I might arrange for some coffee as I went.

They were both in dressing gowns, the strong aroma of that fresh coffee just arrived. They appeared haunted, weak and weary. I went over what I knew once more as Nancy cried softly. Richard said we still did not know for sure, that he could not turn his mind to believing Sandra was dead until she had been identified. He seemed to flip into lawyer-mode, began talking in a matter of fact way about the circumstances, saying that the whole business had been a mess, that the US State Department had shunned his early request for help and that had led him to contacting a PI. I listened as Richard, a partner in the New York city law firm of Seward & Kissel, went through it all, talked it all out. It was his way of coping with the news that had broken his heart.

It took three hours as passengers in our hotel's courtesy car to reach Newara Eliya. Around midday we met with the duty pathologist who led us to the mortuary building and unlocked the door. Inside, a small waiting lobby area with a few chairs. He said the body had been found submerged in a mountain stream of ice-cold running water and was, in relative terms, well preserved. Richard was invited to enter the examination room but clammed up. Tears came into his eyes and he walked towards then stepped back from the door. I looked him in the eye, asked if he would like me to go. He said he would. Nancy was relieved.

There was just one slab. A white sheet had been draped over the body. A brown-paper tag was fixed to one of the exposed toes. The doctor pulled the sheet back. The woman was white, about thirty, had sun tan around her neck and legs. The hairstyle was as I had seen in the photographs, the general shape of the face matching too. I was as sure as I could be that this lost life was Sandra Valentine. For the most part her skin had that strange wax doll quality, something I had seen before on my Asian journey. But an unsightly decomposition had begun, the indications clear that she had been unsheltered for some time. Her mouth was open, her tongue swollen and protruding in a hideous way. It was hard, out and down towards her chin. I asked the doctor if he might be able to put it back into her mouth. Richard and Nancy were on my mind. I wanted to do whatever I could to avoid adding anything to their pain.

The doctor tried to move her tongue, gently pushing and prodding it back into her open mouth with a mortician's implement. But it seemed as if something was in its way, as if there was a blockage further back. It was an awful thing to watch, but he kept trying, carefully, respectfully doing what he could to return the tongue.

As he worked, I noticed something on her neck. It was a faint line, like a scar across the throat. My eyes fixed on it. I became sure this was not anything natural, not any kind of adornment. I pointed it out to the good doctor. He was immediately curious. Using his instrument he started to explore this line, moving the tool along it. And he gasped.

'It's a nylon cord!' he told me. 'It's embedded in the skin!'

As he pulled to lift it from deep in the flesh, he said her skin had puffed up from the lengthy exposure to water. As such, the nylon line had been hidden on the flesh. He said he would update the police given it seemed now that Sandra had been killed. For the time being, as her parents were just yards away, he said he would cut the cord in order to get the tongue back inside her mouth. He gently pushed one blade of a long pair of scissors under the line to the right side of her throat. It was clear in my eyes now that this was a nylon line, similar to a fishing line. This poor, cheerful, kind, adventurous girl had been strangled and her body dumped naked into the fast-flowing mountain stream. One could only imagine what the last moments of her life might have involved.

The doctor snipped the cord and, as if her body was a balloon, air hissed from inside, a long, loud, deathly exhale. Dirty water spilled from her mouth and nose and a horrific smell took over the room. The doctor handed me a surgical mask, but it did little to neutralise the stench.

Yet worse was to come. The release of gas had shrunk her abdomen and I could see movement on her chest, as if she was attempting to draw breath. I watched as the skin began to separate, splits forming as if some rapid, horrific disease was tearing through her. Maggots were writhing around within the breaks.

I was cold with the horror and tragedy of it all as the doctor put her tongue back into her mouth. He pulled the sheet over and asked if I might bring her parents in. Nancy did not want to enter and Richard, walking slowly, held my arm as he moved towards his dead daughter. The doctor rolled the sheet down, revealing just her face. I remember the grip, how hard Richard squeezed as the realisation of his worst nightmare came real. Tears filled his eyes and he nodded, whispering to her, 'Why did you continue?'

The doctor said the body would have to be sent to the central mortuary in Colombo for forensic examination given that her status had changed from possible drowning victim to possible murder victim. We met with the police afterwards and followed their vehicle the next day as Sandra was taken to the capital. It was a desperately quiet journey, barely a word spoken, just occasional sobs from the rear seat.

Richard and Nancy later invited me to dinner, perhaps to help one another absorb the events of recent days, recent weeks. Richard said, his lawyer's mindset reemerging, that after lunch in Nuwara Eliya with the German doctor and his wife, Sandra must have left for Adam's Peak, a mountain of mystical attraction to Sri Lankans who stay overnight to see the sunrise. I'd been there with the taxi driver but no one could remember seeing the American.

Searching around for facts, Richard said, 'Sandy was probably killed on the 28th. She may have been offered a ride to or from the mountain, and she must have been killed before she could return to the guest house in Kandy.'

I had no answers, no real response at all. I was pleased when the meal was over and glad to get to my room. I found it challenging dealing with such raw, open grief.

Unfortunately the police pathologist we met the next morning was as much of an idiot as he was an insensitive prick. He said in his opinion the body was unlikely to be Sandra, that he believed it might be a local girl. In the midst of his misery, Richard was forced to secure dental records via fax from New York to prove his daughter was dead. We compared them with images taken from the corpse when they arrived at our hotel that night. They were a strong match. The next day, we brought them back to the police pathologist. Incredibly, he said that no comparison could be carried out—the body had been cremated.

I exploded. I couldn't believe what he had just told me. He went sheepish, said it was normal for unidentified bodies to be photographed then cremated in Sri Lanka. I said he had known we were getting dental records, but he seemed to think he had done nothing wrong at all. Richard and Nancy were inconsolable.

I filed a complaint at the police HQ. I was beyond outraged. It was an act so unprofessional, so inconsiderate, so callous, that it can still infuriate me to this day.

On Thursday morning, July 22, 1989, Richard received a call at the hotel from the office of the Sri Lankan president inviting us for tea. We went along as he told us how sorry he was and promised a thorough investigation.

About a week later, back in Seychelles, I received a long fax from one of the journalists on a Sri Lankan Newspaper that had assisted me with the appeals. He said police had conducted searches around the river where Sandra was recovered and four more female bodies had been found. Sandra's small backpack, holding an empty camera case, American Express card, a crumpled letter, a map and a copy of *Lonely Planet*, had also been found. Her passport, some of her traveller's checks and her camera were never located. Nor was the little doll she had bought for her niece at the tea plantation on what was probably her last day alive.

Some time later a gang of men were arrested and admitted murdering two of the five young women, but there is nothing to say for sure that they killed Sandra. The truth is that what happened to her remains a mystery. She was a victim of murder in as much as she was a victim of where she was at the time. The complex and bitter political divisions of the region had turned it into something of a lawless pocket where life was, for some, cheaper than it should ever be.

In the aftermath the US State Department warned Americans to avoid unnecessary travel in Sri Lanka. Citing the ongoing civil war, a spokesman said, 'There's no area of the country that we would indicate people should go to without taking appropriate precautions.'

Sadly, in 2003, Richard H Valentine passed on, his final years filled with questions that would never be answered.

URGENT/URGENT/URGENT/URGENT

MISSING PERSON US$ 1,000
==========================

REWARD FOR ANY

INFORMATION

LEADING TO THE LOCATING

SANDRA VALENTINE
=================

AGED 31 YEARS-USA CITIZEN

PASSPORT USA NO. 0605-92742

LAST HEARD OF ON APRIL 2 1989

TRAVELLING COLUMBO-TRIVANDRUM

AND BY ROAD/RAIL TO BOMBAY

5'6" - 167 CMS SLIM DARK COMPLEXION

IN POSSESSION OF AMERICAN EXPRESS CARD

AND CITIBANK TRAVELLERS CHEQUES

PLEASE DISPLAY PHOTOGRAPH

ANY INFORMATION TO

BOMBAY POLICE-CID/MISSING PERSON BUREAU

REFERENCE 213/89 (UP COUNTRY)

USA CONSULATE OFFICE BOMBAY/MADRAS

OR DIRECT TO

IAN D WITHERS - PRIVATE INVESTIGATOR
MARYLAND INVESTIGATOR INC USA
301-627-1124/FAX-202-861-0621 TELEX-289124

at Hilton Hotel, Tel: 544644 - Room 1105

THIRTY-NINE

Wronged Russians and the Vanished Broker (1995/96)

I WAS in a fine restaurant in the beautiful city of Moscow. My host Alexander Marichev introduced me to an elderly man. I shook his hand, said I was delighted to meet him, but I'd no idea who he was.

'This is Mikhail Kalashnikov,' said Alexander.

'Kalashnikov?' I said, taken aback, immediately aware of his most famous work.

I'd expected Russia might be a thrilling place and, no matter where I was, I was never disappointed. I took a number of trips there in the nineties, often to the capital and also to some of the surrounding regions. There were lots of meetings, lots of dinners, lots of interesting people with interesting backgrounds who were curious about my services.

The nation, freshly freed up from the restraints from communism, was soaring in so many ways. Ambition was everywhere. I could feel it crackling in the air. As part of this brave new dawn for the Great Bear of the east, business people were seeking background checks on all sorts of European and American investors and partners. They wanted help with due diligence for fear of falling victim to a capitalist trick or two. They were quite right. And a UK investigator who knew a trick or two was the right man for the job.

The law there required any foreigner involved in commercial activity to have a Russian associate. On more than one occasion we found that the westerners were indeed up to no good. One common feature was known as 'skimming,' whereby the westerners would collect bills for goods or services delivered from the Russians, delay payment to the Russians, generate an advantage by the declining exchange rates, buy roubles at a lower price and trouser the difference. As a result, the demand for services around industrial espionage were required like never before.

The work in Russia came about in the first place after I was hired by a firm with an office in Dublin. Alexander Marichev and his wife Tatyana Kirillova were the main figures in the Russia Corporation. They had become convinced they were the victim of some dodgy dealings by an oil exploration company called Bula, based in the Irish capital.

When I'd first met them I'd said how I had limited experience of their country. I'd said how I'd known two Russian doctors, a married couple based at Seychelles hospital when I lived there. Their English wasn't good but we had muddled along by speaking what limited Kreol we were picking up at the same language class. As for my Russian, I'd explained, I had literally four or five words to work with. In fact, I'd been about to use those four or five words with the stranger Alexander had just introduced when it hit me. I knew one other Russia word.

'Kalashnikov?' I said.

'Kalashnikov,' he said.

It was an extraordinary little moment to find myself talking with the inventor of the world's best known assault rifle, the AK-47, among other weapons. Mr Kalashnikov himself was a highly decorated hero in Russia, although all his work had taken place in another era. His only bonus for all that military engineering prowess had been an upgraded community house and a slight increase in his monthly allowance.

No such financial modesty was at play in terms of what Alexander and his wife had been dealing with in 1995. Their Russia Corporation had an agreement to help finance the development of a Siberian oil field. To make it all work, they had struck up a deal with Irish public limited company Bula Resources and its Chief Executive Officer Jim Stanley. But Bula, and Mr Stanley, were behaving oddly, not settling into the deal and raising problems that were impacting progress. Alexander Marichev had an inkling all was not as it seemed.

I did some exploring of my own and, with the help of intercepted phone calls, confirmed that Jim Stanley had created a secret 'competitive' company on the British Virgin Islands. Through this, he had engineered a complex deal which involved Bula giving 100M shares, worth £2M, to his own competitive company for a stake in the oil field. He was using the private intelligence he had obtained as a result of insight into the Russian Corporation throughout.

The whole thing ended up in court in both London and Dublin and was subject to inquiry by the Irish Stock Exchange, during which my final report was requested. In fact the final report produced by the Irish Stock Exchange was, give or take the odd word or two, a mirror image of my report. I suppose I should have been flattered.

A couple of years later there were some dodgy financial dealings rooted closer to home. Tony Taylor was a well-known figure in insurance circles and chair of the Insurance Brokers Association. He was clean as a whistle in the eyes of the nation given he had drawn up the code of ethics governing his trade. That same code had largely been enshrined in Irish law.

In August 1996, he and his wife Shirley vanished from their high-end Dublin home leaving behind little more than their pet dog. Early theories among a shocked public were that they might have been kidnapped. Yet it emerged that Taylor's investment business, Taylor Asset Management Group, had been falling apart. In fact it had collapsed altogether in 1996 and Taylor had ensured that a batch of documents were destroyed before he legged it. And at the time he did go, accompanied by his wife, about £1.7M of investors' funds was missing.

Time passed, Gardai kept investigating and the press reported on the case many times. Yet what had become of Taylor and his wife remained a mystery. His Mercedes Benz had been spotted parked up in the Dublin port area, the assumption being that he had caught a ferry to England, but that was about it.

My involvement began with a call to my Dame Street office from an accountant by the name of Eddie Hobbs. He was a well-known figure in Ireland himself, a popular broadcaster on financial matters. I had often appeared with him on panel shows discussing issues around locating debtors. He asked me to meet him at his office in Naas, Co Kildare, about twenty miles from the city. Once there he introduced me to half a dozen men. All had invested their savings with Tony Taylor's company, a combined total of about £1M. Among them were individuals who had been hiding undeclared savings and, as a result, did not want to file complaints with the police. They were unlikely to ever get their money back but they wanted Tony Taylor to face justice.

Eddie retained me on behalf of his clients. We agreed, in those pre-Euro days, that I would take a flat fee in Irish Punts. A separate fee would follow, but only if I located Taylor.

Office staff assisted as we ran all the available sources. I prepared a clip-board questionnaire for agents before sending them off to knock neighbours' doors. We spent a lot of time in the area, making sure we were not missing anything. We even did a dumpster dive, emptying the bins at his abandoned house, sifting through the awful rubbish checking for anything of interest. It was there that we found some old phone bills. Lots of calls had been made before the Taylors disappeared. Back in the office, we spent hours calling each, asking who was who, seeing how far we might get.

We went on to collect details on all of his extended family all over Ireland, Britain and various parts of the world via official records. We put in calls where it was appropriate and engaged a number of agencies to knock doors, to ask discreet questions.

We tracked his son Paul to an address in London and, instead of making our presence known, began round-the-clock surveillance. Paul was found to be working with an insurance broker in the city. We were sure that at some point he would engage with his missing parents. And then one day, as spotted by the surveillance team, he began packing up the contents of his home giving every indication he was moving out.

I arranged for a very smart female operative to call at the property. She pretexted that she was a neighbour, chatted easily with him and found out he had landed a job in Washington DC. My immediate thought was that maybe that's where Taylor senior might be? I called on my office in Maryland, only an hour from downtown DC. Very quickly they had a name and date of birth match for an Anthony Taylor living in North Carolina, four or five hours away.

A few days later and an agent was staking out the address but did not see anyone that came close to matching the description of my missing Irishman. I sent him on over to the house, asked him to pose as a journalist. And indeed Tony Taylor was there. He answered the door. But this Tony Taylor was black. So it was back to the drawing board.

I kept my focus on Paul and established an address for him in George-town, a part of DC. Database records listed his newly-created Social Security Number which in turn enabled us to establish where he was working and his landline number. A local researcher managed to secure copies of his phone bills and sent them to me in Dublin. But, once again, nothing of interest.

Months passed. Christmas 1999 was coming and Tony Taylor had been offside for some two years. I needed a break in the case. Then a call from a journalist at a Dublin Sunday newspaper. They were working on a centre page spread listing Ireland's most wanted persons and, knowing I had been searching for Taylor, asked if I had any news. I sensed an opportunity. I helped the reporter out, gave them as much information as I could, asked if they would highlight his case within the story. I said I felt the publicity could move it all forward. My plan was, after publication, to courier a copy to our Maryland office. They would immediately take it to the son's address in DC with a message reading, *'Sorry, to hear your father got arrested.'*

A few days later the newspaper carried the goods under the headline *"Ireland's Most Wanted"*. I sent it by FedEx to my partner agent Terry. He wrote the anonymous note, pinned it to the newspaper and delivered the package as if it had all just arrived from Ireland. Surveillance watched as junior picked up the package and brought it inside.

My idea had been to keep tabs on the phone calls that immediately followed. But, frustratingly, we had to wait a month for the latest bill. When the time came, a researcher secured a copy from the phone company and faxed it over. On the very date the paper was delivered, four separate calls to a UK number. The area code was for Eastbourne in East Sussex, about twenty miles from my office in Brighton. The excitement among our staff was building.

I called Brighton office manager Brian Lewis. He established the number was an unlisted landline in the name of a Mr T Taylor at an address in Eastbourne town. It seemed our man had not changed his name. Yet we had to be absolutely certain it was him. I was the one with the English accent so I took a chance, cobbled some pretext together and dialled. After a couple of rings, it went to an answering machine.

'You have reached the Taylor household. There's no one around so please leave a message.'

An Irish accent. I called Eddie Hobbs right away, asked him to dial the same number and listen. Ten minutes later he got back to me.

'Congratulations, Ian,' he said, 'you found him. I'd recognise that voice anywhere.'

So the last leg of a long journey began. Brian Lewis and his team launched into the surveillance the next morning. Within a few hours they had sightings of a man, matching Taylor's description, coming and going. Eddie requested a round-the-clock watch as Irish police went about arranging for an extradition warrant with the help of their counterparts in Eastbourne.

Three days later and a two-strong surveillance team, parked up in a van, had a knock on the back door. A man in a commercial vehicle had pulled up. The visitor showed them his Sussex Police warrant card. He wanted to know what they were up to. They said to call me. My phone duly rang and a detective sergeant told of his curiosity about the men in the van. I explained saying his office would likely be hearing from Dublin police when the court clears an extradition warrant.

The policeman said, 'I'll put my cards on the table. We have already received a request from the Garda asking that we set up police surveillance on this man pending the issue of a warrant. There's no point in the two of us doing it and getting under each other's feet.'

It made perfect sense that he and his team take over. I arranged for pictures, videos and other details to be handed over and my guys left. Among all that had been some receipts for computers, sourced from his bins, which were significant. For Taylor had started up in business once again, investing other people's money.

Within a few days the fifty-four-year-old was arrested. The story made headlines in Britain and Ireland given he went on to fight the extradition proceedings. It took a few months but eventually he was heading back to Ireland for a date at Dublin Circuit Criminal Court. He pleaded guilty to five charges involving fraud and the destruction of documents. It was reported that investors lost sums of between £30,000 and £100,000. Some of them had entrusted him with their life savings but had no hope of getting the money back. He was given five years in jail.

FORTY

The Paedophile Priest and the Priory of Sion (2000s)

THOUGHTS of retirement came my way once more in 1999, or at least thoughts of stepping back. In that year I sold my six franchised agencies to the franchisees and took on a consultative and back-up role for them all. I wanted to spend more time at home, to finally begin winding down. But I knew quite quickly that it didn't suit me, that I wasn't yet ready to hang up the gumshoes. I got bored. It was something I wasn't used to and something I didn't care to proceed with.

Fortunately the demand for my services had not waned and, around this time, even began to increase. It wasn't in my nature to ignore such a thing. One aspect of the rising demand was the amount of approaches my firm, *Priority Investigations*, was getting from the USA. Indeed those approaches would remain constant to the point that, in the years ahead, seventy-five percent of the company's revenue would come from across the pond.

One such approach came via a Californian law firm which got in touch seeking the location of a paedophile priest. It was understood that he had returned to his native Ireland. But the lawyers there were worried. They knew Ireland was a largely Catholic country and feared an agency such as mine might not want to rock the boat.

Fr Oliver O'Grady had been sentenced to fourteen years for a series of sex assaults on about twenty-five children, beginning in 1973. The details were horrific, his victims scarred mentally and physically. He committed his crimes while based at California's Diocese of Stockton, about ninety minutes east of San Francisco. His was a particularly well-known case

341

given it emerged his Cardinal, Roger Mahony, had tried to keep details of his crimes under wraps. Unfortunately for him, everything was brought into the cold light of day. In 2006, three years before the approach to my office, a documentary on the scandal by Amy J Berg called *Deliver Us From Evil* had shocked viewers across America to the core.

This O'Grady person had served seven years, was paroled in 2000 and duly booted out of the USA. He was back in Ireland and, rumour had it, in the care of the Roman Catholic Church. But in effect, given the outrage directed at him, O'Grady had disappeared from sight.

The law firm was acting on behalf of a group of his victims in a class action lawsuit. They had got together to sue the Catholic Church in California for the immense damage caused to them and their families. So, despite being based in Ireland, might I go in search of the disgraced sixty-four-year-old? Would I serve him with legal process from the California Court? I assured them I'd be happy to do so.

O'Grady hailed from Limerick in Ireland's south west. George Richter, our franchisee there, wasted no time. He put a team together and got stuck into some old-fashioned legwork. They knocked doors of old friends and relatives, visited clergy, phoned everyone they couldn't physically reach. A few members of the church came on board to assist, clearly not wanting anything to do with suggestions that their employer was sheltering a man the tabloids had called a "*monster*". And the Irish police were also happy to help out behind the scenes.

It took about two weeks for Richter to track the paedophile to a Catholic Retreat in Co Limerick. In line with good practice, he began surveilling the property to photograph O'Grady in advance of getting his identity confirmed. And he also wanted to ensure he didn't vanish. After a few days George had some good pictures in the bag which we emailed to the lawyers in California. In turn, they got to double checking everything with the victims in question.

Funny enough, while waiting to hear back from the Americans, George went off to answer a call of nature at the retreat. On his way back he very nearly bumped straight into O'Grady. The rarely seen child rapist was out for a walk in the grounds. George was certain this was the right man although we had still not heard back from the US. But an opportunity had presented itself and George didn't miss a beat. He introduced himself to O'Grady and O'Grady introduced himself to George. The ID was right. The men chatted for a while. Religion came into the conversation quite quickly with O'Grady suggesting he was a very holy bloke and wanted to know all about George's worshipping habits. The paedophile went on to say he was staying at the retreat for a while and was hopeful of a posting in mainland Europe in the near future.

George let him prattle on, feigning fascination to the point that O'Grady, his ego boosted, asked George to drop round for a cup of tea some time. Our agent was only too happy to agree and asked for the details of his lodgings in the large retreat.

Unfortunately things went a little pear-shaped from there. George had called me to advise about the chance meeting and I had called California to do the same. The lawyers were delighted, but they were not exactly moving at warp speed. I had not yet even received the court documents that we would need to physically hand to O'Grady. They asked me to sit tight but to call off the surveillance in the meantime. Their reasoning was that the priest had suggested he would be at the retreat for a while. This turned out to be a mistake.

A few days passed before a sizable FedEx package arrived at my office in Belfast. The bundle of papers cited every detail O'Grady was entitled to know about the class action relating to his crimes. I forwarded the lot to George in Limerick and he made his way back to the retreat. But there was no answer at O'Grady's door. And, a while later, still no answer. George approached a few priests to find out where he might be. They didn't know. What they did know was that he had moved on. We were crestfallen.

A second search began. We got back onto the police who very helpfully circulated O'Grady's image around stations saying he was being sought in terms of the serving of legal papers from victims. We spoke too with Irish journalists and others in hope of getting word out about our slippery priest. And all the while we couldn't help wondering if he had landed that post he spoke of and sloped off to some unfortunate parish somewhere in Europe. The church contacts in Ireland just did not know. Whatever had happened, it was suggested, it was being kept top secret.

We rang and wrote to Catholic organisations in France, Belgium, Holland, Luxembourg and elsewhere. We said this man was a dangerous predator who should not be allowed anywhere near children, that there were fears the church in Ireland might have sent him their way.

We were stunned when the first result came back. O'Grady had been spotted working in a pastoral role under the name of Brother Francis at a Catholic Church Children's School in Rotterdam. An incredible discovery and an unfathomable, despicable decision to place him there in the first place. He'd been recognised by people who had seen the documentary. They were horrified to learn such a man had been anonymously let loose among their kids.

An Irish newspaper got the story as the outrage in Holland surfaced. It reported *"Monster Irish Paedophile Priest discovered working with kids in Holland."*

His cover blown, O'Grady was off and running again. He dashed to the airport, apparently in disguise, catching an Aer Lingus back to Dublin. He was arrested on landing and we were alerted that he was being held. We arranged for someone to get the papers in Limerick and bolt over to Dublin to serve him pronto. But he was gone again by the time they arrived. The coppers had no choice but to let him go. O'Grady had committed no offences in Ireland (none that had been recorded anyway). So where had he gone? Once again, we were stumped.

All staff were manning the phones, doing what we could to get some useful feedback from various church-linked hostels, training centres, retreats and all the rest of it. A breakthrough came when Gardai got in touch with a tip-off. They had heard he might have checked into a B&B near Dublin's Connolly Station. Off our agent went, that bulky file under his tired arm once more, and he entered the B&B. He asked the landlady if one Fr O'Grady, aka Brother Francis, was a guest there. She confirmed that he was. She seemed to have some insight into what it was all about. Indeed she was a little concerned that our agent, although exhausted, might be about to attack and perhaps even kill the paedophile. Our man said he would do no such thing. The lady said she would arrange for Fr O'Grady to meet him in a small room which served as part of the bar.

The men met, at last, and our agent described O'Grady as appearing 'extremely depressed' and a little 'humble.' He said he was polite and expressed his concern about the press and others being on his case, which I'm sure was terrible for him.

He took the documents, placed the package into a plastic carrier bag and said he would look at everything later. We advised Gardai he had been served and thanked them for their help.

We learned later that O'Grady had left a bag on the plane during his flight back to Dublin from Amsterdam. When police examined items inside, they found child porn photos and videos on a hard drive and a USB key. Some of those featured were aged as young as two. In December 2010, O'Grady was arrested in Dublin for his latest sex offence and later sentenced to three years.

In 2012 the law firm in California was in touch once more. They needed me to arrange for the serving of a further batch of legal process. Luckily on this occasion we knew where our man was. He was banged up in jail.

After serving his time it seems Fr O'Grady, a clearly relentless pervert, got straight back to his old tricks and built up another collection of child porn. Yet when Gardai were alerted and went to get him, they learned he had fled Ireland. In 2019 a European Arrest Warrant was issued and, after a time, he was tracked down to the Algarve, Portugal. He was deported back to face the charges in Dublin. In October 2020, aged seventy-five, he was sentenced to twenty-two months at Waterford Circuit Court for possession of child porn.

Matters of religion came up once more in the aftermath of the hit 2003 Dan Brown novel *The Da Vinci Code*. Its elaborate ideas around an old legend, that a child was born to Jesus Christ and Mary Magdalene, captured the imagination of millions. A film starring Tom Hanks followed three years later and the story reached a yet wider audience.

In the aftermath of that movie, as the public continued to devour every fanciful notion linked to the plot, a US-based British director approached me with a query. Bruce Burgess explained he was researching a documentary to be entitled *Bloodline* which was exploring some of the matters touched on in the book. The story goes that Jesus survived the crucifixion, escaped by boat to France, married Mary Magdalene and fathered her child. And, it is said, the details of all that information, including what became of Christ's descendants to the present day, have been protected for many centuries by a secret organisation called *Priory of Sion.*

Thrilling stuff indeed, but what could a private investigator bring to this holiest of matters? Burgess said, as was known at the time, that rumours of the existence of *Priory of Sion* had persisted over the years and that they had been re-energised as a result of the book and movie. There was talk of ancient documents knocking around, of influential members being freshly sworn to silence in various parts of the world. He and his team had spent months attempting to make contact with those in-the-know in order to determine if the *Priory* existed in any real form. If it did, they hoped to get a sense of its structure, its membership, its secrets.

Burgess explained that nothing had come from any of their investigations until a Paris-based producer for *Bloodline,* by the name of Edwardo Flaherty, struck lucky. He managed to get feedback from a contact who pointed him in the direction of a UK-based bloke called Nicolas Haywood. He was advised that Mr Haywood was a representative of the splendidly-titled Inner Circle of the Priory of Sion. Flaherty had reached him by email and they went on to meet in London. Yet the inscrutable and slightly scary Haywood had seemingly given nothing away. My job was to look into this chap and see if I could lift the lid on him and perhaps in some way lift the lid on the organisation to which he apparently belonged.

I launched into it by checking out addresses which the client had established were linked to this mystery man. These were in Derby in England, in the Oakwood area and in Darley Abbey. I found several potential variants to the name and quite a few titles as well. There were listings for a Nicolas Andre Haywood, for Nicholas T Haywood, for Nicolas St Levan and for Nic T. Haywood. And connected to these were the titles—D. PSy, Hyp.D (UCL) MRCPsy, FRCPsych, FRC, FRS and FRSA. But that was as far as it went. Unusually there were no other details available for these names, nothing allowing me to look into family history, no links to a business or professional status. Myself and my team went on to explore the Priory of Sion idea, researching every name ever linked to it, researching all the locations and notions and hearsay we could pick up on. There were a few angry responses along the way, a number of implied threats too, but we came across nothing at all that firmed up any of what was claimed. It was rare indeed that I would report back so empty-handed to a client, but Haywood and his alleged organisation had left very little in the way of a trail.

In the conversations that followed Burgess told me of another name that had come up in Paris, that of a Gino Sandri. Their source had alleged he was General Secretary of the Priory of Sion and they had managed to make contact. Indeed, Mr Sandri had agreed to meet with the production team for an interview at a hotel in the French capital. During filming a messenger had arrived out-of-the-blue and approached to have a quiet word with Mr Sandri. The alleged general secretary seemed horrified at even just seeing the messenger and was horrified yet more by what was said in his ear. He left immediately afterwards. My clients had never been able to reach him again, saying that they too had faced a number of implied threats along the way.

It all sounded fascinating and a little frightening and gave all of us food for thought. But, to be honest, I couldn't help wonder if it was a load of horseshit, a theatrical set-up designed to spook the documentary team and create the illusion there really was a Priory of Sion and that they were at the edge of something extraordinary, mystical and unsettling.

The filmmakers went on to work their sources and make their film. As the production revealed in 2008, they visited the French church where a bloke called Ben Hammott claimed to have discovered what he said were the mummified remains of Mary Magdalene. Various other related artefacts, it was claimed, had been hidden away in the building's dungeons, as Hammott eagerly explained on camera. The filmed material did not disappoint viewers but, in truth, raised more questions than answers. They reported that a Priory of Sion had been formally registered in France in 1956, describing itself as a fraternal organisation. It was registered and dissolved by a man called Pierre Plantard in that same year. His aim had been to create an association, albeit with a fake pedigree, for influential people. It seems he was not even an advocate of the theory that Christ had living descendants.

In March 2012, Ben Hammott came forward to own up to talking a lot of nonsense. His real name was Bill Wilkinson and his fake name was an anagram of *The Tombman*. Wilkinson had been a figure in some fantastical corners of the internet for some time. He had been rumbled, knew he was to be outed and instead spoke first. He said everything to do with the tomb and the related artefacts had been, lo and behold, a hoax.

FORTY-ONE

Sir Mark Thatcher and the Wonga Coup (2004)

My late good friend and supremely talented journalist Barrie Penrose had the finest of instincts and most impeccable of sources. That combination ensured he knew where to look, when to do so and how hard to put the pressure on. And he always knew when it was time to call me. I always enjoyed hearing from him, was always aware that the topic for discussion could be anything up to and including an issue of international significance. Or at least it would be a quality chat. I was happy in either case.

At the turn of the century, and for a few years beyond, Barrie developed an interest in a mysterious and hugely wealthy Lebanese oil dealer. According to *The Sunday Times Rich List* in 2010, British citizen Ely Calil was worth an eye-watering £350M. He was extremely private, rarely photographed yet quite well-known in high-end London circles. He had bought himself Sloane House, an 18ᵗʰ century listed mansion off Chelsea's upmarket King's Road, and lived there with his family.

Barrie's sources directed him towards Mr Calil and, in turn, Barrie engaged me. It was already known that, in 2002, Calil had been arrested over alleged illegal payments in relation to contracts between the French Elf Aquitaine oil company and the Nigerian government. It came to nothing and Calil was never charged, yet further questions were emerging fast.

At Barrie's instruction, my first investigation into this curious gentleman led to confirmation he had rented a luxury flat in London's Holland Park to Peter Mandelson, the European Commissioner for Trade, former Labour minister and close friend to Prime Minister Tony Blair. Mandelson took it on after he quit the cabinet in the wake of revelations of an undeclared home loan from a fellow minister. It was a big story for Barrie in 2004, given the links to the oil dealer. But that was only the beginning.

Barrie talked again of Mr Calil. He said he had information that our man was the source of funding for a planned coup in the small, oil rich west African nation of Equatorial Guinea. And, it was suggested, the son of former Prime Minister Margaret Thatcher was involved in putting the plan together too.

This was startling stuff. The plotters' goal was to replace the sitting president and dictator Teodoro Obiang with exiled opposition politician Severo Moto in exchange for a large chunk of cash and juicy rights to the oil. Barrie had been told this funding was linked to Sir Mark Thatcher and a bloke called Simon Mann, a former British army officer and SAS operative turned adventurous mercenary. But Barrie had only information. He needed evidence.

He connected me with a Paris-based English lawyer who was likewise exploring those with an interest in the planned overthrow. Indeed the lawyer was acting on behalf of the sitting president of Equatorial Guinea. He asked me to locate and track Severo Moto, known to be residing in Spain. I arranged it. We found him at a secret location and, at the lawyer's direction, I engaged my Spanish-based colleague Rick Howatson to set-up surveillance. The lawyer was keen to know when Mr Moto was planning to head homeward, given such a departure might signal the coup was imminent.

Meanwhile, back in London, Barrie instructed me to task my agents in Cape Town, South Africa, with keeping an eye on Sir Mark Thatcher. They established he was living in a substantial home with his family and that he managed his business dealings from the property. And, being typically thorough, they began to gather information on calls he was making from his many phones.

As work continued, a call came in from the south of Spain. It was March 6, 2004. My agent said Moto was on the move and wasn't just going to the shop. They had tracked him as he was chauffeured to a private airfield and they had watched as he boarded a private jet and took to the sky. They had discovered that the flight plan filed by the pilot indicated Moto was en route to an airport near Equatorial Guinea, with a refuelling stop on the way. I passed on the information.

The next day was a big one. March 7, 2004. The plotters were about to launch their coup. And, as with so many coups in my experience, it didn't work out. Simon Mann and sixty-seven mercenaries touched down in Harare, Zimbabwe, in a Boeing 727 and were promptly arrested. Their plan had been to load it with £100,000 worth of weapons and other military hardware but local security forces acting on intelligence put paid to that. The men were later charged with violating immigration, firearms and security laws and with engaging in an attempt to stage a coup d'état. Mann and the others amusingly claimed they had been en route to the Democratic Republic of Congo to provide security for diamond mines but it didn't wash. Mann was found guilty of attempting to buy arms for the plot and sentenced to seven years.

He told later how Calil had recruited him to lead the misadventure. He alleged too that Sir Mark Thatcher had been part of the 'management team' of it all. When in jail, Mann had asked for both Calil and Thatcher to help get him out suggesting in writing that *a large splodge of wonga* would do the trick. However, as he said later, no one came to his aid.

Five months after the collapse of what became known as the *Wonga Coup*, Sir Mark Thatcher was arrested at his home in Cape Town, South Africa. His house and cars had been up for sale and he had a plan to resettle his family in America. The tickets had already been bought, the suitcases packed. The police believed he was about to leg it. He was charged with contravening mercenary laws, denied the lot and was bailed.

One morning, thanks to my diligent old friends at BOSS, a package arrived by courier to my home in Belfast. It was a CD listing Sir Mark Thatcher's entire itemised billing for all his phones for a three month period around the *Wonga Coup*. Those bills very much told a story all of their own concerning a man who denied any part in the attempted military intervention. Indeed Mr Thatcher denied everything right up until January 2005, just before his trail. It was then that he admitted investing in an aircraft without taking proper investigations into what it would be used for. He said he thought it was to help the poor and had no idea it was for use in a coup. As part of a plea bargain he received a four-year suspended sentence. It seemed that copies of the same telephone records I had received had found their way to his defence team and forced their hand.

Mann served four years in Zimbabwe before he was extradited to Equatorial Guinea. He served fifteen months of a thirty-four year sentence before he was pardoned by President Obiang.

As for Mr Calil, he passed away in 2018 aged seventy-two. He had broken his neck after falling down stairs at his home in London.

The Sunday Times:
January 23, 2005:

Insight: Coup plotters wanted a colony of their own

THE FAILED coup attempt involving Sir Mark Thatcher was to have made Equatorial Guinea a private colony run for the benefit of the British plotters, leaked documents reveal...
Another named conspirator is Thatcher, son of the former prime minister. Although he claims to have been drawn into the plot inadvertently after agreeing to finance an air ambulance, the documents suggest otherwise.

EPILOGUE

Thursday August 2, 2018. 14.30.
Metropolitan Police Counterintelligence
Interrogation Unit, London.

THEY ask about my time as National Security Advisor. They want to know who recruited me, what I did, how close I was to the key figures of the time.

I say President France-Albert René gave me the job, that I tracked dissidents all over the world, that I often met the president and his ministers for cigars, espressos, Cognac.

They say they have a warrant for René, not that it's much use. Besides, I've heard he's extremely ill and the end is close.

Former Defence Minister Ogilvy Berlouis is on the warrant too, they say. I tell them he tried to oust René, but didn't get away with it. Anyway, I say, he died months back.

Mario Ricci is listed as well, another one they'd like to speak with. But they already know they're too late. His funeral was ten years ago.

And there's two others, besides myself. One is Bill Underwood, the electronics contractor I introduced to the Seychelles government. They had tasked him with installing the Edgware eavesdropping equipment. The other name is John Dutcher.

'What do you know of Mr Dutcher?' they ask.

'Nothing,' I say. 'I've never heard of him.'

They tell me he's dead. He had been, they explain, a CIA operative loaned to British Intelligence during the Falklands War. It seems he settled in the UK. They tell me his fingerprint was found at the house.

They show me a photograph and ask, 'Could this man have been in the property in Edgware?'

I don't recognise him. I give them the only answer I can.

'I don't know,' I say.

They raise the theory of US involvement, of America seeking regime change via a black operation to disgrace René's government. I hear them out and I know they don't really believe I played any part in the murder of Gérard Horeau. Yet they hold me for two days and we go over it all again and again.

What was I doing that day?

What do I know of the murder?

Who was involved?

I take a break and reflect back on it all, think of how myself, my wife and children were happy where the clock chimes twice, that it broke our hearts to leave.

I think how young Jamie, wrenched away from his first love Natalie, met her again by chance in London while working for our now family business, *Priority Investigations*. They went on to marry, to set up home in Northern Ireland. They have a beautiful daughter, my youngest grandchild.

Scuba instructor Johnnie went on to join the British Antarctic Survey. He spent ten years working in frozen climes, starting out as an under ice diver and becoming Base Commander and Territory Magistrate. He became father to a little boy and, after marrying Leanne, brought another little fella and little girl into our family. Phyl and I were so proud to be invited to Buckingham Palace to see him awarded the Polar Medal by Prince Charles. He went on to work with the agency, manages it now. It's flourishing on both sides of the Atlantic.

My first born, Debbie, worked in banking, brought my first grandchild into the world, and lived for a time in Budapest. Her son Jeremy is a fine actor, and has got himself parts on the big screen. Debbie's back in the UK now. Here's hoping she settles in Northern Ireland.

Andy, my eldest son, worked in banking and became an artist. His work is superb. He spent five years in Seychelles before making a home in Spain. He helps out with *Priority Investigations*, handles assignments along the Mediterranean coast and around the region.

In 2000, myself, Stuart and a colleague called John Edwards founded the *World Association of Professional Investigators*. Its code of ethics maps out the range of work we do, clarifies our practices and acts as an assurance to clients that we always aim to do our best. I'm proud to say it has many hundreds of members across the globe. Sadly my co-founder, little brother and co-adventurer on so many cases in so many locations is no longer with us. Stuart passed away from lung cancer in 2019.

In 2005, after developing chest pains, I was sent off to the GP at Phyl's insistence. Rather surprisingly, he dialled 999 then and there while telling me I was about to have a heart attack. He was absolutely right. A full-blown cardiac arrest was prevented and I spent the following week in hospital. A host of angina attacks, often at the most inconvenient times, would follow in the months ahead. I went on to become a regular ambulance user and, to give them a break, I eventually had bypass surgery at Belfast's Royal Victoria Hospital to circumvent five blockages. My most sincere thanks to the surgeon.

In 2015, a decade or more after buying a holiday home in Cyprus, I finally decided to call it a day. I stepped away from the management of what was now a family business to spend more time with Phyl and the sunshine.

We were in Cyprus in 2016 when Phyl complained of stomach pains, and it was clearly serious. I rushed her to the Blue Cross Hospital in Paphos and, once she stablised, we flew back to Northern Ireland. But severe pains struck again. She was taken to Antrim Area Hospital in August where we were told she needed life saving surgery. The initial pains, it emerged, had been the result of a clot in an artery to the stomach. Phyl's organs and intestines had effectively died and gangrene had set in. It was dreadful news. And the doctors were clear they were running low on hope. They kept us informed all the way as her condition, I'm sorry to say, showed no improvement. On December 5th, after four months of care, she lost consciousness. And on the 19th, she slipped away forever. Phyl was eight years my junior, sixty-eight when she died. It seems unfair she was taken at that age. I think of her all the time, remembering that vivacious, popular, courageous, gorgeous dark-haired girl I met way back in 1966…

And my inquisitors begin again, drilling into my memories, searching hard for a sign I'm holding something back. But they know they won't find one. They know that they can fish forever and catch nothing new.

After a while they pull back and ask who I think killed Gérard Horeau. I talk of his many dangerous contacts, of how his fellow dissident Paul Chow spoke on TV recently of a dispute with some South Africans around oil rights. I suggest that whoever did it must have stood to benefit. I tell them I am not that person. And again, it's clear they know I'm right on this.

They say they're letting me go for now, that they'll arrange for a hotel tonight and a flight tomorrow. And I'm relieved. I've had more than enough of this. I'm cheered by the thought of this ending, *cesspits and roses* on my mind. But they tell me I remain under investigation. They give no good reason why.

My solicitor addresses the detectives.

'I have to ask,' he says, 'why did it take thirty-three years for you to arrest Ian Withers over this case?'

We wait in silence.

They give no answer.

About the Author

Ian Withers was born in 1941, growing up during the Second World War, late forties and fifties. Destined to follow a career in the family building business when, as if by design, tracking down a debtor for the business led to becoming a trainee in a PI Agency. A short stint as a police officer before becoming the general manager of a sizeable commercial investigation agency. Following this contract, along with brother Stuart, they grew and managed their own Agency until 1977. They then split the Agency, each brother following their own dreams. Ian landed a contract with the Republic of Seychelles as National Security Adviser. He headed a comprehensive external intel service until 1986, when the agreement with Seychelles ended following the cold-blooded murder of the leader of the dissidents in London. Together with his family, Ian settled in the Seychelles, where he operated several businesses whilst still managing his Agency in the USA.

In 1991 following the decision by the Seychelles Government to reintroduce multi-party democracy, Ian packed his bags. He returned to Ireland, and restarted his Agencies, trading as Priority Investigations.

A founder member of the World Association of Professional Investigations and Chairman for seven years, Ian gave evidence to both the Leveson Tribunal and the Home Affairs Committee, before retiring to a consultancy role in the family Investigation Business.

Biography of the Author

School finished (aged 15):	1956
Apprenticeship:	1956/1959
Family Business	1959/1960
Army:	1960/1962
Building Joinery Services:	1959/1962
Kingston Detective Agency:	1962/1964
Surrey Police:	1964/1966
Southern Provincial Investigations:	1966/1967
Christopher Robert & Co / Nationwide:	1968/1978
Maryland Investigators (USA):	1972/2010
The Agency split:	1978
T/As Intercity Investigations:	1978/1979
Bought Reliant Business Services—Jersey:	1979
Seychelles Contract:	1979/1986
T/As Intercity Reliant Ltd:	1980/1986
Priority Services:	1980/1986
Seychelles Resident:	1986/1992
Priority (Dublin):	1987/2015
Priority (Belfast):	1980/DATE

TV Documentaries

World in Action Documentary	Circa 1968	"Spies for hire"
Southern TV Documentary	Circa 1974	"For the love of Helen"
Southern TV Documentary	Circa 1976	"The rise & rise of Withers & Withers"
World in Action Documentary	Circa 1978	"Kidnapped, Escape from Salonika"
Sixty Minutes	Circa 1989	"Spies Island"

Truth & Reconciliation Hearing – Seychelles

TRNUC Hearing- Monday 14-OCT-2019—Session 1—Jemmy Marengo / Donald Bertin / Christian Lionnet / Ian Withers
https://www.youtube.com/watch?v=SX9YE3Gd66E

Published Books Quoting/Mentioning the Author

The Political Police in Britain	1976	Tony Bunyon
The Pencourt File	1978	Barrie Penrose
Inside Boss	1981	Gordan Winter
Children in the Crossfile	1983	Sally Abrams
Enemies of the State	1993	Gary Murray
No Place That Far	2001	Jacques Vankirk
On South Africa's Secret Service	2002	Riaan Labuschagne
Covert	2005	Ian Lumley
Hack Attack	2014	Nick Davies
Spooked	2021	Barry Meier

Lightning Source UK Ltd.
Milton Keynes UK
UKHW030451011021
391460UK00002B/75